WEIGHT WATCHERS ®

QUICK MEALS

WEIGHT WATCHERS ®
QUICK MEALS

Macmillan ■ USA

MACMILLAN
A Simon & Schuster Macmillan Company
1633 Broadway
New York, NY 10019-6785

Library of Congress Cataloging-in-Publication Data
Weight Watchers quick meals.
    p.   cm.
  Includes index
  ISBN 0–02–860351–6
  1. Reducing diets—Recipes.   2. Quick and easy cookery.
 I. Weight Watchers International.
 RM222.2.W325   1995
613.2'5-dc20   94-24255
                  CIP

Manufactured in the United States of America
10 9 8 7 6 5 4 3 2

Our thanks to the following dedicated people who were instrumental in creating this book: Recipe developers Barbara Posner Beltrami, Luli Gray and Tamara Holt; recipe editors Patricia Barnett and Joyce Hendley, M.S.; nutrition consultant Lynne S. Hill, M.S., R.D., L.D. Photography by Martin Jacobs; prop styling by Linda Johnson; food styling by William Smith.

Contents

Master Staples List

VEGETABLES

Carrots
Celery
Garlic

Onions
Potatoes
Shallots

FRUIT

Lemons
Limes

Oranges
Raisins, black and golden

DAIRY

Eggs, large
Margarine, regular stick and
   reduced-calorie tub

Plain nonfat yogurt
Skim milk

CANNED AND BOTTLED GOODS

Chicken broth, low-sodium
Evaporated skimmed milk
Seltzer, plain
Sparkling mineral water, plain
   and flavored

Tomatoes, plum, crushed and stewed
Tomato paste
Tuna, water-packed
Wine, dry red and white

SUGARS, FLOURS, SYRUPS, OILS, CONDIMENTS AND GRAINS

Baking powder, double-acting

Baking soda

Bouillon cubes

Bread crumbs, plain and seasoned

Broth and seasoning mix

Cocoa powder, unsweetened

Coffee, regular and decaffeinated, ground and instant

Cornmeal, yellow

Cornstarch

Flour, all-purpose

Gelatin, unflavored

Honey

Hot pepper sauce

Ketchup

Maple syrup

Mustard, yellow and Dijon-style

Nonfat dry milk powder, instant

Nonstick cooking spray

Oil, vegetable and olive

Rice, long-grain, regular, converted and instant

Soy sauce, reduced-sodium

Sugar, granulated and light and dark brown

Sugar substitute

Tea bags, regular and decaffeinated, assorted varieties

Vanilla extract

Vinegar, cider, red wine and balsamic

Worcestershire sauce

HERBS AND SPICES

Allspice, ground and whole

Anise seeds

Basil

Bay leaves

Caraway seeds

Chili powder, mild or hot

Cinnamon, ground and stick

Cloves, ground and whole

Cream of tartar

Cumin, ground and seeds

Curry powder, mild and hot

Dill

Fennel seeds

Garlic powder

Ginger

Marjoram

Nutmeg

Oregano

Paprika

Peppercorns, black

Red pepper, ground and flakes

Rosemary

Sage

Salt

Sesame seeds

Tarragon

Thyme

Turmeric

White pepper

Master Equipment List

COOKWARE

Crêpe pan or skillet, 8" nonstick

Dutch oven

Griddle or cast-iron skillet, heavy large

Heavy-bottom pot with cover, large

Saucepans with covers, heavy large, medium and small (preferably nonstick)

Skillets with covers, heavy large, medium and small (preferably nonstick)

Steamer rack

Wok

BAKEWARE AND BOWLS

Baking sheets, large and small (preferably nonstick)

Broiler pan with rack

Casserole dishes, 1-, 2- and 3-quart

Cooling racks

Custard cups or ramekins, 6- and 8-ounce

Decorative paper or foil baking cups

Glass and stainless-steel mixing bowls, large, medium and small

Gratin dishes, individual (optional)

Jelly-roll pans, large and small

Metal baking pans, 8" and 9" square

Metal baking pans, 13 × 9"

Metal cake pans, 8" and 9" round

Metal pie pans, 9" and 10"

Metal roasting pans, small and large

Muffin pans with six and twelve $2^3/_4$" cups (preferably nonstick)

Roasting rack

Shallow baking dishes with covers, 1- and 2-quart

Shallow bowl

APPLIANCES

Blender

Coffeemaker

Electric mixer, stationary or portable

Food processor

Food scale

Teapot

UTENSILS

Apple corer

Bamboo and metal skewers, 12" and 6"

Baster

Bottle opener

Brushes, basting and pastry

Can opener

Colander

Corkscrew

Cutting boards

Garlic press

Grater, 4-sided

Grater, small, for whole nutmeg (optional)

Ice-cream scoop

Juicer

Knife, chef's

Knife, paring

Knife, slicing

Knives, serrated

Knives, utility

Ladle

Measuring cups for dry ingredients

Measuring cups for liquid ingredients

Meat mallet

Melon baller

Mortar and pestle

Pancake turner

Pepper mill

Potato masher

Ruler

Salad spinner (optional)

Sieves

Spatulas, metal and rubber

Spice mill (optional)

Spoons, measuring

Spoons, mixing

Spoons, slotted

Spoons, wooden

Tongs

Vegetable grater

Utensils, coated or nylon, to use in nonstick pans

Wire whisks

Zester (optional)

MISCELLANEOUS

Aluminum foil, heavy duty and regular

Cheesecloth

Paper bags

Paper plates

Parchment paper (optional)

Plastic bags, gallon-size sealable

Plastic wrap

Pot holders and oven mitts

Storage containers with covers

Toothpicks

Wax paper

SERVING PIECES AND TABLEWARE

Cups, mugs and glassware, individual

Decorative bowls, large, medium and small

Decorative platters, large and medium

Dessert dishes, individual

Dinner, luncheon and salad plates, individual

Flatware, individual

Napkins

Salad bowl, large
Salad servers
Salt and pepper shakers
Serving forks
Serving spoons
Soup bowls, individual
Tablecloths

Weight Watchers

Since 1963, Weight Watchers has grown from a handful of people to millions of enrollments annually. Today, Weight Watchers is the recognized leading name in safe and sensible weight control. Weight Watchers members form a diverse group, from youths ten years old and older to senior citizens, attending meetings virtually around the globe.

Growing numbers of people purchase and enjoy our popular, expanding line of convenience foods, best-selling cookbooks, personal calendar planners and audio and video tapes. Weight-loss and weight-management results vary by the individual, but we recommend that you attend Weight Watchers meetings, follow the Weight Watchers food plan and participate in regular physical activity. For the Weight Watchers meeting nearest you, call 1-800-651-6000.

1

Poultry

CHICKEN DINNER WITH A FOREIGN FLAIR

The unexpected flavors of caraway and cumin make this pretty pilaf exotic and delicious; pile it onto a bed of lightly steamed spinach for color. Tart-sweet cherry tomatoes provide a contrast of flavor and texture—you'll be surprised at how good they are cooked.

Menu serves 4

- **Walnut Chicken with Bulgur Pilaf, 1 serving**
- **Steamed Spinach, 1 cup per serving**
- **Hot Cherry Tomatoes, 1 serving**
- **Apricot Mousse, 1 serving**
- **Herbal Tea**

One serving of this meal provides: 1 Fat, $1^1/_4$ Fruits, $4^1/_2$ Vegetables, $2^1/_4$ Proteins, 2 Breads, 85 Optional Calories; 12 g Fat, 19 g Fiber

Market List

12 medium apricots	Chopped walnuts
4 whole strawberries	Bulgur
One 10-ounce bag fresh spinach	Frozen light whipped topping
36 cherry tomatoes	(8 calories per tablespoon)
10 ounces skinless boneless	Apricot-flavored brandy
chicken breasts	

Preparation Schedule

Note: For maximum efficiency, assemble all ingredients and equipment before starting preparation.

1. Prepare Apricot Mousse; freeze.
2. Prepare Walnut Chicken with Bulgur Pilaf; simmer.
3. While chicken is simmering, prepare Hot Cherry Tomatoes.
4. Prepare Steamed Spinach.
5. Heat water for tea.
6. While water is heating, beat mousse; divide among dessert dishes. Top with strawberries.

WALNUT CHICKEN WITH BULGUR PILAF

Makes 4 servings

1 teaspoon vegetable oil	$1/2$ teaspoon cumin seeds
10 ounces skinless boneless chicken breasts, cut into chunks	2 cups low-sodium chicken broth
1 cup chopped onions	8 ounces bulgur
1 cup chopped carrots	2 tablespoons golden raisins
1 ounce chopped walnuts	$1/8$ teaspoon cinnamon
$1/2$ teaspoon caraway seeds	Pinch salt

1. In medium nonstick saucepan, heat oil; add chicken, onions, carrots, walnuts, caraway seeds and cumin seeds. Cook over medium heat, stirring frequently, 4–5 minutes, until onions are golden brown.
2. Add broth, bulgur, raisins, cinnamon and salt to chicken mixture; bring liquid to a boil. Reduce heat to low; simmer, covered, 15 minutes, until chicken is cooked through and bulgur is tender.

Each serving (1 cup) provides: $3/4$ Fat, $1/4$ Fruit, 1 Vegetable, $2^1/4$ Proteins, 2 Breads, 10 Optional Calories

Per serving: 385 Calories, 8 g Total Fat, 1 g Saturated Fat, 41 mg Cholesterol, 128 mg Sodium, 55 g Total Carbohydrate, 12 g Dietary Fiber, 26 g Protein, 57 mg Calcium

HOT CHERRY TOMATOES

Makes 4 servings

1 teaspoon olive oil	2 teaspoons granulated sugar
36 cherry tomatoes	1 teaspoon fresh lemon juice

In medium skillet, heat oil; add tomatoes, sugar and juice. Cook over medium heat, stirring gently, 3 minutes, until tomatoes are heated but still firm.

Each serving ($1^1/2$ cups) provides: $1/4$ Fat, $1^1/2$ Vegetables, 10 Optional Calories

Per serving: 37 Calories, 1 g Total Fat, 0 g Saturated Fat, 0 mg Cholesterol, 8 mg Sodium, 6 g Total Carbohydrate, 1 g Dietary Fiber, 1 g Protein, 5 mg Calcium

Apricot Mousse

Makes 4 servings

12 medium apricots, pared and pitted
 1 fluid ounce (2 tablespoons) apricot-
      flavored brandy *
 1 cup thawed frozen light whipped
      topping (8 calories per tablespoon)

1 teaspoon granulated sugar
4 whole strawberries

1. In food processor or blender, purée apricots until very smooth; transfer to medium metal mixing bowl.
2. Add brandy, whipped topping and sugar to apricots; freeze, covered, 30 minutes, just until firm.
3. Just before serving, with wire whisk, beat apricot mixture until smooth. Divide mixture evenly among 4 dessert dishes; top each portion with a strawberry.

Each serving provides: 1 Fruit, 65 Optional Calories

Per serving: 113 Calories, 2 g Total Fat, 0 g Saturated Fat, 0 mg Cholesterol, 1 mg Sodium, 20 g Total Carbohydrate, 2 g Dietary Fiber, 2 g Protein, 17 mg Calcium

   * *2 tablespoons apricot nectar may be substituted for the brandy; reduce Optional Calories to 50.*

Per serving with apricot nectar: 97 Calories, 2 g Total Fat, 0 g Saturated Fat, 0 mg Cholesterol, 1 mg Sodium, 19 g Total Carbohydrate, 2 g Dietary Fiber, 2 g Protein, 18 mg Calcium

A TASTE OF INDIA

This wonderfully easy Indian meal is made up of a beautiful array of flavors, fragrances and colors. Just breathe deeply and you'll feel like you've been taken on a magic carpet ride to a culinary delight!

Menu serves 4

- **Chicken in Spinach-Curry Sauce, 1 serving**
- **Raita, 1 serving**
- **Spiced Rice Pilaf with Raisins, 1 serving**
- **Mango Chutney, 2 tablespoons per serving**
- **Spiced Tea**

One serving of this meal provides: 1 Fat, $1/2$ Fruit, $2^{1}/2$ Vegetables, 3 Proteins, $1^{1}/2$ Breads, 110 Optional Calories; 8 g Fat, 5 g Fiber

Market List

1 large European cucumber
Fresh cilantro
Fresh ginger root
Four 4-ounce skinless boneless
    chicken breasts

Low-fat (1.5%) buttermilk
Long-grain or basmati rice
Mango chutney
One 10-ounce package frozen
    chopped spinach

Preparation Schedule

Note: For maximum efficiency, assemble all ingredients and equipment before starting preparation.

1. Prepare Raita; refrigerate.
2. Prepare Spiced Rice Pilaf with Raisins; simmer.
3. While rice is simmering, coat and brown chicken.
4. When rice is completed, prepare Spinach-Curry Sauce.
5. Heat water for tea.
6. Complete Chicken in Spinach-Curry Sauce.

CHICKEN IN SPINACH-CURRY SAUCE

Makes 4 servings

2   tablespoons all-purpose flour
³/₄ teaspoon salt
¹/₂ teaspoon freshly ground black pepper
Four 4-ounce skinless boneless chicken
     breasts
2   teaspoons vegetable oil
2   teaspoons mild or hot curry powder

¹/₂ teaspoon ground cumin
1   garlic clove, minced
2   cups well-drained thawed frozen
     chopped spinach
1   cup low-sodium chicken broth
¹/₄ cup low-fat (1.5%) buttermilk

1. In gallon-size sealable plastic bag, combine flour, ¹/₄ teaspoon of the salt and the pepper; add 1 chicken breast. Seal bag; shake to coat thoroughly. Transfer chicken to plate; repeat with remaining chicken breasts.
2. In large nonstick skillet, heat oil; add chicken. Cook over medium-high heat, turning once, 2–3 minutes on each side, until lightly browned. Transfer chicken to clean plate; set aside.
3. In same skillet, combine curry powder, cumin and garlic; cook over medium heat, stirring constantly, 1 minute, until fragrant. Stir in spinach and broth; bring liquid to a boil. Reduce heat to low; simmer, stirring occasionally, 10 minutes, until flavors are blended. Cool slightly.
4. Transfer spinach mixture to food processor; purée until smooth. Return mixture to skillet; stir in buttermilk and remaining ¹/₂ teaspoon salt.
5. Return chicken to skillet; cook over low heat about 15 minutes until chicken is cooked through and mixture is heated.

Each serving provides: ¹/₂ Fat, 1 Vegetable, 3 Proteins, 25 Optional Calories

Per serving: 205 Calories, 5 g Total Fat, 1 g Saturated Fat, 66 mg Cholesterol, 595 mg Sodium, 9 g Total Carbohydrate, 3 g Dietary Fiber, 31 g Protein, 162 mg Calcium

RAITA

Makes 4 servings

2   cups coarsely grated European cucumber
¹/₂ cup plain nonfat yogurt

¹/₃ cup chopped cilantro
Pinch ground red pepper (optional)

In medium bowl, combine cucumber, yogurt, cilantro and red pepper; refrigerate, covered, until ready to serve.

Each serving provides: 1 Vegetable, 15 Optional Calories

Per serving: 23 Calories, 0 g Total Fat, 0 g Saturated Fat, 1 mg Cholesterol, 23 mg Sodium, 4 g Total Carbohydrate, 1 g Dietary Fiber, 2 g Protein, 65 mg Calcium

Spiced Rice Pilaf with Raisins

Makes 4 servings

2 teaspoons vegetable oil
1 cup chopped onions
6 ounces long-grain or basmati rice
2 teaspoons grated pared fresh ginger root
$^1/_2$ teaspoon ground turmeric

$^1/_4$ teaspoon ground cloves
2 cups low-sodium chicken broth
$^1/_4$ cup raisins
$^1/_2$ teaspoon salt

1. In medium saucepan, heat oil; add onions. Cook over medium heat, stirring frequently, 2–3 minutes, until softened.
2. Add rice, ginger, turmeric and cloves to onion mixture; stir to coat. Stir in broth, raisins and salt; bring liquid to a boil. Reduce heat to low; simmer, covered, 20 minutes, until rice is tender and broth is absorbed.

Each serving provides: $^1/_2$ Fat, $^1/_2$ Fruit, $^1/_2$ Vegetable, $1^1/_2$ Breads, 10 Optional Calories

Per serving: 235 Calories, 4 g Total Fat, 1 g Saturated Fat, 0 mg Cholesterol, 305 mg Sodium, 46 g Total Carbohydrate, 2 g Dietary Fiber, 5 g Protein, 28 mg Calcium

MEXICAN MEAL IN MINUTES

In Mexican cooking, the condiments are as exciting as the main dish, and this menu (which is shown on the cover) features three enticing condiments. For a 30-minute dinner, make just one; for a festive buffet, make all three. Chipotle peppers in adobo sauce is a wonderfully versatile product that is available in Hispanic grocery stores; purée it in a blender or food processor and store it in the refrigerator. Add a spoonful or two to sauces, chili and dressings; its smoky heat is instantly addictive.

Menu serves 4

- Chicken Fajitas, 1 serving
- Cucumber Relish, 1 serving
- Mango Salsa, 1 serving
- Pico de Gallo, 1 serving
- Sangria, 1 serving

One serving of this meal provides: $1/4$ Milk, 1 Fat, $1^3/4$ Fruits, $6^1/2$ Vegetables, 3 Proteins, 2 Breads, 95 Optional Calories; 10 g Fat, 9 g Fiber

Market List

2 small nectarines	3 medium red onions
1 small mango	Fresh cilantro
Orange juice	15 ounces skinless boneless
1 medium avocado	chicken breasts
2 medium cucumbers	Flour tortillas (6" diameter)
1 bunch scallions	Canned chipotle peppers in
4 medium tomatoes	adobo sauce
1 medium red bell pepper	Pickled jalapeño peppers
1 head iceberg lettuce	Curaçao

Special Equipment

1-quart pitcher
4 wine glasses

Mexican Meal in Minutes

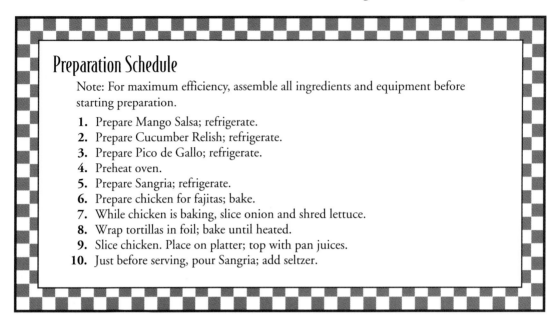

Preparation Schedule

Note: For maximum efficiency, assemble all ingredients and equipment before starting preparation.

1. Prepare Mango Salsa; refrigerate.
2. Prepare Cucumber Relish; refrigerate.
3. Prepare Pico de Gallo; refrigerate.
4. Preheat oven.
5. Prepare Sangria; refrigerate.
6. Prepare chicken for fajitas; bake.
7. While chicken is baking, slice onion and shred lettuce.
8. Wrap tortillas in foil; bake until heated.
9. Slice chicken. Place on platter; top with pan juices.
10. Just before serving, pour Sangria; add seltzer.

CHICKEN FAJITAS

Makes 4 servings

15 ounces skinless boneless chicken breasts
One 7-ounce can chipotle peppers in
    adobo sauce
1 tablespoon fresh lime juice
2 garlic cloves, pressed

$^1/_2$ teaspoon dried oregano leaves
8 flour tortillas (6" diameter)
2 cups sliced red onion
2 cups shredded iceberg lettuce

1. Preheat oven to 400° F. Spray an 8" square baking pan with nonstick cooking spray.
2. Place chicken in prepared baking pan; set aside.
3. In food processor or blender, purée chipotle peppers with sauce until smooth. Transfer 2 teaspoons pureed mixture to small bowl; refrigerate remaining mixture, covered, for use at another time.
4. Add lime juice, garlic and oregano to pureed peppers; stir to combine. Brush mixture over chicken breasts; bake, covered, 20 minutes, until chicken is cooked through. Remove chicken from oven; leave oven on.
5. Wrap tortillas in foil; bake 5 minutes, until heated.
6. Meanwhile, slice chicken crosswise. Arrange sliced chicken on medium decorative platter; top with pan juices. Serve with warm tortillas, sliced onion and shredded lettuce.

Each serving provides: 2 Vegetables, 3 Proteins, 2 Breads

Per serving: 303 Calories, 5 g Total Fat, 1 g Saturated Fat, 62 mg Cholesterol, 382 mg Sodium, 34 g Total Carbohydrate, 3 g Dietary Fiber, 30 g Protein, 113 mg Calcium

Cucumber Relish

Makes 4 servings

2 cups pared, seeded and diced cucumbers
2 medium tomatoes, blanched, peeled, seeded and diced
3/4 cup plain nonfat yogurt
1/2 cup sliced scallions

1 medium pickled jalapeño pepper, drained, seeded and minced (reserve 1 tablespoon liquid)
1/2 teaspoon dried oregano leaves

In small bowl, combine cucumbers, tomatoes, yogurt, scallions, jalapeño pepper and reserved liquid and oregano; refrigerate, covered, until chilled.

Each serving (3/4 cup) provides: 1/4 Milk, 2 1/2 Vegetables

Per serving: 56 Calories, 0 g Total Fat, 0 g Saturated Fat, 1 mg Cholesterol, 119 mg Sodium, 10 g Total Carbohydrate, 2 g Dietary Fiber, 4 g Protein, 114 mg Calcium

Mango Salsa

Makes 4 servings

1/2 teaspoon cumin seeds
1 small mango, peeled, pitted and diced *
1/2 cup diced red bell pepper

1/4 cup minced red onion
1 tablespoon fresh lime juice
1/4 teaspoon hot pepper sauce

1. In small nonstick skillet, toast cumin seeds over low heat, stirring constantly, 3 minutes, until fragrant; transfer to small bowl.
2. Add mango, red pepper, onion, lime juice and hot pepper sauce to toasted seeds; stir well to combine. Refrigerate, covered, until chilled.

Each serving (1/2 cup) provides: 1/2 Fruit, 1/2 Vegetable

Per serving: 35 Calories, 0 g Total Fat, 0 g Saturated Fat, 0 mg Cholesterol, 11 mg Sodium, 9 g Total Carbohydrate, 1 g Dietary Fiber, 1 g Protein, 11 mg Calcium

* If desired, substitute 2 cups diced cantaloupe or 2 medium peaches or small nectarines, peeled, pitted and diced, for the mango.

Per serving with cantaloupe: 37 Calories, 0 g Total Fat, 0 g Saturated Fat, 0 mg Cholesterol, 17 mg Sodium, 9 g Total Carbohydrate, 1 g Dietary Fiber, 1 g Protein, 15 mg Calcium

Per serving with peaches: 37 Calories, 0 g Total Fat, 0 g Saturated Fat, 0 mg Cholesterol, 10 mg Sodium, 9 g Total Carbohydrate, 1 g Dietary Fiber, 1 g Protein, 10 mg Calcium

Per serving with nectarines: 35 Calories, 0 g Total Fat, 0 g Saturated Fat, 0 mg Cholesterol, 10 mg Sodium, 8 g Total Carbohydrate, 1 g Dietary Fiber, 1 g Protein, 9 mg Calcium

PICO DE GALLO

Makes 4 servings

2 medium tomatoes, blanched, peeled, seeded and diced
$^1/_2$ medium avocado, peeled and diced
$^1/_2$ cup diced onion
1 medium pickled jalapeño pepper, drained, seeded and minced (reserve 1 tablespoon liquid)

2 tablespoons minced fresh cilantro
1 tablespoon fresh lime juice

In small bowl, combine tomatoes, avocado, onion, pepper and reserved liquid, cilantro and lime juice; refrigerate, covered, until chilled.

Each serving ($^1/_2$ cup) provides: 1 Fat, $1^1/_2$ Vegetables

Per serving: 71 Calories, 5 g Total Fat, 1 g Saturated Fat, 0 mg Cholesterol, 84 mg Sodium, 8 g Total Carbohydrate, 2 g Dietary Fiber, 2 g Protein, 13 mg Calcium

SANGRIA

Makes 4 servings

2 small nectarines, pitted and sliced
1 small navel orange, sliced
$^1/_2$ lime, sliced
10 fluid ounces ($1^1/_4$ cups) dry red wine
1 cup orange juice

1 fluid ounce (2 tablespoons) curaçao (orange-flavored liqueur)
2 tablespoons fresh lime juice
2 teaspoons granulated sugar
Plain seltzer

1. In 1-quart pitcher, combine nectarines, orange and lime, slightly crushing fruit with back of large spoon. Stir in wine, orange juice, curaçao, lime juice and sugar; refrigerate, covered, until chilled.
2. Just before serving, fill 4 wine glasses with ice. Pour wine mixture into glasses, dividing liquid and fruit evenly; add enough seltzer to fill glasses.

Each serving provides: $1^1/_4$ Fruits, 95 Optional Calories

Per serving: 154 Calories, 0 g Total Fat, 0 g Saturated Fat, 0 mg Cholesterol, 5 mg Sodium, 24 g Total Carbohydrate, 2 g Dietary Fiber, 1 g Protein, 31 mg Calcium

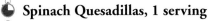

LA COMIDA MEXICANA

This south-of-the-border meal is so easy and can be whipped up instantly! Prepare extra portions of the salad; you'll find it tastes even better the second day!

Menu serves 4

- Spinach Quesadillas, 1 serving
- Salsa Chicken, 1 serving
- Black Bean Salad, 1 serving
- Double Coffee, 1 serving

One serving of this meal provides: $^3/_4$ Fat, 2 Vegetables, $3^1/_2$ Proteins, $1^3/_4$ Breads, 100 Optional Calories; 10 g Fat, 3 g Fiber

Market List

1 medium jalapeño pepper	$1^1/_2$ ounces Monterey Jack or
One 10-ounce bag fresh spinach	cheddar cheese
1 medium tomato	Flour tortillas (6" diameter)
1 medium red bell pepper	Salsa, mild or hot
1 medium red onion	White vinegar
Fresh cilantro	Black beans
Four 4-ounce skinless boneless	Coffee-flavored liqueur
chicken breasts	

Preparation Schedule

Note: For maximum efficiency, assemble all ingredients and equipment before starting preparation.

1. Prepare Salsa Chicken; bake.
2. While chicken is baking, prepare Spinach Quesadillas.
3. Prepare Black Bean Salad.
4. Prepare coffeemaker.
5. Just before serving, pour coffee into cups or mugs; add liqueur.

SPINACH QUESADILLAS

Makes 4 servings

1 medium jalapeño pepper, seeded and minced	4 flour tortillas (6" diameter)
2 cups packed spinach leaves, well rinsed, drained and chopped	1¹/₂ ounces shredded Monterey Jack or cheddar cheese
	1 medium tomato, thinly sliced

1. In large nonstick skillet, cook pepper over medium heat, stirring occasionally, 2 minutes, until soft. Add spinach; cook, stirring occasionally, just until wilted. Remove skillet from heat; transfer mixture to medium bowl.
2. To prepare quesadillas, place 1 tortilla into same skillet. Sprinkle one-fourth of the cheese onto one half of the tortilla. Top cheese with one-fourth of the spinach mixture and one-fourth of the tomato slices. Fold tortilla in half, covering tomato slices; press down with back of spatula until even. Place skillet over medium heat; cook filled tortilla 2 minutes on each side, pressing down with spatula, until golden brown on both sides and cheese is melted. Transfer quesadilla to cutting board; cut into wedges.
3. Repeat, making 3 more quesadillas.

Each serving (1 quesadilla) provides: 1³/₄ Vegetables, ¹/₂ Protein, 1 Bread

Per serving with Monterey Jack cheese: 122 Calories, 5 g Total Fat, 2 g Saturated Fat, 11 mg Cholesterol, 184 mg Sodium, 15 g Total Carbohydrate, 2 g Dietary Fiber, 6 g Protein, 142 mg Calcium

Per serving with cheddar cheese: 125 Calories, 5 g Total Fat, 2 g Saturated Fat, 11 mg Cholesterol, 193 mg Sodium, 15 g Total Carbohydrate, 2 g Dietary Fiber, 6 g Protein, 139 mg Calcium

SALSA CHICKEN

Makes 4 servings

Preheat oven to 375° F. Place *four 4-ounce skinless boneless chicken breasts* in a 2-quart shallow baking dish; top with *1 cup mild or hot salsa.* Bake 30 minutes, until cooked through.

Each serving (1 chicken breast) provides: 3 Proteins

Per serving: 141 Calories, 1 g Total Fat, 0 g Saturated Fat, 66 mg Cholesterol, 434 mg Sodium, 4 g Total Carbohydrate, 0 g Dietary Fiber, 26 g Protein, 12 mg Calcium

Black Bean Salad

Makes 4 servings

2 teaspoons ground cumin
2 tablespoons fresh lemon juice
1 tablespoon vegetable oil
1 teaspoon white vinegar
$^1/_4$ teaspoon salt

6 ounces drained cooked black beans
$^1/_2$ cup finely diced red bell pepper
$^1/_4$ cup chopped fresh cilantro
2 tablespoons chopped red onion

1. To prepare dressing, in small skillet, heat cumin over low heat, stirring constantly, 1 minute, until fragrant; transfer to large decorative bowl. Add lemon juice, oil, vinegar and salt; with wire whisk, blend until smooth.
2. Add beans, red pepper, cilantro and onion to dressing; toss to combine.

Each serving provides: $^3/_4$ Fat, $^1/_4$ Vegetable, $^3/_4$ Bread

Per serving: 98 Calories, 4 g Total Fat, 0 g Saturated Fat, 0 mg Cholesterol, 138 mg Sodium, 13 g Total Carbohydrate, 1 g Dietary Fiber, 4 g Protein, 26 mg Calcium

Double Coffee

For each serving, in coffee cup or mug, combine $^3/_4$ *cup hot decaffeinated coffee* and *1 fluid ounce (2 tablespoons) coffee-flavored liqueur.*

Each serving provides: 100 Optional Calories

Per serving: 100 Calories, 0 g Total Fat, 0 g Saturated Fat, 0 mg Cholesterol, 4 mg Sodium, 10 g Total Carbohydrate, 0 g Dietary Fiber, 0 g Protein, 4 mg Calcium

MEXICAN SOUP SUPPER

On a cool spring night, a light hot soup is very refreshing. This one is extra special when served with crisp, spicy Tortilla Chips. For a tropical fruit shake that's sure to please everyone, make sure the fruit for the Batido is ripe and fragrant.

Menu serves 4

- **Mexican Chicken Soup, 1 serving**
- **Tortilla Chips, 1 serving**
- **Cucumber Salad, 1 serving**
- **Batido, 1 serving**

One serving of this meal provides: $^1/_2$ Milk, $1^1/_4$ Fats, $1^1/_2$ Fruits, $3^1/_2$ Vegetables, 2 Proteins, $1^1/_2$ Breads, 25 Optional Calories; 11 g Fat, 7 g Fiber

Market List

2 small mangoes	2 medium cucumbers
1 medium banana	10 ounces skinless boneless
1 medium red bell pepper	chicken breasts
1 medium jalapeño pepper	Corn tortillas (6" diameter)
1 head iceberg lettuce	Corn oil

Preparation Schedule

Note: For maximum efficiency, assemble all ingredients and equipment before starting preparation.

1. Preheat oven.
2. Prepare Cucumber Salad; refrigerate.
3. Prepare Tortilla Chips; let stand in oven.
4. While chips are standing, prepare Mexican Chicken Soup.
5. Cut up lime for soup.
6. Just before serving, add lettuce and lime juice to soup.
7. Just before serving, prepare Batido.

MEXICAN CHICKEN SOUP

Makes 4 servings

1 teaspoon corn oil	10 ounces skinless boneless chicken breasts,
1 cup diced onions	thinly sliced into strips
1 cup diced red bell pepper	1 bay leaf
1 medium jalapeño pepper, seeded and	$^1/_2$ teaspoon dried marjoram leaves
minced	$^1/_4$ teaspoon dried thyme leaves
2 garlic cloves, minced	1 cup shredded iceberg lettuce
3 cups low-sodium chicken broth	1 tablespoon fresh lime juice
$1^1/_2$ cups canned stewed tomatoes, coarsely	1 lime, cut into wedges
chopped	Hot pepper sauce to taste

1. In medium saucepan, heat oil; add onions, red pepper, jalapeño pepper and garlic. Cook over medium-high heat, stirring frequently, 3–4 minutes, until very tender.
2. Add broth and tomatoes to vegetable mixture; bring to a boil. Add chicken, bay leaf, marjoram and thyme; cook, stirring occasionally, 5 minutes, until heated through and flavors are blended. Remove and discard bay leaf.
3. Just before serving, stir lettuce and lime juice into soup; serve with lime wedges and hot pepper sauce.

Each serving provides: $^1/_4$ Fat, $2^1/_2$ Vegetables, 2 Proteins, 15 Optional Calories

Per serving: 171 Calories, 3 g Total Fat, 1 g Saturated Fat, 41 mg Cholesterol, 333 mg Sodium, 16 g Total Carbohydrate, 3 g Dietary Fiber, 20 g Protein, 74 mg Calcium

TORTILLA CHIPS

Makes 4 servings

6 corn tortillas (6" diameter)	$^1/_2$ teaspoon ground cumin
1 teaspoon mild or hot chili powder	

1. Preheat oven to 350° F. Spray baking sheet with nonstick cooking spray.
2. Lightly spray one side of each tortilla with nonstick cooking spray; rub evenly with chili powder and cumin.
3. Cut tortillas in half, then into $3 \times ^1/_4$" strips; place in a single layer on prepared baking sheet. Bake 10–15 minutes. Turn oven off; do not remove tortillas. Let tortillas cool in turned-off oven until crispy.

Each serving provides: $1^1/_2$ Breads

Per serving: 93 Calories, 2 g Total Fat, 0 g Saturated Fat, 0 mg Cholesterol, 67 mg Sodium, 18 g Total Carbohydrate, 2 g Dietary Fiber, 2 g Protein, 70 mg Calcium

CUCUMBER SALAD

For each serving, in small bowl, combine *¹/₂ cup pared sliced cucumber, 1 teaspoon olive oil* and *red wine vinegar to taste.*

Each serving provides: 1 Fat, 1 Vegetable

Per serving: 50 Calories, 5 g Total Fat, 1 g Saturated Fat, 0 mg Cholesterol, 4 mg Sodium, 2 g Total Carbohydrate, 0 g Dietary Fiber, 0 g Protein, 12 mg Calcium

BATIDO

Makes 4 servings

2   cups ice-cold skim milk
1   cup crushed ice or ice cubes (optional) *
2   small mangoes, peeled, pitted and sliced

1   medium banana, peeled and cut into chunks
2   teaspoons granulated sugar

In blender, combine milk, ice, mangoes, banana and sugar; purée until smooth and frothy. Serve immediately.

Each serving (1¹/₂ cups) provides: ¹/₂ Milk, 1¹/₂ Fruits, 10 Optional Calories

Per serving: 127 Calories, 1 g Total Fat, 0 g Saturated Fat, 2 mg Cholesterol, 66 mg Sodium, 28 g Total Carbohydrate, 1 g Dietary Fiber, 5 g Protein, 160 mg Calcium

* Crushed ice will help make the drink thicker.

SHORTCAKE SUPPER

Homey and delicious, this menu gets a touch of glamour with rum-flavored pineapple for dessert. If you prefer, you can bake the shortcake as individual biscuits or, if you are *really* rushed, serve the filling over noodles or crisp toast.

Menu serves 4

- **Chicken Shortcake, 1 serving**
- **Celery with Peas, 1 serving**
- **Broiled Pineapple, 1 serving**
- **Café au Lait, 1 serving**

One serving of this meal provides: $^1/_2$ Milk, 1 Fat, 1 Fruit, 2 Vegetables, 2 Proteins, $1^1/_2$ Breads, 80 Optional Calories; 10 g Fat, 4 g Fiber

Market List

One 12-ounce package fresh mushrooms
1 medium red bell pepper
8 ounces skinless boneless cooked
    chicken breast
Low-fat (1.5%) buttermilk
Nonfat sour cream

Canned pineapple slices
    (no sugar added)
White wine vinegar
One 10-ounce package frozen
    green peas
Dark rum

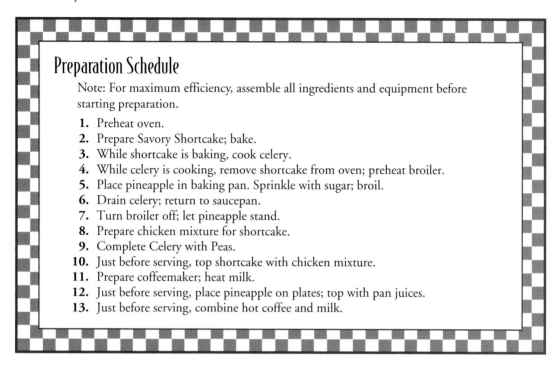

Preparation Schedule

Note: For maximum efficiency, assemble all ingredients and equipment before starting preparation.

1. Preheat oven.
2. Prepare Savory Shortcake; bake.
3. While shortcake is baking, cook celery.
4. While celery is cooking, remove shortcake from oven; preheat broiler.
5. Place pineapple in baking pan. Sprinkle with sugar; broil.
6. Drain celery; return to saucepan.
7. Turn broiler off; let pineapple stand.
8. Prepare chicken mixture for shortcake.
9. Complete Celery with Peas.
10. Just before serving, top shortcake with chicken mixture.
11. Prepare coffeemaker; heat milk.
12. Just before serving, place pineapple on plates; top with pan juices.
13. Just before serving, combine hot coffee and milk.

Shortcake Supper

CHICKEN SHORTCAKE

Makes 4 servings

1 teaspoon vegetable oil	8 ounces diced skinless cooked
1 cup sliced mushrooms	chicken breast
$^1/_2$ cup sliced onion	$^1/_2$ cup nonfat sour cream
$^1/_2$ cup minced red bell pepper	$^1/_4$ teaspoon salt
$^1/_2$ cup low-sodium chicken broth	$^1/_8$ teaspoon freshly ground black pepper
1 tablespoon fresh lemon juice	Savory Shortcake (recipe follows)
$^1/_2$ teaspoon cornstarch	

1. In medium skillet, heat oil; add mushrooms, onion and red pepper. Cook over medium-high heat, stirring frequently, 4–5 minutes, until liquid is evaporated and vegetables are golden.
2. In small bowl, with wire whisk, combine broth, lemon juice and cornstarch, blending until cornstarch is dissolved; stir into onion mixture. Reduce heat to low; simmer, stirring constantly, 1 minute, until slightly thickened. Stir in chicken, sour cream, salt and black pepper; simmer, stirring constantly, 2 minutes longer.
3. Just before serving, place Savory Shortcake on large platter; top with chicken mixture.

Each serving (including shortcake) provides: 1 Fat, 1 Vegetable, 2 Proteins, $1^1/_4$ Breads, 35 Optional Calories

Per serving (including shortcake): 311 Calories, 10 g Total Fat, 2 g Saturated Fat, 52 mg Cholesterol, 736 mg Sodium, 30 g Total Carbohydrate, 2 g Dietary Fiber, 23 g Protein, 133 mg Calcium

SAVORY SHORTCAKE

Makes 4 servings

1 cup minus 1 tablespoon all-purpose flour	$^1/_4$ teaspoon dried thyme leaves
$^1/_2$ teaspoon double-acting baking powder	$^1/_4$ teaspoon dried marjoram leaves
$^1/_2$ teaspoon baking soda	$^1/_8$ teaspoon dried sage leaves
$^1/_2$ teaspoon salt	$^1/_2$ cup low-fat (1.5%) buttermilk
$^1/_2$ teaspoon freshly ground black pepper	1 tablespoon vegetable oil

1. Preheat oven to 400° F. Spray baking sheet with nonstick cooking spray.
2. In medium bowl, combine flour, baking powder, baking soda, salt, pepper, thyme, marjoram and sage. Add buttermilk and oil; mix just until combined.
3. Transfer dough to prepared baking sheet; pat into a 7" circle about $^1/_2$" thick. Bake 15–20 minutes, until golden brown and firm.

Each serving ($^1/_4$ shortcake) provides: $^3/_4$ Fat, $1^1/_4$ Breads, 10 Optional Calories

Per serving: 152 Calories, 4 g Total Fat, 1 g Saturated Fat, 1 mg Cholesterol, 524 mg Sodium, 24 g Total Carbohydrate, 1 g Dietary Fiber, 4 g Protein, 79 mg Calcium

CELERY WITH PEAS

Makes 4 servings

   8 medium celery stalks, cut into 2" sticks   2 tablespoons white wine vinegar
 $^1/_2$ cup frozen green peas $^1/_2$ teaspoon dried dill

1. In medium saucepan, bring 1 quart water to a boil; add celery. Cook 10–12 minutes, just until tender; drain.
2. Return celery to saucepan; add peas, vinegar and dill. Cook over medium heat, stirring gently, 1 minute, until peas are heated and most of the liquid has evaporated.

Each serving (1 heaping cup) provides: 1 Vegetable, $^1/_4$ Bread

Per serving: 25 Calories, 0 g Total Fat, 0 g Saturated Fat, 0 mg Cholesterol, 73 mg Sodium, 5 g Total Carbohydrate, 2 g Dietary Fiber, 1 g Protein, 30 mg Calcium

BROILED PINEAPPLE

Makes 4 servings

   8 drained canned pineapple slices (no sugar added)
   1 tablespoon + 1 teaspoon firmly packed dark brown sugar
 $1^1/_2$ fluid ounces (3 tablespoons) dark rum

1. Preheat broiler. Spray an 8" square metal baking pan with nonstick cooking spray.
2. Place pineapple slices in a single layer in prepared baking pan. Sprinkle pineapple evenly with sugar, then rum. Broil 4" from heat 5–7 minutes, until topping is bubbly. Turn broiler off; serve immediately or let pineapple stand in oven until ready to serve.
3. Just before serving, place 2 pineapple slices on each of 4 plates; drizzle each portion with an equal amount of pan juices.

Each serving provides: 1 Fruit, 45 Optional Calories

Per serving: 117 Calories, 0 g Total Fat, 0 g Saturated Fat, 0 mg Cholesterol, 3 mg Sodium, 24 g Total Carbohydrate, 1 g Dietary Fiber, 1 g Protein, 21 mg Calcium

CAFÉ AU LAIT

For each serving, in coffee cup, combine $^1/_2$ *cup hot decaffeinated coffee* and $^1/_2$ *cup hot skim milk.*

Each serving provides: $^1/_2$ Milk

Per serving: 45 Calories, 0 g Total Fat, 0 g Saturated Fat, 2 mg Cholesterol, 66 mg Sodium, 6 g Total Carbohydrate, 0 g Dietary Fiber, 4 g Protein, 153 mg Calcium

COZY AUTUMN DINNER

People will rave about this creamy chowder that looks like it took hours to make; thanks to the food processor, only you will know how easy it was to prepare. Crunchy popovers and slightly sweet cucumber salad are perfect accompaniments. Then top off the meal with a refreshing fresh fruit salad made with the best the season has to offer.

Menu serves 4

- 🕐 **Chicken and Corn Chowder, 1 serving**
- 🕐 **Cheese Popovers, 1 serving**
- 🕐 **Lemony Cucumber Salad, 1 serving**
- **Fresh Fruit Salad, $^1/_2$ cup per serving**
- **Mint Tea**

One serving of this meal provides: $^3/_4$ Milk, 1 Fat, 1 Fruit, $3^1/_4$ Vegetables, 2 Proteins, 2 Breads, 90 Optional Calories; 19 g Fat, 8 g Fiber

Market List

Fresh fruit for salad
5 ounces red potatoes
1 medium red bell pepper
1 medium green bell pepper
2 cups corn kernels, fresh or frozen
3 medium cucumbers
Fresh flat-leaf parsley

Fresh dill
3 slices bacon
4 ounces skinless boneless cooked
      chicken breast
$1^1/_2$ ounces extra-sharp cheddar cheese
Corn oil
Grated Parmesan cheese

Special Equipment

Twelve $2^3/_4$" shiny aluminum muffin
      or popover cups

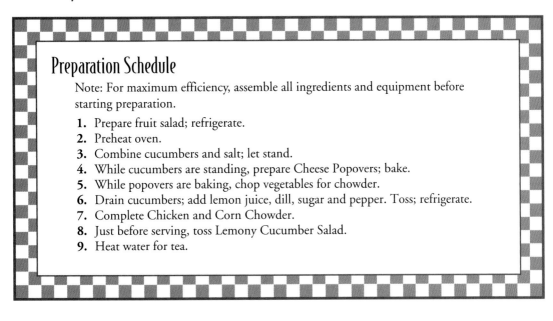

Preparation Schedule

Note: For maximum efficiency, assemble all ingredients and equipment before starting preparation.

1. Prepare fruit salad; refrigerate.
2. Preheat oven.
3. Combine cucumbers and salt; let stand.
4. While cucumbers are standing, prepare Cheese Popovers; bake.
5. While popovers are baking, chop vegetables for chowder.
6. Drain cucumbers; add lemon juice, dill, sugar and pepper. Toss; refrigerate.
7. Complete Chicken and Corn Chowder.
8. Just before serving, toss Lemony Cucumber Salad.
9. Heat water for tea.

CHICKEN AND CORN CHOWDER

Makes 4 servings

2 medium onions, cut into chunks
5 ounces red potatoes, cut into chunks
2 medium celery stalks, cut into chunks
1 medium carrot, cut into chunks
$1/2$ medium red bell pepper, seeded and cut into chunks
$1/2$ medium green bell pepper, seeded and cut into chunks
2 tablespoons packed flat-leaf parsley sprigs
2 teaspoons corn oil

2 cups fresh or frozen corn kernels
2 cups low-sodium chicken broth
$1^1/2$ cups evaporated skimmed milk
4 ounces finely diced skinless cooked chicken breast
3 slices crisp-cooked bacon, crumbled
1 teaspoon salt
$1/2$ teaspoon freshly ground black pepper
Hot pepper sauce to taste

1. In food processor, one at a time, finely chop onions, potatoes, celery, carrot, red and green peppers and parsley; set aside.
2. In large saucepan, heat oil; add chopped onions. Cook over medium-high heat, stirring frequently, 10 minutes, until golden brown. Add potatoes, celery, carrot, red and green peppers, corn, broth, milk, chicken and bacon; bring liquid to a boil. Reduce heat to low; simmer, stirring occasionally, 10 minutes, until vegetables are tender.
3. Add parsley, salt, black pepper and hot pepper sauce to chowder; stir to combine.

Each serving (2 cups) provides: $3/4$ Milk, $1/2$ Fat, $1^3/4$ Vegetables, 1 Protein, $1^1/4$ Breads, 40 Optional Calories

Per serving: 323 Calories, 9 g Total Fat, 2 g Saturated Fat, 33 mg Cholesterol, 826 mg Sodium, 41 g Total Carbohydrate, 5 g Dietary Fiber, 22 g Protein, 314 mg Calcium

CHEESE POPOVERS

Makes 4 servings

$^2/_3$ cup skim milk
$^1/_2$ cup + 2 tablespoons all-purpose flour
2 teaspoons olive oil
$^1/_4$ teaspoon salt
$^1/_4$ teaspoon freshly ground black pepper

Pinch ground red pepper
2 eggs, beaten
$1^1/_2$ ounces extra-sharp cheddar cheese, grated
2 tablespoons grated Parmesan cheese

1. Preheat oven to 450° F. Spray twelve $2^3/_4$" shiny aluminum muffin or popover cups * with nonstick cooking spray.
2. In medium bowl, with wire whisk, combine milk, flour, oil, salt, black pepper and red pepper, blending until combined; blend in eggs.
3. Spoon 1 tablespoon batter into each prepared cup; sprinkle evenly with cheddar and Parmesan cheese. Top with remaining batter. Bake 15 minutes; reduce oven temperature to 350° F. Bake 15 minutes longer, until sides of popovers are firm. Serve warm.

Each serving (3 popovers) provides: $^1/_2$ Fat, 1 Protein, $^3/_4$ Bread, 40 Optional Calories

Per serving: 203 Calories, 10 g Total Fat, 4 g Saturated Fat, 120 mg Cholesterol, 301 mg Sodium, 18 g Total Carbohydrate, 1 g Dietary Fiber, 10 g Protein, 179 mg Calcium

   * *Use shiny aluminum cups; if dark cups are used, popovers may burn.*

LEMONY CUCUMBER SALAD

Makes 4 servings

3 cups pared, seeded and sliced cucumbers
$^1/_2$ teaspoon salt
$^1/_4$ cup fresh lemon juice

1 tablespoon minced fresh dill
2 teaspoons granulated sugar
$^1/_4$ teaspoon freshly ground black pepper

1. In medium bowl, combine cucumbers and salt, tossing to combine. Let stand 15 minutes.
2. Drain accumulated liquid from cucumbers, pressing cucumbers with back of wooden spoon to release as much liquid as possible. Add lemon juice, dill, sugar and pepper; toss to combine. Refrigerate, covered, until chilled. Just before serving, toss again.

Each serving ($^3/_4$ cup) provides: $1^1/_2$ Vegetables, 10 Optional Calories

Per serving: 27 Calories, 0 g Total Fat, 0 g Saturated Fat, 0 mg Cholesterol, 214 mg Sodium, 7 g Total Carbohydrate, 1 g Dietary Fiber, 1 g Protein, 24 mg Calcium

QUICK AND EASY CHICKEN DINNER

This quick and pretty meal is sophisticated enough to serve to company. Crown the meal with a prune compote laced with sweet vermouth and a glass of crisp, cold white wine.

Menu serves 4

- **Lemon-Broiled Chicken, 1 serving**
- **Tomato-Basil Crostini, 1 serving**
- **Arugula Salad, 1 serving**
- **Prunes in Vermouth, 1 serving**
- **Dry White Wine, 4 fluid ounces per serving**

One serving of this meal provides: $1^{1}/_{2}$ Fats, 2 Fruits, $5^{1}/_{2}$ Vegetables, $3^{1}/_{4}$ Proteins, $1^{1}/_{2}$ Breads, 125 Optional Calories; 15 g Fat, 9 g Fiber

Market List

2 bunches arugula
6 medium tomatoes
Fresh basil
Four 6-ounce chicken breasts
1 loaf French or Italian bread

Chopped walnuts
Walnut oil
Pitted prunes, medium
Sweet red vermouth

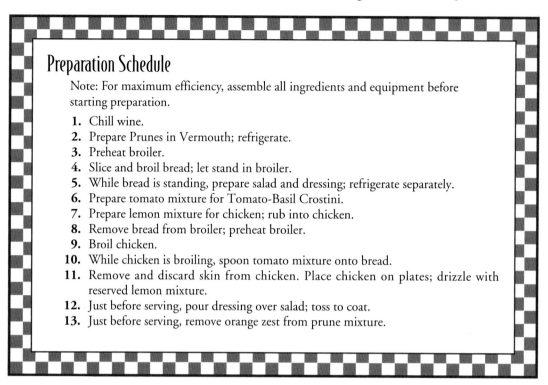

Preparation Schedule

Note: For maximum efficiency, assemble all ingredients and equipment before starting preparation.

1. Chill wine.
2. Prepare Prunes in Vermouth; refrigerate.
3. Preheat broiler.
4. Slice and broil bread; let stand in broiler.
5. While bread is standing, prepare salad and dressing; refrigerate separately.
6. Prepare tomato mixture for Tomato-Basil Crostini.
7. Prepare lemon mixture for chicken; rub into chicken.
8. Remove bread from broiler; preheat broiler.
9. Broil chicken.
10. While chicken is broiling, spoon tomato mixture onto bread.
11. Remove and discard skin from chicken. Place chicken on plates; drizzle with reserved lemon mixture.
12. Just before serving, pour dressing over salad; toss to coat.
13. Just before serving, remove orange zest from prune mixture.

LEMON-BROILED CHICKEN

Makes 4 servings

¹/₄ cup fresh lemon juice
¹/₂ teaspoon dried thyme leaves
¹/₂ teaspoon dried rosemary leaves

¹/₂ teaspoon coarsely ground black pepper
Four 6-ounce chicken breasts

1. Preheat broiler. Spray rack in broiler pan with nonstick cooking spray.
2. In small bowl, combine lemon juice, thyme, rosemary and pepper.
3. Carefully loosen skin of chicken. Rub half of the lemon mixture on chicken under skin; reserve remaining mixture. Place chicken skin side up on prepared broiler rack; broil 4" from heat, turning once, 10 minutes, until browned and cooked through.
4. To serve, remove and discard skin from chicken breasts; place one breast on each of 4 plates. Drizzle each with an equal amount of reserved lemon mixture.

Each serving provides: 3 Proteins

Per serving: 147 Calories, 3 g Total Fat, 1 g Saturated Fat, 72 mg Cholesterol, 63 mg Sodium, 2 g Total Carbohydrate, 0 g Dietary Fiber, 26 g Protein, 20 mg Calcium

Tomato-Basil Crostini

Makes 4 servings

6 ounces French or Italian bread, cut into 12 equal slices	$^1/_2$ cup packed fresh basil leaves, slivered
6 medium tomatoes, blanched, peeled, seeded and diced	1 teaspoon olive oil
	1 teaspoon fresh lemon juice
	Pinch salt

1. Preheat broiler.
2. Place bread slices on baking sheet; broil 1–2 minutes on each side, until golden brown. Turn broiler off; do not remove bread. Let bread cool in broiler until crispy.
3. In small bowl, combine tomatoes, basil, oil, lemon juice and salt; set aside.
4. Just before serving, spoon an equal amount of tomato mixture onto each slice of bread.

Each serving (3 crostinis) provides: $^1/_4$ Fat, 3 Vegetables, $1^1/_2$ Breads

Per serving: 184 Calories, 3 g Total Fat, 1 g Saturated Fat, 0 mg Cholesterol, 314 mg Sodium, 35 g Total Carbohydrate, 4 g Dietary Fiber, 6 g Protein, 115 mg Calcium

Arugula Salad

Makes 4 servings

5 cups shredded arugula	1 tablespoon balsamic vinegar
1 ounce finely chopped walnuts	Pinch salt
1 tablespoon walnut oil	Pinch freshly ground black pepper

1. In large salad bowl, combine arugula and walnuts.
2. To prepare dressing, in small bowl, combine oil, vinegar, salt and pepper.
3. Just before serving, pour dressing over salad; toss to coat.

Each serving ($1^1/_4$ cups) provides: $1^1/_4$ Fats, $2^1/_2$ Vegetables, $^1/_4$ Protein

Per serving: 81 Calories, 8 g Total Fat, 1 g Saturated Fat, 0 mg Cholesterol, 51 mg Sodium, 2 g Total Carbohydrate, 1 g Dietary Fiber, 2 g Protein, 58 mg Calcium

PRUNES IN VERMOUTH

Makes 4 servings

24 medium pitted prunes
2 fluid ounces (¹/₄ cup) sweet red
    vermouth

2 × ¹/₂" strip orange zest *
1 teaspoon granulated sugar

1. In small saucepan, combine prunes, ¹/₂ cup water, the vermouth, orange zest and sugar; bring liquid to a boil. Reduce heat to low; simmer, covered, 10 minutes, until prunes are tender.
2. Cool prune mixture slightly, then refrigerate, covered, until chilled. Remove orange zest before serving.

Each serving provides: 2 Fruits, 25 Optional Calories

Per serving: 130 Calories, 0 g Total Fat, 0 g Saturated Fat, 0 mg Cholesterol, 2 mg Sodium, 30 g Total Carbohydrate, 3 g Dietary Fiber, 1 g Protein, 24 mg Calcium

* *The zest of the orange is the peel without any of the pith (white membrane). To remove zest from orange, use a zester or vegetable grater; wrap orange in plastic wrap and refrigerate for use at another time.*

SIMPLE SPRINGTIME SUPPER

This menu says, "Welcome to spring!" Fragrant and flavorful, these wonderful springtime dishes take such a short time to cook that you'll have plenty of time to enjoy the coming of the new season.

Menu serves 4

- **Asparagus Vinaigrette, 1 serving**
- **Orange-Broiled Chicken Thighs, 1 serving**
- **New Potatoes with Rosemary-Dijon Dressing, 1 serving**
- **Fresh Fruit Salad, $^1/_2$ cup per serving**
- **Sparkling Mineral Water with Lime Wedge**

One serving of this meal provides: $^1/_4$ Fat, $1^1/_4$ Fruits, 1 Vegetable, 3 Proteins, $^3/_4$ Bread, 30 Optional Calories; 11 g Fat, 5 g Fiber

Market List

Fresh fruit for salad
15   ounces tiny new potatoes
24   asparagus spears
 1   medium red onion
Fresh thyme

Fresh rosemary
Four 6-ounce chicken thighs
Extra-virgin olive oil
Frozen orange juice concentrate

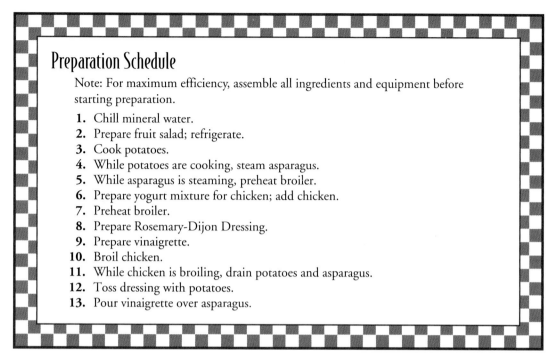

Preparation Schedule

Note: For maximum efficiency, assemble all ingredients and equipment before starting preparation.

1. Chill mineral water.
2. Prepare fruit salad; refrigerate.
3. Cook potatoes.
4. While potatoes are cooking, steam asparagus.
5. While asparagus is steaming, preheat broiler.
6. Prepare yogurt mixture for chicken; add chicken.
7. Preheat broiler.
8. Prepare Rosemary-Dijon Dressing.
9. Prepare vinaigrette.
10. Broil chicken.
11. While chicken is broiling, drain potatoes and asparagus.
12. Toss dressing with potatoes.
13. Pour vinaigrette over asparagus.

ASPARAGUS VINAIGRETTE

Makes 4 servings

24 asparagus spears, trimmed	1 teaspoon extra-virgin olive oil
3 tablespoons balsamic vinegar	1 garlic clove, minced
2 tablespoons minced red onion	$^1/_4$ teaspoon freshly ground black pepper

1. Fill large saucepan with 1" water; set steamer rack in saucepan. Place asparagus on rack. Bring water to a boil; reduce heat to low. Steam asparagus over simmering water, covered, until tender.
2. Meanwhile, in small bowl, combine vinegar, onion, oil, garlic and pepper.
3. Transfer asparagus to medium decorative platter; top with vinegar mixture.

Each serving provides: $^1/_4$ Fat, 1 Vegetable

Per serving: 34 Calories, 1 g Total Fat, 0 g Saturated Fat, 0 mg Cholesterol, 3 mg Sodium, 4 g Total Carbohydrate, 1 g Dietary Fiber, 3 g Protein, 22 mg Calcium

Simple Springtime Supper

ORANGE-BROILED CHICKEN THIGHS

Makes 4 servings

$^1/_2$ cup plain nonfat yogurt
3 tablespoons thawed frozen orange juice
     concentrate
2 teaspoons chopped fresh thyme

2 teaspoons grated orange zest *
$^1/_2$ teaspoon freshly ground black pepper
Four 6-ounce chicken thighs, skinned

1. Preheat broiler.
2. In an 8" square baking pan, combine yogurt, orange juice concentrate, thyme, orange zest and pepper. Add chicken; turn to coat thoroughly. Let stand 5 minutes.
3. Broil chicken mixture 5" from heat, turning once, about 15 minutes or until chicken is browned and cooked through. Serve with yogurt mixture.

Each serving provides: $^1/_4$ Fruit, 3 Proteins, 25 Optional Calories

Per serving: 217 Calories, 9 g Total Fat, 3 g Saturated Fat, 81 mg Cholesterol, 97 mg Sodium, 8 g Total Carbohydrate, 0 g Dietary Fiber, 24 g Protein, 77 mg Calcium

   * *The zest of the orange is the peel without any of the pith (white membrane). To remove zest from orange, use a zester or fine side of a vegetable grater; wrap orange in plastic wrap and refrigerate for use at another time.*

NEW POTATOES WITH ROSEMARY-DIJON DRESSING

Makes 4 servings

15 ounces tiny new potatoes
2 tablespoons plain nonfat yogurt
1 teaspoon chopped fresh rosemary

1 teaspoon Dijon-style mustard
$^1/_2$ teaspoon fresh lemon juice

1. In medium saucepan, cover potatoes with water. Bring water to a boil; reduce heat to low. Simmer 12 minutes, until potatoes are tender; drain.
2. In medium bowl, combine yogurt, rosemary, mustard and lemon juice. Add potatoes; toss to coat.

Each serving provides: $^3/_4$ Bread, 5 Optional Calories

Per serving: 92 Calories, 0 g Total Fat, 0 g Saturated Fat, 0 mg Cholesterol, 51 mg Sodium, 20 g Total Carbohydrate, 2 g Dietary Fiber, 2 g Protein, 15 mg Calcium

A SUMMER LUNCHEON

With its three luncheon favorites—creamy pasta, salad topped with tasty bits of chicken, then a light finale with just enough chocolate to make it a real dessert—this is the kind of meal you'd expect to eat only in a trendy restaurant.

Menu serves 4

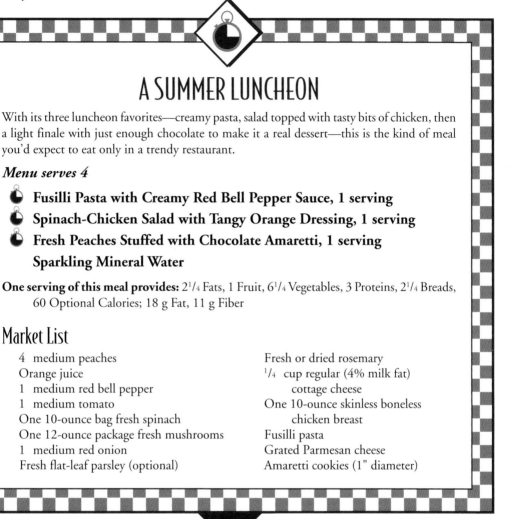

🕐 **Fusilli Pasta with Creamy Red Bell Pepper Sauce, 1 serving**

🕐 **Spinach-Chicken Salad with Tangy Orange Dressing, 1 serving**

🕐 **Fresh Peaches Stuffed with Chocolate Amaretti, 1 serving**

Sparkling Mineral Water

One serving of this meal provides: $2^1/_4$ Fats, 1 Fruit, $6^1/_4$ Vegetables, 3 Proteins, $2^1/_4$ Breads, 60 Optional Calories; 18 g Fat, 11 g Fiber

Market List

4 medium peaches	Fresh or dried rosemary
Orange juice	$^1/_4$ cup regular (4% milk fat)
1 medium red bell pepper	cottage cheese
1 medium tomato	One 10-ounce skinless boneless
One 10-ounce bag fresh spinach	chicken breast
One 12-ounce package fresh mushrooms	Fusilli pasta
1 medium red onion	Grated Parmesan cheese
Fresh flat-leaf parsley (optional)	Amaretti cookies (1" diameter)

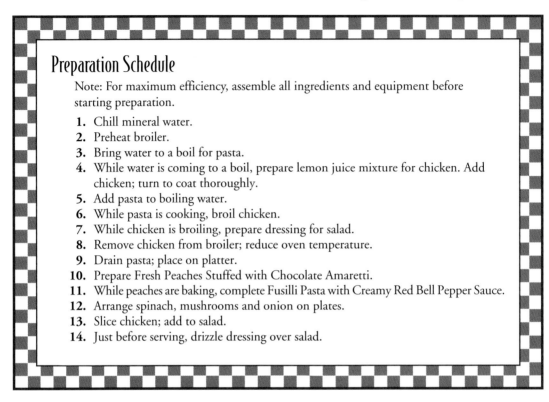

Preparation Schedule

Note: For maximum efficiency, assemble all ingredients and equipment before starting preparation.

1. Chill mineral water.
2. Preheat broiler.
3. Bring water to a boil for pasta.
4. While water is coming to a boil, prepare lemon juice mixture for chicken. Add chicken; turn to coat thoroughly.
5. Add pasta to boiling water.
6. While pasta is cooking, broil chicken.
7. While chicken is broiling, prepare dressing for salad.
8. Remove chicken from broiler; reduce oven temperature.
9. Drain pasta; place on platter.
10. Prepare Fresh Peaches Stuffed with Chocolate Amaretti.
11. While peaches are baking, complete Fusilli Pasta with Creamy Red Bell Pepper Sauce.
12. Arrange spinach, mushrooms and onion on plates.
13. Slice chicken; add to salad.
14. Just before serving, drizzle dressing over salad.

FUSILLI PASTA WITH CREAMY RED BELL PEPPER SAUCE

Makes 4 servings

6 ounces fusilli pasta
1 medium red bell pepper, cored, seeded and cut into $^1/_4$" slices
$^1/_2$ cup blanched, peeled, seeded and chopped tomato
$^1/_4$ cup chopped onion
2 teaspoons olive oil

Pinch salt
Freshly ground black pepper to taste
$^1/_4$ cup regular (4% milk fat) cottage cheese
1 tablespoon + 1 teaspoon grated Parmesan cheese
Fresh flat-leaf parsley sprigs to garnish (optional)

1. In large pot of boiling water, cook fusilli 10–12 minutes, until tender. Drain and place on large decorative platter; keep warm.
2. Meanwhile, in large nonstick skillet, combine red pepper, tomato, onion, oil, salt, black pepper and $^1/_2$ cup water; cook over medium-low heat, covered, stirring frequently, 15 minutes, until liquid has evaporated and vegetables are tender, adding more water, 1 tablespoon at a time, just to keep mixture from sticking.

3. Transfer vegetable mixture to food processor or blender; add cottage cheese. Purée until smooth.
4. Top pasta with vegetable mixture; sprinkle with Parmesan cheese. Serve garnished with parsley if desired.

Each serving (2 cups) provides: $1/2$ Fat, 1 Vegetable, $1/4$ Protein, 2 Breads, 10 Optional Calories

Per serving: 214 Calories, 4 g Total Fat, 1 g Saturated Fat, 3 mg Cholesterol, 123 mg Sodium, 36 g Total Carbohydrate, 2 g Dietary Fiber, 8 g Protein, 44 mg Calcium

SPINACH-CHICKEN SALAD WITH TANGY ORANGE DRESSING

Makes 4 servings

2 tablespoons fresh lemon juice
1 tablespoon + 1 teaspoon olive oil
1 tablespoon + 1 teaspoon prepared yellow mustard
1 tablespoon chopped fresh rosemary leaves or $1/2$ teaspoon dried
2 garlic cloves, minced
$1/4$ teaspoon salt
$1/4$ teaspoon freshly ground black pepper
One 10-ounce skinless boneless chicken breast, butterflied and pounded thin

2 tablespoons orange juice
1 tablespoon red wine vinegar
Granulated sugar substitute to equal 1 tablespoon sugar
1 teaspoon balsamic vinegar
8 cups packed spinach leaves, well rinsed, dried and torn into bite-size pieces
2 cups sliced mushrooms
1 medium red onion, thinly sliced

1. Preheat broiler. Spray broiler pan with nonstick cooking spray.
2. In shallow bowl, with wire whisk, combine lemon juice, 1 teaspoon of the oil, the mustard, rosemary, garlic, $1/8$ teaspoon of the salt and $1/8$ teaspoon of the pepper. Add chicken; turn to coat.
3. Transfer chicken to prepared broiler pan, reserving remaining lemon juice mixture; broil 4" from heat 3–4 minutes, until golden brown. Turn chicken; top with reserved lemon juice mixture. Broil 3–4 minutes longer, until golden brown and cooked through.
4. Meanwhile, to prepare dressing, in small bowl, combine the remaining 1 tablespoon oil, the orange juice, wine vinegar, sugar substitute, balsamic vinegar, remaining $1/8$ teaspoon salt and remaining $1/8$ teaspoon pepper.
5. Divide spinach, mushrooms and onion evenly among 4 plates, arranging vegetables in a circle.
6. Cut chicken into $1/4$" slices; place one-fourth of the chicken slices in center of each salad. Drizzle each salad with one-fourth of the dressing.

Each serving (4 cups) provides: 1 Fat, $5^{1}/4$ Vegetables, 2 Proteins, 5 Optional Calories

Per serving: 182 Calories, 6 g Total Fat, 1 g Saturated Fat, 41 mg Cholesterol, 361 mg Sodium, 11 g Total Carbohydrate, 4 g Dietary Fiber, 22 g Protein, 166 mg Calcium

FRESH PEACHES STUFFED WITH CHOCOLATE AMARETTI

Makes 4 servings

1 egg, beaten
4 amaretti cookies (1" diameter), crumbled
3 tablespoons plain dried bread crumbs
2 tablespoons unsweetened cocoa powder

Granulated sugar substitute to equal
   1 tablespoon + 1$^1/_2$ teaspoons sugar
4 medium peaches, halved and pitted

1. Preheat oven to 400° F.
2. In small bowl, combine egg, cookie crumbs, bread crumbs, cocoa powder and sugar substitute.
3. Fill each peach half with an equal amount of crumb mixture, mounding as necessary. Place in 2-quart shallow baking dish; bake 20 minutes, until peaches are soft and crumb mixture forms a light crust. Serve warm or at room temperature.

Each serving (2 filled peach halves) provides: $^3/_4$ Fat, 1 Fruit, $^3/_4$ Protein, $^1/_4$ Bread, 45 Optional Calories

Per serving: 207 Calories, 7 g Total Fat, 1 g Saturated Fat, 53 mg Cholesterol, 70 mg Sodium, 33 g Total Carbohydrate, 4 g Dietary Fiber, 7 g Protein, 56 mg Calcium

SUMMER HARVEST MEAL

Make this meal after a trip to the farmers' market. The menu shows off the best of summer produce: fresh peaches, tomatoes, greens, zucchini and brilliant, flavorful herbs.

Menu serves 4

- **Cold Tomato-Basil Soup, 1 serving**
- **Summer Vegetable Chicken Salad, 1 serving**

  Crusty French Roll, 1 ounce per serving
- **Peaches with Mint, 1 serving**

  Lemonade, 8 fluid ounces per serving

One serving of this meal provides: $1^{1}/_{4}$ Fats, 1 Fruit, $6^{1}/_{4}$ Vegetables, $1^{1}/_{2}$ Proteins, 1 Bread, 100 Optional Calories; 11 g Fat, 8 g Fiber

Market List

4 medium peaches	Fresh tarragon
Orange juice	Fresh basil
1 medium red bell pepper	6 ounces skinless boneless cooked
1 medium zucchini	chicken breast
1 medium red onion	Extra-virgin olive oil
6 medium tomatoes	Crusty French rolls
Assorted salad greens	Lemonade
Fresh mint	Sauternes or other sweet wine

Preparation Schedule

Note: For maximum efficiency, assemble all ingredients and equipment before starting preparation.

1. Prepare chicken mixture and salad dressing; combine and refrigerate.
2. Prepare Cold Tomato-Basil Soup; refrigerate.
3. Prepare Peaches with Mint.
4. Just before serving, combine chicken-dressing mixture with greens.

Cold Tomato–Basil Soup

Makes 4 servings

6 medium tomatoes, blanched, peeled, seeded and cut into chunks
$^1/_4$ cup packed fresh basil leaves, chopped
1 tablespoon red wine vinegar

2 teaspoons extra-virgin olive oil
$^1/_2$ teaspoon salt
$^1/_4$ teaspoon freshly ground black pepper

1. In food processor, combine tomatoes, basil, vinegar, oil, salt and pepper; with on-off motion, pulse processor 2–3 times, until mixture is chunky-smooth (do not purée).
2. Transfer mixture to large bowl; refrigerate, covered, until chilled.

Each serving provides: $^1/_2$ Fat, 3 Vegetables

Per serving: 72 Calories, 3 g Total Fat, 0 g Saturated Fat, 0 mg Cholesterol, 295 mg Sodium, 12 g Total Carbohydrate, 3 g Dietary Fiber, 2 g Protein, 38 mg Calcium

Summer Vegetable Chicken Salad

Makes 4 servings

6 ounces shredded skinless cooked chicken breast
1 medium red bell pepper, cored, seeded and slivered
1 medium zucchini, thinly sliced
$^1/_2$ cup thinly sliced red onion
2 tablespoons chopped fresh tarragon

2 tablespoons fresh lemon juice
2 tablespoons orange juice
1 tablespoon extra-virgin olive oil
1 garlic clove, minced
$^1/_2$ teaspoon freshly ground black pepper
$^1/_4$ teaspoon salt
4 cups torn assorted salad greens

1. In large bowl, combine chicken, red pepper, zucchini and onion; set aside.
2. In small bowl, with wire whisk, combine tarragon, lemon and orange juices, oil, garlic, black pepper and salt. Pour over chicken mixture; toss to combine. Refrigerate, covered, until chilled.
3. Just before serving, place greens in large salad bowl. Top greens with chicken mixture; toss to combine.

Each serving provides: $^3/_4$ Fat, $3^1/_4$ Vegetables, $1^1/_2$ Proteins, 5 Optional Calories

Per serving: 149 Calories, 7 g Total Fat, 1 g Saturated Fat, 38 mg Cholesterol, 181 mg Sodium, 8 g Total Carbohydrate, 2 g Dietary Fiber, 14 g Protein, 61 mg Calcium

Summer Harvest Meal

Peaches with Mint

Makes 4 servings

4 medium peaches, pitted and cut into
   thin wedges
1 tablespoon chopped fresh mint

$^1/_2$ fluid ounce (1 tablespoon) sauternes or
   other sweet wine

In medium bowl, combine peaches, mint and sauternes; let stand 15 minutes before serving.

Each serving provides: 1 Fruit, 5 Optional Calories

Per serving: 58 Calories, 0 g Total Fat, 0 g Saturated Fat, 0 mg Cholesterol, 0 mg Sodium, 14 g Total Carbohydrate, 2 g Dietary Fiber, 1 g Protein, 7 mg Calcium

FAST AND EASY MIDWEEK DINNER

Make this bright salad with leftovers from Sunday's roast chicken, or use leftover turkey. If you bake a double batch of these savory biscuits, you can freeze and reheat them for an even faster meal next time. The Bittersweet Fruit uses Italian bitters, an aperitif that has a natural affinity for fruit; for a change of taste, try it with ruby-red grapefruit instead of oranges.

Menu serves 4

- **Roast Chicken Salad, 1 serving**
  Sliced Tomatoes, ¹/₂ cup per serving
- **Herb and Cheese Biscuits, 1 serving**
- **Bittersweet Fruit, 1 serving**
- **White Wine Spritzer, 1 serving**

One serving of this meal provides: ¹/₄ Milk, 1 Fat, 1 Fruit, 3 Vegetables, 2³/₄ Proteins, 2 Breads, 110 Optional Calories; 13 g Fat, 6 g Fiber

Market List

1 large bunch seedless green grapes
Tomatoes
1 medium red bell pepper
1 bunch arugula or 1 small head radicchio
8 ounces skinless boneless roast chicken breasts

Pitted black olives, large
Grated Parmesan cheese
One 10-ounce package frozen cut green beans
Club soda
Italian bitters
Nonalcoholic dry white wine

Preparation Schedule

Note: For maximum efficiency, assemble all ingredients and equipment before starting preparation.

1. Prepare Bittersweet Fruit; refrigerate.
2. Prepare Herb and Cheese Biscuits; bake.
3. Prepare Roast Chicken Salad.
4. Slice tomatoes.
5. Just before serving, line platter with arugula; top with chicken salad.
6. Just before serving, prepare White Wine Spritzer.

ROAST CHICKEN SALAD

Makes 4 servings

1 tablespoon olive oil	2 cups cooked frozen cut green beans
1 cup finely diced red bell pepper	1/4 cup fresh lemon juice
2 garlic cloves, pressed	6 large pitted black olives, sliced
1/4 teaspoon dried red pepper flakes	8 arugula or radicchio leaves
8 ounces skinless boneless roast chicken breasts, slivered	

1. In medium skillet, heat oil; add red bell pepper, garlic and red pepper flakes. Cook over medium heat, stirring frequently, 1–2 minutes, until bell pepper is softened and garlic is lightly golden. Remove from heat; stir in chicken, green beans, lemon juice and olives.
2. Just before serving, arrange arugula leaves on large decorative platter; top with chicken mixture.

Each serving provides: 1 Fat, 2 Vegetables, 2 Proteins

Per serving: 165 Calories, 7 g Total Fat, 1 g Saturated Fat, 48 mg Cholesterol, 115 mg Sodium, 9 g Total Carbohydrate, 2 g Dietary Fiber, 19 g Protein, 61 mg Calcium

HERB AND CHEESE BISCUITS

Makes 4 servings

1 1/2 cups all-purpose flour	1/2 teaspoon fennel seeds
2 1/4 ounces grated Parmesan cheese	1/4 teaspoon salt
1 teaspoon double-acting baking powder	1/4 teaspoon freshly ground black pepper
1/2 teaspoon baking soda	Pinch ground red pepper
1/2 teaspoon dried oregano leaves	1 cup plain nonfat yogurt

1. Preheat oven to 425° F. Spray baking sheet with nonstick cooking spray.
2. In medium bowl, combine all but 2 tablespoons of the flour, the Parmesan cheese, baking powder, baking soda, oregano, fennel, salt, black pepper and red pepper; stir in yogurt and 2 tablespoons water.
3. Sprinkle work surface and hands with remaining 2 tablespoons flour; turn dough out onto prepared surface. Lightly pat dough into a 7 × 6" rectangle. With sharp knife, cut dough into 8 equal pieces; transfer pieces to prepared baking sheet. Bake 15 minutes; with spatula, carefully turn biscuits over. Bake 5–10 minutes longer, until biscuits are golden brown and crispy.

Each serving (2 biscuits) provides: 1/4 Milk, 3/4 Protein, 2 Breads, 10 Optional Calories

Per serving: 279 Calories, 6 g Total Fat, 3 g Saturated Fat, 14 mg Cholesterol, 755 mg Sodium, 41 g Total Carbohydrate, 1 g Dietary Fiber, 15 g Protein, 414 mg Calcium

BITTERSWEET FRUIT

Makes 4 servings

2 small navel oranges, peeled and thinly sliced	2 fluid ounces ($^1/_4$ cup) Italian bitters *
24 large seedless green grapes, halved	

1. Arrange orange slices on medium decorative platter.
2. In small bowl, combine grapes and bitters; spoon over orange slices. Refrigerate, covered, until chilled.

Each serving provides: 1 Fruit, 50 Optional Calories

Per serving: 99 Calories, 0 g Total Fat, 0 g Saturated Fat, 0 mg Cholesterol, 1 mg Sodium, 19 g Total Carbohydrate, 2 g Dietary Fiber, 1 g Protein, 32 mg Calcium

* Italian bitters, such as Campari®, is available in most liquor stores.

WHITE WINE SPRITZER

For each serving, in tall glass, combine *4 fluid ounces ($^1/_2$ cup) nonalcoholic dry white wine* and enough *club soda* and *ice cubes* to fill glass.

Each serving provides: 50 Optional Calories

Per serving: 50 Calories, 0 g Total Fat, 0 g Saturated Fat, 0 mg Cholesterol, 25 mg Sodium, 7 g Total Carbohydrate, 0 g Dietary Fiber, 0 g Protein, 6 mg Calcium

SPECIAL CHICKEN SALAD SUPPER

If you have time, make extra pita chips and store them in a canister for snacking, or serve them with soups and other salads. This salad is also delicious made with plain cooked chicken breast instead of smoked chicken.

Menu serves 4

- Smoked Chicken Salad, 1 serving
- Spicy Pita Chips, 1 serving
- Honey-Broiled Grapefruit, 1 serving
- Iced Tea with Mint

One serving of this meal provides: 1 Fat, 1 Fruit, 3 Vegetables, 2 Proteins, 2 Breads, 55 Optional Calories; 7 g Fat, 6 g Fiber

Market List

2 medium grapefruits	
12 cherry tomatoes	Four 2-ounce pitas
1 medium yellow bell pepper	Tomato juice
1 medium red onion	One 10-ounce package frozen
1 small head radicchio	artichoke hearts
Fresh basil	Onion powder
Fresh mint	Garlic salt
8 ounces skinless boneless	Dry mustard
smoked chicken	Italian bitters

Preparation Schedule

Note: For maximum efficiency, assemble all ingredients and equipment before starting preparation.

1. Prepare iced tea; refrigerate.
2. Preheat oven.
3. Prepare Spicy Pita Chips; let stand in oven.
4. While pita chips are standing, prepare Smoked Chicken Salad; refrigerate.
5. Cut grapefruits; prepare honey mixture and drizzle over grapefruits.
6. Remove chips from oven; preheat broiler.
7. Line platter with radicchio leaves; top with chicken mixture.
8. Broil grapefruits.
9. Place grapefruits on plates; drizzle with pan juices and remaining honey mixture.

SMOKED CHICKEN SALAD

Makes 4 servings

 8 ounces diced skinless smoked chicken
 2 cups drained cooked frozen artichoke
       hearts, quartered
12 cherry tomatoes, halved
 1 cup diced yellow bell pepper
$^1/_2$ cup diced red onion
$^1/_2$ cup packed fresh basil leaves, slivered

 2 tablespoons fresh lemon juice
 1 tablespoon olive oil
$^1/_4$ teaspoon freshly ground black pepper
$^1/_4$ teaspoon dry mustard
Pinch salt
 8 radicchio leaves

1. In large bowl, combine chicken, artichoke hearts, cherry tomatoes, yellow pepper, onion and basil.
2. In small bowl, with wire whisk, combine lemon juice, oil, black pepper, mustard and salt. Pour lemon juice mixture over chicken mixture; toss to coat. Refrigerate, covered, until chilled.
3. Just before serving, line large decorative platter with radicchio leaves; top with chicken mixture.

Each serving (1$^1/_2$ cups) provides: $^3/_4$ Fat, 2$^3/_4$ Vegetables, 2 Proteins

Per serving: 150 Calories, 5 g Total Fat, 1 g Saturated Fat, 24 mg Cholesterol, 650 mg Sodium, 14 g Total Carbohydrate, 5 g Dietary Fiber, 16 g Protein, 87 mg Calcium

SPICY PITA CHIPS

Makes 4 servings

$^1/_4$ cup tomato juice
 1 teaspoon onion powder
 1 teaspoon dried oregano leaves
 1 teaspoon olive oil

$^1/_2$ teaspoon garlic salt
$^1/_2$ teaspoon freshly ground black pepper
$^1/_4$ teaspoon salt
Four 2-ounce pitas

1. Preheat oven to 350° F. Line baking sheet with foil; spray with nonstick cooking spray.
2. In small bowl, combine tomato juice, onion powder, oregano, oil, garlic salt, pepper and salt.
3. With pastry brush, brush both sides of each pita with an equal amount of tomato juice mixture. Cut pitas into eighths; place on prepared baking sheet. Bake 15 minutes. Turn oven off; do not remove pitas. Let pitas remain in oven until cool and crispy.

Each serving (8 chips) provides: $^1/_4$ Fat, $^1/_4$ Vegetable, 2 Breads

Per serving: 174 Calories, 2 g Total Fat, 0 g Saturated Fat, 0 mg Cholesterol, 674 mg Sodium, 33 g Total Carbohydrate, 1 g Dietary Fiber, 5 g Protein, 60 mg Calcium

Honey-Broiled Grapefruit

Makes 4 servings

2 medium grapefruits, halved   2 tablespoons honey
1 fluid ounce (2 tablespoons) Italian
   bitters *

1. Preheat broiler.
2. Cut a thin slice off bottom of each grapefruit half so it stands upright; place in broiler pan.
3. In small bowl, combine bitters and honey; drizzle half of the honey mixture over grapefruit halves. Broil grapefruits 6" from heat 5–7 minutes, until heated.
4. Place 1 grapefruit half on each of 4 plates; drizzle evenly with pan juices and remaining honey mixture.

Each serving provides: 1 Fruit, 55 Optional Calories

Per serving: 89 Calories, 0 g Total Fat, 0 g Saturated Fat, 0 mg Cholesterol, 0 mg Sodium, 20 g Total Carbohydrate, 1 g Dietary Fiber, 1 g Protein, 14 mg Calcium

   * *Italian bitters, such as Campari®, is available in most liquor stores.*

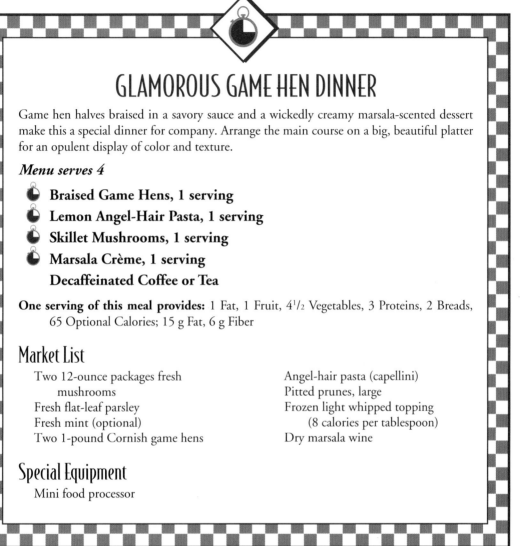

GLAMOROUS GAME HEN DINNER

Game hen halves braised in a savory sauce and a wickedly creamy marsala-scented dessert make this a special dinner for company. Arrange the main course on a big, beautiful platter for an opulent display of color and texture.

Menu serves 4

- **Braised Game Hens, 1 serving**
- **Lemon Angel-Hair Pasta, 1 serving**
- **Skillet Mushrooms, 1 serving**
- **Marsala Crème, 1 serving**
  Decaffeinated Coffee or Tea

One serving of this meal provides: 1 Fat, 1 Fruit, $4^1/_2$ Vegetables, 3 Proteins, 2 Breads, 65 Optional Calories; 15 g Fat, 6 g Fiber

Market List

Two 12-ounce packages fresh
   mushrooms
Fresh flat-leaf parsley
Fresh mint (optional)
Two 1-pound Cornish game hens

Angel-hair pasta (capellini)
Pitted prunes, large
Frozen light whipped topping
   (8 calories per tablespoon)
Dry marsala wine

Special Equipment

Mini food processor

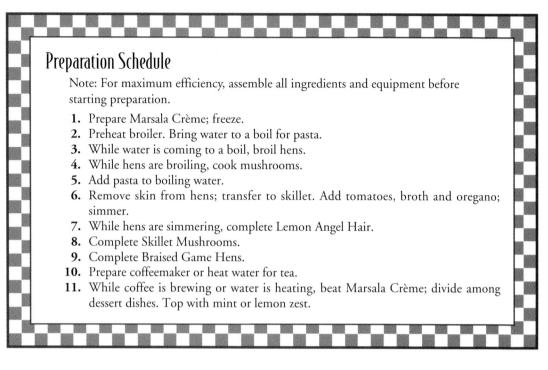

Preparation Schedule

Note: For maximum efficiency, assemble all ingredients and equipment before starting preparation.

1. Prepare Marsala Crème; freeze.
2. Preheat broiler. Bring water to a boil for pasta.
3. While water is coming to a boil, broil hens.
4. While hens are broiling, cook mushrooms.
5. Add pasta to boiling water.
6. Remove skin from hens; transfer to skillet. Add tomatoes, broth and oregano; simmer.
7. While hens are simmering, complete Lemon Angel Hair.
8. Complete Skillet Mushrooms.
9. Complete Braised Game Hens.
10. Prepare coffeemaker or heat water for tea.
11. While coffee is brewing or water is heating, beat Marsala Crème; divide among dessert dishes. Top with mint or lemon zest.

BRAISED GAME HENS

Makes 4 servings

Two 1-pound Cornish game hens, halved *
1 cup canned stewed tomatoes
$^1/_4$ cup low-sodium chicken broth
$^1/_2$ teaspoon dried oregano leaves

1. Preheat broiler. Line broiler pan with foil.
2. Carefully loosen skin of hens. Place hens, skin-side up, in prepared broiler pan; broil 4" from heat 7–10 minutes, until browned. Remove and discard skin.
3. Transfer hens to large skillet; discard pan juices in broiler pan. Add tomatoes, broth and oregano to hens; bring liquid to a boil. Reduce heat to low; simmer, covered, basting frequently, 10 minutes, until hens are cooked through and flavors are blended.
4. Transfer hens to large decorative platter; set aside and keep warm.
5. Increase heat to high. Cook tomato mixture, stirring frequently, until reduced in volume to about $^3/_4$ cup; pour over hens.

Each serving provides: $^1/_2$ Vegetable, 3 Proteins

Per serving: 181 Calories, 7 g Total Fat, 2 g Saturated Fat, 76 mg Cholesterol, 238 mg Sodium, 4 g Total Carbohydrate, 1 g Dietary Fiber, 25 g Protein, 37 mg Calcium

* A 1-pound Cornish game hen will yield about 6 ounces cooked poultry.

Glamorous Game Hen Dinner

LEMON ANGEL-HAIR PASTA

Makes 4 servings

6 ounces angel-hair pasta (capellini)	2 tablespoons fresh lemon juice
2 teaspoons olive oil	$^1/_4$ teaspoon salt
1 large garlic clove, crushed	Freshly ground black pepper to taste
$^1/_4$ cup minced fresh flat-leaf parsley	

1. In large pot of boiling water, cook angel hair 3 minutes, until tender. Drain; set aside.
2. Meanwhile, in medium skillet, heat oil; add garlic. Cook over low heat, crushing garlic with fork, 2 minutes, until tender. Add cooked angel hair, parsley, lemon juice and salt; toss to coat. Serve sprinkled with pepper.

Each serving provides: $^1/_2$ Fat, 2 Breads

Per serving: 183 Calories, 3 g Total Fat, 0 g Saturated Fat, 0 mg Cholesterol, 140 mg Sodium, 33 g Total Carbohydrate, 1 g Dietary Fiber, 6 g Protein, 16 mg Calcium

SKILLET MUSHROOMS

Makes 4 servings

2 teaspoons olive oil	$^1/_4$ teaspoon salt
8 cups sliced or small whole mushrooms	Pinch nutmeg
1 tablespoon Worcestershire sauce	Pinch ground red pepper

1. In large nonstick skillet, heat oil; add mushrooms. Cook over medium-high heat, stirring occasionally, 7 minutes, until mushrooms release their liquid.
2. Add Worcestershire sauce, salt, nutmeg and red pepper; cook, stirring frequently, 3–4 minutes, until liquid is evaporated.

Each serving provides: $^1/_2$ Fat, 4 Vegetables

Per serving: 59 Calories, 3 g Total Fat, 0 g Saturated Fat, 0 mg Cholesterol, 182 mg Sodium, 7 g Total Carbohydrate, 2 g Dietary Fiber, 3 g Protein, 8 mg Calcium

MARSALA CRÈME

Makes 4 servings

8 large pitted prunes
1¹/₂ cups thawed frozen light whipped
    topping (8 calories per tablespoon)
2 fluid ounces (¹/₄ cup) dry marsala wine

1 teaspoon granulated sugar
Fresh mint leaves or strips of
    lemon zest* to garnish (optional)

1. In small bowl, combine prunes and hot water to cover; let stand 5 minutes, until prunes are softened. Drain, reserving liquid.
2. Transfer prunes to mini food processor; purée until smooth, adding reserved liquid, if necessary, until smooth but still thick.
3. Transfer prune purée to medium metal mixing bowl. Add whipped topping, wine and sugar to prune purée; with wire whisk, beat until smooth. Freeze, covered, 30 minutes, just until firm.
4. Just before serving, with wire whisk, beat prune mixture until smooth. Divide mixture evenly among 4 dessert dishes; top each portion with a mint leaf or strip of lemon zest if desired.

Each serving provides: 1 Fruit, 65 Optional Calories

Per serving: 126 Calories, 3 g Total Fat, 0 g Saturated Fat, 0 mg Cholesterol, 3 mg Sodium, 22 g Total Carbohydrate, 2 g Dietary Fiber, 1 g Protein, 12 mg Calcium

   The zest of the lemon is the peel without any of the pith (white membrane). To remove zest from lemon, use a zester or vegetable grater; wrap lemon in plastic wrap and refrigerate for use at another time.

FABULOUS FALL FARE

This game hen dinner is perfect for cooler autumn temperatures. Creamy carrot soup will warm you from the inside out. The hens are drenched with fragrant gravy, and the Maple Baked Apples will put a smile on your face and fortify you for winter.

Menu serves 4

- 🕐 **Spiced Carrot Soup, 1 serving**
- 🕐 **Rosemary Game Hens, 1 serving**
- 🕐 **Sauteed Kale, 1 serving**
- 🕐 **Maple Baked Apples, 1 serving**
- 🕐 **Cinnamon Tea with Honey, 1 serving**

One serving of this meal provides: $^1/_4$ Milk, $^1/_2$ Fat, 1 Fruit, $3^1/_4$ Vegetables, 3 Proteins, 80 Optional Calories; 9 g Fat, 5 g Fiber

Market List

Two 8-ounce apples	Fresh rosemary
1 pound fresh kale	Two 1-pound Cornish game hens
Fresh ginger root	Low-fat (1%) milk

Preparation Schedule

Note: For maximum efficiency, assemble all ingredients and equipment before starting preparation.

1. Preheat oven.
2. Prepare rosemary mixture for hens; coat hens.
3. Place hens in roasting pan and add broth; roast.
4. While hens are roasting, prepare Maple Baked Apples; bake along with hens.
5. Combine ingredients for Spiced Carrot Soup; simmer.
6. Prepare Sauteed Kale.
7. Transfer hens to platter; cook pan juices.
8. Purée soup with milk; heat.
9. Pour pan juices over hens.
10. Heat water for tea.
11. Just before serving, add honey and cinnamon stick to tea.

Spiced Carrot Soup

Makes 4 servings

2¹/₂ cups thinly sliced carrots
2 cups low-sodium chicken broth
2 teaspoons minced pared fresh ginger root
2 garlic cloves, minced

1 teaspoon ground cumin
¹/₄ teaspoon freshly ground black pepper
¹/₄ teaspoon ground allspice
1 cup low-fat (1%) milk

1. In large saucepan, combine carrots, broth, ginger, garlic, cumin, pepper and allspice; bring liquid to a boil. Reduce heat to low; simmer 10 minutes, until carrots are tender.
2. Transfer mixture to food processor; add milk. Purée mixture until smooth.
3. Return carrot mixture to saucepan; cook over medium heat, stirring occasionally, until heated.

Each serving provides: ¹/₄ Milk, 1¹/₄ Vegetables, 10 Optional Calories

Per serving: 76 Calories, 2 g Total Fat, 1 g Saturated Fat, 2 mg Cholesterol, 83 mg Sodium, 12 g Total Carbohydrate, 2 g Dietary Fiber, 4 g Protein, 103 mg Calcium

Rosemary Game Hens

Makes 4 servings

1 tablespoon chopped fresh rosemary
1 tablespoon prepared yellow mustard
2 teaspoons fresh lemon juice
¹/₂ teaspoon freshly ground black pepper

Two 1-pound Cornish game hens, skinned and quartered *
¹/₂ cup low-sodium chicken broth

1. Preheat oven to 400° F.
2. In large bowl, combine rosemary, mustard, lemon juice and pepper. Add hen pieces; turn to coat thoroughly.
3. Transfer hen pieces and any remaining rosemary mixture to large metal roasting pan; add broth. Roast, basting occasionally, 20 minutes, until hens are cooked through and thigh juices run clear when pierced with a fork. Transfer hen pieces to large decorative platter; keep warm.
4. Place roasting pan over medium heat; add ¹/₂ cup water. Cook, scraping up browned bits from bottom of pan, 3 minutes, until mixture is brown and thickened. Pour over hens.

Each serving provides: 3 Proteins, 5 Optional Calories

Per serving: 170 Calories, 7 g Total Fat, 2 g Saturated Fat, 76 mg Cholesterol, 129 mg Sodium, 1 g Total Carbohydrate, 0 g Dietary Fiber, 25 g Protein, 20 mg Calcium

A 1-pound Cornish game hen will yield about 6 ounces cooked poultry.

SAUTEED KALE

Makes 4 servings

2   teaspoons olive oil
4   cups packed kale leaves, rinsed well
     and dried
1   tablespoon + 1 teaspoon fresh
     lemon juice

Pinch salt
Pinch freshly ground black pepper

In large skillet, heat oil; add kale. Cook, stirring frequently, until kale is tender; sprinkle with lemon juice, salt and pepper.

Each serving provides: $^1/_2$ Fat, 2 Vegetables

Per serving: 64 Calories, 3 g Total Fat, 0 g Saturated Fat, 0 mg Cholesterol, 70 mg Sodium, 9 g Total Carbohydrate, 6 g Dietary Fiber, 3 g Protein, 115 mg Calcium

MAPLE BAKED APPLES

Makes 4 servings

Two 8-ounce apples, halved lengthwise
     and cored
$^1/_4$ cup maple syrup

2   tablespoons fresh lemon juice
$^1/_2$ teaspoon cinnamon

1. Preheat oven to 400° F. Line baking sheet with foil.
2. Place apple halves, cut-sides up, on prepared baking sheet. In small bowl, combine syrup, lemon juice and cinnamon; pour evenly over apples. Bake 12–15 minutes, until apples are tender.

Each serving provides: 1 Fruit, 45 Optional Calories

Per serving: 116 Calories, 0 g Total Fat, 0 g Saturated Fat, 0 mg Cholesterol, 2 mg Sodium, 30 g Total Carbohydrate, 2 g Dietary Fiber, 0 g Protein, 24 mg Calcium

CINNAMON TEA WITH HONEY

For each serving, in teacup, combine *$^3/_4$ cup hot tea* and *1 teaspoon honey*, stir with *1 cinnamon stick.*

Each serving provides: 20 Optional Calories

Per serving: 20 Calories, 0 g Total Fat, 0 g Saturated Fat, 0 mg Cholesterol, 6 mg Sodium, 7 g Total Carbohydrate, 0 g Dietary Fiber, 0 g Protein, 7 mg Calcium

EASY INDOOR BARBECUE

These meaty kabobs will remind you of summertime barbecues all year long. Keep a close eye on the sweet potatoes; their sugar content is so high that they burn easily.

Menu serves 4

- **Oven-Barbecued Turkey Kabobs, 1 serving**
- **Baked Sweet Potato Sticks, 1 serving**
- **Carrot and Apple Salad, 1 serving**
- **Sparkling Apple Cider, $^1/_2$ cup per serving**

One serving of this meal provides: $^3/_4$ Fat, $1^3/_4$ Fruits, 6 Vegetables, 3 Proteins, 1 Bread, 20 Optional Calories; 10 g Fat, 10 g Fiber

Market List

2 small Granny Smith apples
Apple cider
Sparkling apple cider
16 large whole mushrooms
16 cherry tomatoes
2 medium red bell peppers
2 medium yellow bell peppers
1 pound sweet potatoes

1 bunch scallions
15 ounces skinless boneless
    turkey thighs
Steak sauce
Frozen orange juice concentrate
One 10-ounce package frozen
    baby onions
Onion powder

Preparation Schedule

Note: For maximum efficiency, assemble all ingredients and equipment before starting preparation.

1. Chill sparkling cider.
2. Soak skewers.
3. Preheat oven.
4. Prepare Carrot and Apple Salad; refrigerate.
5. Prepare Baked Sweet Potato Sticks; bake.
6. While potatoes are baking, marinate ingredients for Oven-Barbecued Turkey Kabobs. Heat marinade; thread turkey and vegetables onto skewers.
7. Roast kabobs.
8. Turn potatoes; complete baking.
9. Brush kabobs with marinade; complete roasting.
10. Transfer kabobs to platter; top with pan juices.

OVEN-BARBECUED TURKEY KABOBS

Makes 4 servings

3 tablespoons reduced-sodium soy sauce
2 tablespoons red wine vinegar
2 tablespoons steak sauce
1 tablespoon minced fresh garlic
1 tablespoon vegetable oil
15 ounces skinless boneless turkey thighs, cut into 16 equal pieces

16 large whole mushrooms
16 cherry tomatoes
16 frozen baby onions, partially thawed
2 medium red bell peppers, cored, seeded and cut into 16 equal pieces
2 medium yellow bell peppers, cored, seeded and cut into 16 equal pieces

1. Preheat oven to 450° F. Line large roasting pan with foil; spray with nonstick cooking spray.
2. Soak four 12" or eight 6" bamboo skewers in water for 10 minutes.
3. Meanwhile, to prepare marinade, in gallon-size sealable plastic bag, combine soy sauce, vinegar, steak sauce, garlic and oil; add turkey, mushrooms, cherry tomatoes, onions and red and yellow peppers. Seal bag, squeezing out air; turn to coat thoroughly. Let marinate until skewers are ready, turning bag occasionally.
4. Drain marinade into small saucepan; bring to a boil. Thread an equal amount of turkey and vegetables onto each skewer; place skewers in prepared roasting pan. Roast 20 minutes, turning once and brushing with remaining marinade, until turkey is cooked through and vegetables are tender.
5. Transfer skewers to large decorative platter; top with pan juices.

Each serving provides: $3/4$ Fat, $4^3/4$ Vegetables, 3 Proteins, 10 Optional Calories

Per serving: 262 Calories, 9 g Total Fat, 2 g Saturated Fat, 80 mg Cholesterol, 686 mg Sodium, 22 g Total Carbohydrate, 4 g Dietary Fiber, 26 g Protein, 55 mg Calcium

BAKED SWEET POTATO STICKS

Makes 4 servings

2 tablespoons thawed frozen orange
   juice concentrate
1 teaspoon onion powder
$^1/_2$ teaspoon salt

$^1/_8$ teaspoon ground red pepper
1 pound sweet potatoes, pared and
   cut into $^1/_2$" sticks

1. Preheat oven to 450° F. Line baking sheet with foil; spray with nonstick cooking spray.
2. In medium bowl, combine orange juice concentrate, onion powder, salt and red pepper.
   Add potato sticks; turn to coat.
3. Arrange potatoes in a single layer on prepared baking sheet. Bake 10 minutes; turn carefully.
   Bake 10 minutes longer, until tender.

Each serving provides: $^1/_4$ Fruit, 1 Bread

Per serving: 104 Calories, 1 g Total Fat, 0 g Saturated Fat, 0 mg Cholesterol, 285 mg Sodium,
24 g Total Carbohydrate, 3 g Dietary Fiber, 20 g Protein, 25 mg Calcium

CARROT AND APPLE SALAD

Makes 4 servings

2 cups shredded carrots
2 small Granny Smith apples, cored,
   pared and diced
$^1/_2$ cup sliced scallions

$^1/_4$ cup apple cider
2 tablespoons cider vinegar
$^1/_2$ teaspoon salt

In medium bowl, combine carrots, apples, scallions, cider, vinegar and salt; refrigerate,
covered, until chilled.

Each serving provides: $^1/_2$ Fruit, $1^1/_4$ Vegetables, 10 Optional Calories

Per serving: 63 Calories, 0 g Total Fat, 0 g Saturated Fat, 0 mg Cholesterol, 295 mg Sodium,
16 g Total Carbohydrate, 3 g Dietary Fiber, 1 g Protein, 29 mg Calcium

ITALIAN SUMMER BUFFET

This variation on a classic Italian meal makes a brightly flavored and beautiful summer buffet with an orzo salad and basil-scented tomatoes. Add chilled Soave and some plump ripe strawberries to round out the meal.

Menu serves 4

- **Turkey Tonnato, 1 serving**
- **Orzo Salad, 1 serving**
- **Basil Tomatoes, 1 serving**
- **Whole Strawberries, 1 cup per serving**
- **Soave, 4 fluid ounces per serving**

One serving of this meal provides: $^3/_4$ Fat, 1 Fruit, $2^1/_2$ Vegetables, $3^1/_4$ Proteins, 1 Bread, 115 Optional Calories; 6 g Fat, 7 g Fiber

Market List

4 cups whole strawberries	Anchovy paste
1 bunch scallions	Bottled capers
1 medium red bell pepper	Orzo (rice-shaped pasta)
4 medium tomatoes	White wine vinegar
Fresh flat-leaf parsley	Fat-free mayonnaise dressing
Fresh basil	(10 calories per tablespoon)
15 ounces skinless boneless turkey breast	Soave

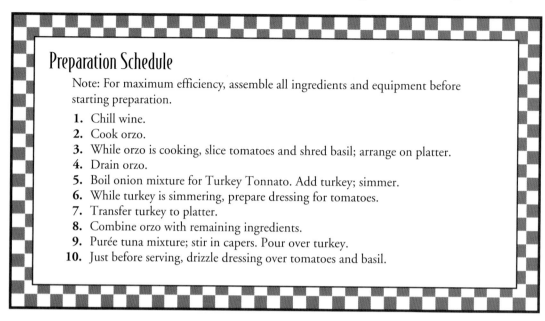

Preparation Schedule

Note: For maximum efficiency, assemble all ingredients and equipment before starting preparation.

1. Chill wine.
2. Cook orzo.
3. While orzo is cooking, slice tomatoes and shred basil; arrange on platter.
4. Drain orzo.
5. Boil onion mixture for Turkey Tonnato. Add turkey; simmer.
6. While turkey is simmering, prepare dressing for tomatoes.
7. Transfer turkey to platter.
8. Combine orzo with remaining ingredients.
9. Purée tuna mixture; stir in capers. Pour over turkey.
10. Just before serving, drizzle dressing over tomatoes and basil.

TURKEY TONNATO

Makes 4 servings

$^1/_4$ cup thinly sliced onion
$^1/_4$ cup low-sodium chicken broth
$^1/_4$ cup white wine vinegar
 1 large whole garlic clove
$^1/_8$ teaspoon dried thyme leaves
15 ounces skinless boneless turkey breast,
     cut into 8 equal pieces
 2 ounces drained canned water-packed
     chunk light tuna

$^1/_4$ cup fat-free mayonnaise dressing
     (10 calories per tablespoon)
 1 tablespoon fresh lemon juice
 1 teaspoon anchovy paste
 1 tablespoon drained capers, rinsed
Lemon slices, fresh flat-leaf parsley sprigs
     and additional capers to garnish
     (optional)

1. In medium skillet, combine onion, broth, vinegar, garlic and thyme; bring liquid to a boil. Add turkey; reduce heat to low. Simmer, covered, 5 minutes, until turkey is cooked through. With slotted spoon, transfer turkey to large decorative platter; set aside and keep warm. Reserve pan juices.
2. In food processor or blender, combine pan juices, tuna, mayonnaise, lemon juice and anchovy paste; purée until smooth. Stir in capers. Pour tuna mixture over turkey; garnish with lemon slices, parsley and additional capers if desired.

Each serving provides: $3^1/_4$ Proteins, 15 Optional Calories

Per serving: 160 Calories, 1 g Total Fat, 0 g Saturated Fat, 73 mg Cholesterol, 321 mg Sodium, 4 g Total Carbohydrate, 0 g Dietary Fiber, 31 g Protein, 21 mg Calcium

ORZO SALAD

Makes 4 servings

3 ounces orzo (rice-shaped pasta),
  cooked and drained
$^1/_2$ cup sliced scallions
$^1/_4$ cup minced celery
$^1/_4$ cup minced red bell pepper

$^1/_4$ cup minced fresh flat-leaf parsley
$^1/_4$ cup low-sodium chicken broth
1 tablespoon fresh lemon juice
$^1/_4$ teaspoon salt
Freshly ground black pepper to taste

In medium bowl, combine orzo, scallions, celery, red pepper, parsley, broth, lemon juice, salt and black pepper.

Each serving provides: $^1/_2$ Vegetable, 1 Bread

Per serving: 90 Calories, 0 g Total Fat, 0 g Saturated Fat, 0 mg Cholesterol, 150 mg Sodium, 18 g Total Carbohydrate, 1 g Dietary Fiber, 3 g Protein, 22 mg Calcium

BASIL TOMATOES

Makes 4 servings

4 medium tomatoes, thickly sliced
$^1/_4$ cup packed fresh basil leaves, slivered
1 tablespoon balsamic vinegar

1 tablespoon olive oil
1 teaspoon red wine vinegar
$^1/_4$ teaspoon salt

1. On medium decorative platter, arrange tomato slices. Sprinkle tomatoes with basil; set aside.
2. To prepare dressing, in small bowl, combine balsamic vinegar, oil, wine vinegar and salt.
3. Just before serving, drizzle dressing over tomatoes and basil.

Each serving provides: $^3/_4$ Fat, 2 Vegetables

Per serving: 66 Calories, 4 g Total Fat, 1 g Saturated Fat, 0 mg Cholesterol, 150 mg Sodium, 8 g Total Carbohydrate, 2 g Dietary Fiber, 2 g Protein, 32 mg Calcium

SOUTHWESTERN SPECTACULAR

People will think you worked for hours to concoct this southwestern supper, but it's lightning-quick to fix; just don't tell them!

Menu serves 4

🕐 **Tex-Mex Turkey, 1 serving**

🕐 **Pepper Rice, 1 serving**

🕐 **Jicama Salad, 1 serving**

Mango, ¹/₂ small per serving

Light Beer, 12 fluid ounces per serving

One serving of this meal provides: 1 Fat, 1³/₄ Fruits, 3¹/₄ Vegetables, 2 Proteins, 1 Bread, 115 Optional Calories; 6 g Fat, 8 g Fiber

Market List

2 small mangoes
Orange juice
1 large jicama
1 medium red onion
1 bunch scallions
1 medium red bell pepper
1 medium green bell pepper
1 medium yellow bell pepper

Fresh cilantro
8 ounces skinless boneless
    turkey breast
Red kidney beans
Salsa, mild or hot
Corn oil
Light beer

Preparation Schedule

Note: For maximum efficiency, assemble all ingredients and equipment before starting preparation.

1. Chill beer.
2. Cook bell peppers for rice. Add water, rice and salt; simmer.
3. While rice is simmering, prepare Jicama Salad; let stand.
4. While salad is standing, cook turkey; transfer to plate.
5. Complete Pepper Rice.
6. Complete Tex-Mex Turkey.
7. Toss salad.

Tex-Mex Turkey

Makes 4 servings

1 teaspoon corn oil	2 tablespoons minced fresh cilantro
8 ounces skinless boneless turkey breast, cut into $1/2$" pieces	2 teaspoons unsweetened cocoa powder, dissolved in 2 tablespoons hot water
1 cup diced onions	1 teaspoon mild or hot chili powder
2 garlic cloves, minced	$1/4$ teaspoon ground cumin
4 ounces drained cooked red kidney beans	$1/8$ teaspoon ground red pepper
$1/2$ cup low-sodium chicken broth	

1. In medium skillet, heat oil; add turkey. Cook over medium heat, stirring frequently, 3–4 minutes, until browned on all sides. Transfer turkey to plate; set aside.
2. In same skillet, combine onions and garlic; cook, stirring constantly, 3–4 minutes, until onions are golden brown. Return turkey to skillet; add beans, broth, cilantro, dissolved cocoa powder, chili powder, cumin and red pepper; reduce heat to low. Simmer, stirring occasionally, 5 minutes, until turkey is cooked through and mixture is heated.

Each serving provides: $1/4$ Fat, $1/2$ Vegetable, 2 Proteins, 5 Optional Calories

Per serving: 135 Calories, 2 g Total Fat, 0 g Saturated Fat, 35 mg Cholesterol, 43 mg Sodium, 11 g Total Carbohydrate, 2 g Dietary Fiber, 17 g Protein, 29 mg Calcium

Pepper Rice

Makes 4 servings

1 teaspoon corn oil	4 ounces converted rice
$1/2$ cup diced red bell pepper	$1/2$ teaspoon salt
$1/2$ cup diced green bell pepper	$1/2$ cup mild or hot salsa
$1/2$ cup diced yellow bell pepper	$1/2$ teaspoon dried oregano leaves

1. In medium saucepan, heat oil; add red, green and yellow peppers. Cook over medium heat, stirring occasionally, 3–4 minutes, until lightly browned.
2. Add 1 cup water, the rice and salt to bell pepper mixture; bring liquid to a boil. Reduce heat to low; simmer, covered, 20 minutes, until rice is tender and liquid is absorbed. Remove from heat.
3. Add salsa and oregano to rice mixture; stir to combine. Let stand, covered, 5 minutes.

Each serving provides: $1/4$ Fat, $3/4$ Vegetable, 1 Bread

Per serving: 134 Calories, 1 g Total Fat, 0 g Saturated Fat, 0 mg Cholesterol, 456 mg Sodium, 28 g Total Carbohydrate, 1 g Dietary Fiber, 2 g Protein, 25 mg Calcium

Jicama Salad

Makes 4 servings

 2 teaspoons corn oil
 2 garlic cloves, minced
 $1/4$ cup orange juice
 1 tablespoon red wine vinegar
 12 ounces pared jicama, cut into $1/8$" sticks
 3 small navel oranges, peeled and sectioned

 $1/2$ cup thinly sliced red onion
 $1/4$ cup sliced scallions (green portion only)
 $1/2$ teaspoon salt
 $1/4$ teaspoon freshly ground black pepper
 Pinch ground red pepper

1. In large skillet, heat oil; add garlic. Cook over medium heat, stirring constantly, 1–2 minutes, until golden brown. Remove from heat; stir in orange juice and vinegar.
2. In medium bowl, combine jicama, oranges, onion, scallions, salt, black pepper and red pepper. Add orange juice mixture; toss to combine. Let stand 15 minutes; toss again.

Each serving provides: $1/2$ Fat, $3/4$ Fruit, 2 Vegetables, 10 Optional Calories

Per serving: 119 Calories, 3 g Total Fat, 0 g Saturated Fat, 0 mg Cholesterol, 282 mg Sodium, 23 g Total Carbohydrate, 4 g Dietary Fiber, 2 g Protein, 70 mg Calcium

THE BETTER BURGER AND BEYOND

Sometimes you just crave simple food: burgers, fries and a creamy milk shake. Add a scoop of coleslaw and you're ready to dig in!

Menu serves 4

- **Turkey Burgers, 1 serving**
- **Oven Fries, 1 serving**
- **Processor Cabbage Slaw, 1 serving**
- **Mocha Milk Shake, 1 serving**

One serving of this meal provides: $3/4$ Milk, $1^1/2$ Fats, $6^1/4$ Vegetables, 3 Proteins, 1 Bread, 95 Optional Calories; 15 g Fat, 10 g Fiber

Market List

1 large head green cabbage	Sugar-free hot cocoa mix
1 medium green bell pepper	16 fluid ounces chocolate, vanilla
15 ounces ground turkey	or coffee nonfat sugar-free
Nonfat sour cream	frozen yogurt
Steak sauce	Onion powder
Mayonnaise	Caraway or poppy seeds

Preparation Schedule

Note: For maximum efficiency, assemble all ingredients and equipment before starting preparation.

1. Prepare Processor Cabbage Slaw; refrigerate.
2. Preheat oven. Prepare baking sheet for potatoes.
3. Combine ingredients for Turkey Burgers; form into patties.
4. Cut potatoes for Oven Fries. Combine broth and seasonings; toss with potatoes. Arrange potatoes on prepared baking sheet; bake.
5. While potatoes are baking, cook burgers.
6. Just before serving, prepare Mocha Milk Shake.

TURKEY BURGERS

Makes 4 servings

15 ounces ground turkey	2 garlic cloves, minced
$^1/_2$ cup minced onion	$^1/_2$ teaspoon salt
2 teaspoons Worcestershire sauce	$^1/_4$ teaspoon freshly ground black pepper
2 teaspoons steak sauce	

1. In medium bowl, combine turkey, onion, Worcestershire sauce, steak sauce, garlic, salt and pepper; form mixture into 4 equal patties, each about $^3/_4$" thick.
2. Heat medium nonstick skillet over medium heat 1 minute; add patties. Cook, turning once, 2–3 minutes on each side, until browned (be careful not to burn).
3. Add $^1/_4$ cup water to skillet; reduce heat to low. Cook, covered, 5 minutes, until patties are cooked through.

Each serving provides: $^1/_4$ Vegetable, 3 Proteins, 5 Optional Calories

Per serving: 166 Calories, 8 g Total Fat, 2 g Saturated Fat, 78 mg Cholesterol, 449 mg Sodium, 3 g Total Carbohydrate, 0 g Dietary Fiber, 19 g Protein, 23 mg Calcium

OVEN FRIES

Makes 4 servings

3 tablespoons low-sodium chicken broth	$^1/_4$ teaspoon freshly ground black pepper
1 teaspoon paprika	1 pound 4 ounces baking potatoes,
1 teaspoon onion powder	cut into $^1/_2$" sticks

1. Preheat oven to 500° F. Line baking sheet with foil; spray with nonstick cooking spray.
2. In medium bowl, combine broth, paprika, onion powder and pepper. Add potato sticks; turn to coat thoroughly.
3. Arrange potatoes in a single layer on prepared baking sheet; spray with nonstick cooking spray. Bake 10 minutes; carefully turn. Bake 10 minutes longer, until tender and crispy.

Each serving provides: 1 Bread

Per serving: 112 Calories, 1 g Total Fat, 0 g Saturated Fat, 0 mg Cholesterol, 13 mg Sodium, 24 g Total Carbohydrate, 3 g Dietary Fiber, 3 g Protein, 22 mg Calcium

Processor Cabbage Slaw

Makes 4 servings

8 cups green cabbage chunks	2 tablespoons cider vinegar
2 cups carrot chunks	1 teaspoon granulated sugar
1 cup onion chunks	1 teaspoon prepared yellow mustard
1 cup green bell pepper chunks	$^1/_2$ teaspoon caraway or poppy seeds
$^1/_4$ cup nonfat sour cream	$^1/_2$ teaspoon salt
2 tablespoons mayonnaise	$^1/_4$ teaspoon freshly ground black pepper

1. In food processor, combine cabbage, carrot, onion, green pepper, sour cream, mayonnaise, vinegar, sugar, mustard, caraway, salt and black pepper; with on-off motion, pulse processor 4–5 times, until mixture is finely chopped and ingredients are blended.
2. Transfer cabbage mixture to large bowl; refrigerate, covered, until chilled.

Each serving provides: $1^1/_2$ Fats, 6 Vegetables, 15 Optional Calories

Per serving: 146 Calories, 6 g Total Fat, 1 g Saturated Fat, 4 mg Cholesterol, 385 mg Sodium, 21 g Total Carbohydrate, 6 g Dietary Fiber, 4 g Protein, 117 mg Calcium

Mocha Milk Shake

Makes 4 servings

16 fluid ounces chocolate, vanilla or coffee nonfat sugar-free frozen yogurt	2 packets sugar-free hot cocoa mix
2 cups skim milk	1 tablespoon instant coffee powder
	2 teaspoons vanilla extract

In blender, combine frozen yogurt, milk, cocoa mix, instant coffee and vanilla; purée on high speed until thick and foamy. Serve immediately.

Each serving provides: $^3/_4$ Milk, 75 Optional Calories

Per serving: 167 Calories, 0 g Total Fat, 0 g Saturated Fat, 2 mg Cholesterol, 209 mg Sodium, 78 g Total Carbohydrate, 0 g Dietary Fiber, 11 g Protein, 427 mg Calcium

MIDDLE EASTERN SAUSAGE AND SALAD SUPPER

Mildly spiced sausages are the centerpiece for this light, savory dinner. Add fresh apricots and iced tea with lemon as cooling complements.

Menu serves 4

- **Middle Eastern Turkey Sausages, 1 serving**
- **Warm Chick-Pea Salad, 1 serving**
- **Cucumbers with Mint, 1 serving**
  Fresh Apricots, 3 medium per serving
  Iced Tea with Lemon

One serving of this meal provides: $1/4$ Milk, $3/4$ Fat, 1 Fruit, 3 Vegetables, 3 Proteins, $1^1/4$ Breads; 12 g Fat, 5 g Fiber

Market List

12 medium apricots	13 ounces ground turkey
One 10-ounce bag fresh spinach	Couscous
3 medium cucumbers	Chick-peas (garbanzo beans)
Fresh flat-leaf parsley	White wine vinegar
Fresh mint	

Preparation Schedule

Note: For maximum efficiency, assemble all ingredients and equipment before starting preparation.

1. Prepare iced tea; refrigerate.
2. Prepare Cucumbers with Mint; refrigerate.
3. Toast seeds for turkey sausages. Prepare sausage mixture; shape into links.
4. Brown sausages; add water. Cook 5 minutes.
5. While sausages are cooking, prepare Warm Chick-Pea Salad.

Middle Eastern Turkey Sausages

Makes 4 servings

¹/₄ teaspoon cumin seeds
¹/₄ teaspoon caraway seeds
¹/₈ teaspoon cinnamon
¹/₈ teaspoon ground red pepper
 3 tablespoons plain dried bread crumbs
 2 cups packed spinach leaves, rinsed well
      and dried

¹/₂ cup coarsely chopped onion
13 ounces ground turkey
¹/₂ teaspoon salt
 1 teaspoon olive oil

1. In medium nonstick skillet, toast cumin and caraway seeds over low heat, stirring constantly, 3 minutes, until fragrant. Stir in cinnamon and red pepper; remove from heat.
2. In food processor, combine cumin mixture and bread crumbs; process until seeds are ground and mixture is combined. Add spinach and onion; with on-off motion, pulse processor 4–5 times, until mixture is finely chopped and ingredients are blended. Add turkey and salt; process just until combined.
3. Form turkey mixture into 8 link-shaped sausages; place on plate.
4. Wipe out same skillet with damp paper towel. Add oil; heat. Add turkey sausages; cook over medium heat, turning occasionally, until browned on all sides. Reduce heat to low; add ¹/₄ cup water. Cook, covered, 5 minutes, until turkey sausages are cooked through.

Each serving provides: ¹/₄ Fat, 1¹/₄ Vegetables, 2¹/₂ Proteins, ¹/₄ Bread

Per serving: 177 Calories, 8 g Total Fat, 2 g Saturated Fat, 67 mg Cholesterol, 432 mg Sodium, 7 g Total Carbohydrate, 1 g Dietary Fiber, 18 g Protein, 67 mg Calcium

WARM CHICK-PEA SALAD

Makes 4 servings

4 ounces couscous	$^1/_4$ cup minced fresh flat-leaf parsley
2 teaspoons olive oil	2 tablespoons fresh lemon juice
$^1/_2$ cup chopped onion	1 teaspoon salt
2 garlic cloves, minced	$^1/_2$ teaspoon freshly ground black pepper
4 ounces drained cooked chick-peas (garbanzo beans)	

1. In small saucepan, bring $1^1/_2$ cups water to a boil; stir in couscous. Remove from heat; let stand, covered, 5 minutes.
2. Meanwhile, in small skillet, heat oil; add onion and garlic. Cook over medium heat, stirring frequently, 3–4 minutes, until golden brown. Add chick-peas and 1 tablespoon water; cook, stirring occasionally, until liquid is evaporated.
3. Transfer chick-pea mixture to medium bowl; stir in couscous, parsley, lemon juice, salt and pepper.

Each serving provides: $^1/_2$ Fat, $^1/_4$ Vegetable, $^1/_2$ Protein, 1 Bread

Per serving: 187 Calories, 3 g Total Fat, 0 g Saturated Fat, 0 mg Cholesterol, 557 mg Sodium, 33 g Total Carbohydrate, 2 g Dietary Fiber, 7 g Protein, 38 mg Calcium

CUCUMBERS WITH MINT

Makes 4 servings

3 cups pared diced cucumbers	1 tablespoon white wine vinegar
$^3/_4$ cup plain nonfat yogurt	$^1/_2$ teaspoon salt
$^1/_4$ cup finely chopped fresh mint	

In medium bowl, combine cucumbers, yogurt, mint, vinegar and salt; refrigerate, covered, 20 minutes. Stir before serving.

Each serving provides: $^1/_4$ Milk, $1^1/_2$ Vegetables

Per serving: 40 Calories, 0 g Total Fat, 0 g Saturated Fat, 1 mg Cholesterol, 312 mg Sodium, 7 g Total Carbohydrate, 1 g Dietary Fiber, 3 g Protein, 106 mg Calcium

SOUP AND SALAD SUPPER

With a food processor, this meal can be assembled with blinding speed. If you have homemade turkey broth in the freezer, you can use it in place of the chicken broth. And if there are any orphan vegetables in the bin, add them to the soup; just be sure to avoid beets, and to add cruciferous vegetables, such as cabbage, broccoli and cauliflower, during the last 5 minutes of cooking.

Menu serves 4

- **Processor Turkey Soup, 1 serving**
- **Beet Salad, 1 serving**
- **Yogurt Biscuits, 1 serving**
- **Broiled Grapefruit, 1 serving**
- **Iced Tea**

One serving of this meal provides: $1/4$ Milk, $3/4$ Fat, $1^1/4$ Fruits, 7 Vegetables, 2 Proteins, $2^3/4$ Breads, 55 Optional Calories; 10 g Fat, 12 g Fiber

Market List

2 grapefruits
1 small Granny Smith apple
2 medium turnips
2 medium zucchini
1 medium red bell pepper
1 cup whole green beans
1 pound beets

1 medium red onion
Fresh flat-leaf parsley
8 ounces skinless boneless cooked
    turkey breast
Orzo (rice-shaped pasta)
Corn oil

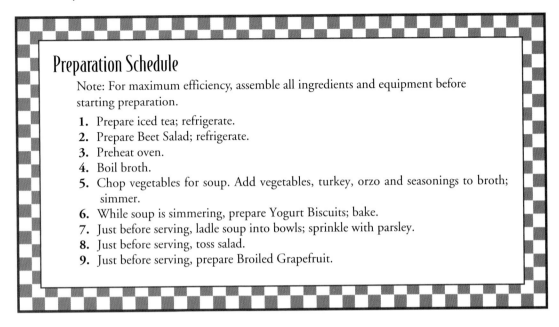

Preparation Schedule

Note: For maximum efficiency, assemble all ingredients and equipment before starting preparation.

1. Prepare iced tea; refrigerate.
2. Prepare Beet Salad; refrigerate.
3. Preheat oven.
4. Boil broth.
5. Chop vegetables for soup. Add vegetables, turkey, orzo and seasonings to broth; simmer.
6. While soup is simmering, prepare Yogurt Biscuits; bake.
7. Just before serving, ladle soup into bowls; sprinkle with parsley.
8. Just before serving, toss salad.
9. Just before serving, prepare Broiled Grapefruit.

PROCESSOR TURKEY SOUP

Makes 4 servings

5 cups low-sodium chicken broth	1 cup trimmed whole green beans
2 cups carrot chunks	8 ounces diced skinless cooked turkey breast
2 cups onion chunks	
2 cups turnip chunks	$1^1/_2$ ounces orzo (rice-shaped pasta)
2 cups zucchini chunks	$^1/_2$ teaspoon dried thyme or oregano leaves
$1^1/_2$ cups celery chunks	$^1/_2$ teaspoon salt
1 medium red bell pepper, cored, seeded and cut into chunks	$^1/_4$ teaspoon freshly ground black pepper
	$^1/_4$ cup minced fresh flat-leaf parsley

1. In large pot, bring broth to a boil.
2. Meanwhile, in food processor, in batches, with on-off motion, chop carrot, onion, turnip, zucchini, celery, red pepper and green beans, pulsing processor as needed, until vegetables are coarsely chopped.
3. Stir chopped vegetables, turkey, orzo, thyme, salt and black pepper into broth; return liquid to a boil. Reduce heat to low; simmer, partially covered, 20 minutes, until vegetables are tender and flavors are blended.
4. Just before serving, ladle soup evenly into 4 soup bowls; sprinkle each portion with 1 tablespoon parsley.

Each serving provides: $5^3/_4$ Vegetables, 2 Proteins, $^1/_2$ Bread, 25 Optional Calories

Per serving: 282 Calories, 5 g Total Fat, 1 g Saturated Fat, 44 mg Cholesterol, 493 mg Sodium, 35 g Total Carbohydrate, 7 g Dietary Fiber, 25 g Protein, 118 mg Calcium

Beet Salad

Makes 4 servings

2 cups sliced cooked beets
$^1/_2$ cup sliced red onion

1 small Granny Smith apple, cored
   and diced
2 tablespoons cider vinegar

1. In medium bowl, combine beets, onion, apple and vinegar; refrigerate, covered, until chilled.
2. Just before serving, toss salad.

Each serving provides: $^1/_4$ Fruit, $1^1/_4$ Vegetables

Per serving: 51 Calories, 0 g Total Fat, 0 g Saturated Fat, 0 mg Cholesterol, 44 mg Sodium, 12 g Total Carbohydrate, 3 g Dietary Fiber, 1 g Protein, 17 mg Calcium

Yogurt Biscuits

Makes 4 servings

$1^3/_4$ cups all-purpose flour
2 teaspoons double-acting baking powder
1 teaspoon baking soda

$^1/_2$ teaspoon salt
1 cup plain nonfat yogurt
1 tablespoon corn oil

1. Preheat oven to 425° F. Spray twelve $2^3/_4$" muffin cups with nonstick cooking spray.
2. In large bowl, combine flour, baking powder, baking soda and salt. Add yogurt and oil; mix well. Divide equally among prepared muffin cups. Bake 15–20 minutes, until firm and browned.

Each serving (3 biscuits) provides: $^1/_4$ Milk, $^3/_4$ Fat, $2^1/_4$ Breads, 15 Optional Calories

Per serving: 267 Calories, 5 g Total Fat, 1 g Saturated Fat, 1 mg Cholesterol, 879 mg Sodium, 47 g Total Carbohydrate, 1 g Dietary Fiber, 9 g Protein, 259 mg Calcium

Broiled Grapefruit

For each serving, sprinkle $^1/_2$ *medium grapefruit* with *1 teaspoon brown sugar*. Place in broiler pan; broil until bubbly.

Each serving provides: 1 Fruit, 15 Optional Calories

Per serving: 54 Calories, 0 g Total Fat, 0 g Saturated Fat, 0 mg Cholesterol, 2 mg Sodium, 14 g Total Carbohydrate, 1 g Dietary Fiber, 1 g Protein, 18 mg Calcium

HOMEY ONE-OVEN BRUNCH

Home-style jams, fresh coffee or tea and a big platter of sweet melon chunks complete this brunch that bakes all together in one oven. Freeze extra corn muffins to enjoy at a later date.

Menu serves 4

- **Smoked Turkey Hash, 1 serving**
- **Baked Tomatoes, 1 serving**
- **Corn Muffins, 1 serving**
- **Strawberry Jam, 1 tablespoon**
- **Assorted Melon Chunks, 1 cup per serving**
- **Decaffeinated Coffee or Tea**

One serving of this meal provides: 1 Fruit, 3 Vegetables, 2 Proteins, 3 Breads, 115 Optional Calories; 6 g Fat, 8 g Fiber

Market List

Assorted melons
8 ounces red potatoes
2 medium turnips
4 medium tomatoes
1 cup corn kernels, fresh or frozen
6 ounces skinless boneless smoked turkey breast

Low-fat (1%) buttermilk
Grated Parmesan cheese
Hot fruit sauce
Strawberry jam
Egg substitute, frozen or refrigerated

Preparation Schedule

Note: For maximum efficiency, assemble all ingredients and equipment before starting preparation.

1. Cut melons into chunks; refrigerate.
2. Prepare Corn Muffins; bake.
3. While muffins are baking, prepare Smoked Turkey Hash; bake.
4. While muffins and hash are baking, prepare Baked Tomatoes; bake.
5. While hash and tomatoes are baking, cool muffins.
6. Prepare coffeemaker or heat water for tea.

SMOKED TURKEY HASH

Makes 4 servings

8 ounces cooked red potatoes, diced
6 ounces diced skinless smoked turkey breast
1¹/₂ cups diced cooked yellow turnips
¹/₂ cup minced onion
¹/₂ cup egg substitute

1 tablespoon hot fruit sauce *
¹/₄ teaspoon salt
¹/₄ teaspoon freshly ground black pepper
Pinch paprika

1. Preheat oven to 425° F. Spray an 8 or 9" square baking pan with nonstick cooking spray.
2. In medium bowl, combine potatoes, turkey, turnips, onion, egg substitute, hot fruit sauce, salt and pepper; transfer to prepared baking pan, pressing down with back of wooden spoon. Sprinkle with paprika. Bake 20–25 minutes, until top is browned.

Each serving provides: 1 Vegetable, 2 Proteins, ¹/₂ Bread, 5 Optional Calories

Per serving: 143 Calories, 2 g Total Fat, 1 g Saturated Fat, 22 mg Cholesterol, 665 mg Sodium, 20 g Total Carbohydrate, 3 g Dietary Fiber, 13 g Protein, 31 mg Calcium

* Hot fruit sauce, such as PickaPeppa™ Sauce, is available in many supermarkets and gourmet stores; if you can't find it, substitute 1 tablespoon steak sauce and a pinch of ground red pepper.

BAKED TOMATOES

Makes 4 servings

4 medium tomatoes, halved
1 tablespoon plain dried bread crumbs
1 tablespoon grated Parmesan cheese

¹/₄ teaspoon dried oregano leaves
Pinch ground red pepper

1. Preheat oven to 425° F. Spray a 13 × 9" baking pan with nonstick cooking spray.
2. Cut a thin slice off bottom of each tomato half so it stands upright; place tomato halves in prepared baking pan.
3. In small bowl, combine bread crumbs, Parmesan cheese, oregano and red pepper; sprinkle an equal amount of mixture over each tomato half. Bake 15 minutes, until topping is golden brown.

Each serving (2 tomato halves) provides: 2 Vegetables, 15 Optional Calories

Per serving: 47 Calories, 1 g Total Fat, 0 g Saturated Fat, 1 mg Cholesterol, 52 mg Sodium, 9 g Total Carbohydrate, 2 g Dietary Fiber, 2 g Protein, 30 mg Calcium

CORN MUFFINS

Makes 6 servings

1¹/₄ cups yellow cornmeal
  1 cup fresh or frozen corn kernels
  ³/₄ cup all-purpose flour
  1 tablespoon granulated sugar
2¹/₂ teaspoons double-acting baking
     powder

  ³/₄ teaspoon salt
  1 cup low-fat (1.5%) buttermilk
  1 egg, beaten

1. Preheat oven to 425° F. Spray twelve 2³/₄" muffin cups with nonstick cooking spray.
2. In medium bowl, combine cornmeal, corn, flour, sugar, baking powder and salt. In small bowl, with wire whisk, combine buttermilk and egg. Add wet ingredients to dry; stir just until combined.
3. Spoon batter into prepared cups, filling each about ²/₃ full. Bake 20–25 minutes, until golden brown and toothpick inserted in center comes out clean. Cool on rack 10 minutes. Remove muffins from pan; cool completely on rack.

Each serving (2 muffins) provides: 2¹/₂ Breads, 50 Optional Calories

Per serving: 225 Calories, 3 g Total Fat, 1 g Saturated Fat, 37 mg Cholesterol, 536 mg Sodium, 44 g Total Carbohydrate, 3 g Dietary Fiber, 7 g Protein, 170 mg Calcium

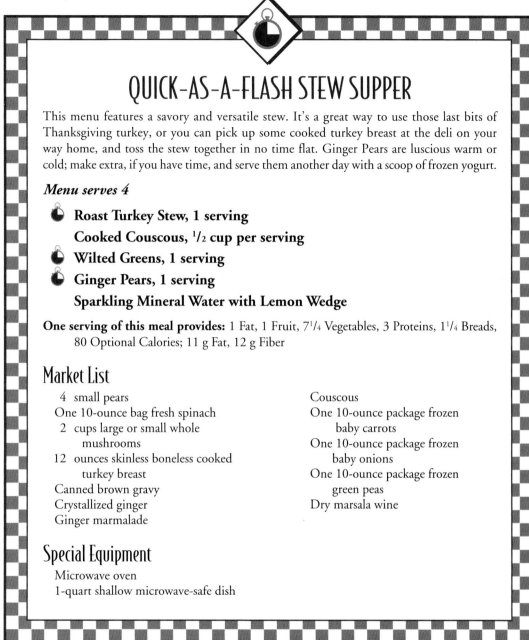

QUICK-AS-A-FLASH STEW SUPPER

This menu features a savory and versatile stew. It's a great way to use those last bits of Thanksgiving turkey, or you can pick up some cooked turkey breast at the deli on your way home, and toss the stew together in no time flat. Ginger Pears are luscious warm or cold; make extra, if you have time, and serve them another day with a scoop of frozen yogurt.

Menu serves 4

- **Roast Turkey Stew, 1 serving**
  Cooked Couscous, $^1/_2$ cup per serving
- **Wilted Greens, 1 serving**
- **Ginger Pears, 1 serving**
  Sparkling Mineral Water with Lemon Wedge

One serving of this meal provides: 1 Fat, 1 Fruit, $7^1/_4$ Vegetables, 3 Proteins, $1^1/_4$ Breads, 80 Optional Calories; 11 g Fat, 12 g Fiber

Market List

4 small pears	Couscous
One 10-ounce bag fresh spinach	One 10-ounce package frozen
2 cups large or small whole	baby carrots
mushrooms	One 10-ounce package frozen
12 ounces skinless boneless cooked	baby onions
turkey breast	One 10-ounce package frozen
Canned brown gravy	green peas
Crystallized ginger	Dry marsala wine
Ginger marmalade	

Special Equipment

Microwave oven
1-quart shallow microwave-safe dish

Preparation Schedule

Note: For maximum efficiency, assemble all ingredients and equipment before starting preparation.

1. Chill mineral water.
2. Prepare Roast Turkey Stew; simmer.
3. While stew is simmering, prepare Ginger Pears; microwave.
4. Add peas to stew; simmer.
5. While stew is simmering, prepare couscous.
6. Baste pears; microwave.
7. Prepare Wilted Greens.

ROAST TURKEY STEW

Makes 4 servings

2 teaspoons vegetable oil	$^{1}/_{2}$ cup canned brown gravy
2 cups halved large or whole small mushrooms	$^{1}/_{2}$ cup low-sodium chicken broth
1 cup chopped onions	2 fluid ounces ($^{1}/_{4}$ cup) dry marsala wine
12 ounces skinless boneless cooked turkey breast, cut into chunks	$^{1}/_{2}$ teaspoon salt
2 cups frozen baby carrots	$^{1}/_{2}$ teaspoon dried thyme leaves
1 cup frozen baby onions	$^{1}/_{4}$ teaspoon freshly ground black pepper
$^{1}/_{2}$ cup chopped celery	$^{1}/_{4}$ teaspoon dried rosemary leaves
	$^{1}/_{2}$ cup frozen green peas

1. In large nonstick skillet, heat oil; add mushrooms and chopped onions. Cook over medium-high heat, stirring frequently, 4–5 minutes, until liquid is evaporated and vegetables are golden brown.
2. Add turkey, carrots, baby onions, celery, gravy, broth, wine, salt, thyme, pepper and rosemary; bring liquid to a boil. Reduce heat to low; simmer, stirring occasionally, 15 minutes, until vegetables are tender.
3. Stir peas into turkey mixture; simmer 10 minutes, until peas are heated through and tender.

Each serving provides: $^{1}/_{2}$ Fat, $3^{1}/_{4}$ Vegetables, 3 Proteins, $^{1}/_{4}$ Bread, 55 Optional Calories

Per serving: 280 Calories, 7 g Total Fat, 2 g Saturated Fat, 65 mg Cholesterol, 593 mg Sodium, 21 g Total Carbohydrate, 3 g Dietary Fiber, 29 g Protein, 76 mg Calcium

WILTED GREENS

Makes 4 servings

2 teaspoons vegetable oil	2 teaspoons balsamic vinegar
8 cups packed spinach leaves, well rinsed, dried and torn into bite-size pieces	$^1/_4$ teaspoon salt Pinch ground nutmeg

In large, heavy-bottom pot, heat oil; add spinach, vinegar, salt and nutmeg. Cook over medium-high heat, tossing constantly, 30–60 seconds, until spinach is wilted.

Each serving provides: $^1/_2$ Fat, 4 Vegetables

Per serving: 51 Calories, 3 g Total Fat, 0 g Saturated Fat, 0 mg Cholesterol, 246 mg Sodium, 5 g Total Carbohydrate, 4 g Dietary Fiber, 4 g Protein, 140 mg Calcium

GINGER PEARS

Makes 4 servings

4 small pears, cored and halved	1 tablespoon ginger marmalade *
1 tablespoon minced crystallized ginger	

1. Cut a thin slice from skin side of each pear half so it lies flat; place in a 1-quart shallow microwave-safe dish.
2. Fill cavity of each pear with an equal amount of ginger and marmalade. Sprinkle pears with 2 tablespoons water; cover dish with wax paper. Microwave on High (100% power) 3 minutes. Baste pears with pan juices; microwave on High 1 minute longer, until pears are tender.
3. Just before serving, place 2 pear halves on each of 4 dishes; drizzle each portion with an equal amount of pan juices.

Each serving provides: 1 Fruit, 25 Optional Calories

Per serving: 118 Calories, 1 g Total Fat, 0 g Saturated Fat, 0 mg Cholesterol, 5 mg Sodium, 30 g Total Carbohydrate, 4 g Dietary Fiber, 1 g Protein, 28 mg Calcium

* *Ginger marmalade is available in most specialty shops and good supermarkets.*

THE PERFECT PICNIC

Fill your picnic basket with this spectacular giant sandwich, piled high with *everything*, zucchini salad and a pale pink sangria that gives you a refreshing drink and dessert in the same glass.

Menu serves 4

- 🕐 **Giant Turkey Sub, 1 serving**
- 🕐 **Zucchini-Mint Salad, 1 serving**
- 🕐 **Pink Sangria, 1 serving**

One serving of this meal provides: $1^1/_2$ Fats, $^1/_2$ Fruit, $3^3/_4$ Vegetables, $1^1/_2$ Proteins, 2 Breads, 90 Optional Calories; 16 g Fat, 5 g Fiber

Market List

1 cup whole strawberries	One 10-ounce loaf French or Italian
1 small head radicchio	bread
2 medium zucchini	Sun-dried tomato halves (not packed
1 medium red onion	in oil)
Fresh mint	Pickled pepperoncini
3 ounces skinless boneless cooked	Nonalcoholic dry white wine
smoked turkey breast	Sweet red vermouth
$2^1/_4$ ounces Fontina cheese	

Special Equipment

1-quart pitcher
4 wine glasses

Preparation Schedule

Note: For maximum efficiency, assemble all ingredients and equipment before starting preparation.

1. Prepare Zucchini-Mint Salad; refrigerate.
2. Prepare Pink Sangria; refrigerate.
3. Prepare Giant Turkey Sub.
4. Just before serving, pour sangria; add seltzer.

GIANT TURKEY SUB

Makes 4 servings

One 10-ounce loaf French or Italian bread,
   split lengthwise
2 teaspoons olive oil
1 teaspoon red wine vinegar
$^1/_4$ teaspoon dried oregano leaves
$^1/_8$ teaspoon salt
$^1/_8$ teaspoon freshly ground black pepper
3 ounces thinly sliced skinless
   smoked turkey breast

$2^1/_4$ ounces sliced Fontina cheese
6 radicchio leaves
8 sun-dried tomato halves (not packed in
   oil), slivered, soaked in hot water until
   tender and drained
$^1/_4$ cup drained pickled pepperoncini, sliced
$^1/_2$ cup sliced red onion

1. Evenly remove 1 ounce of soft bread from cut side of each bread half; reserve for use at another time. Set bread halves aside.
2. In small bowl, combine oil, vinegar, oregano, salt and pepper; set aside.
3. Onto bottom half of bread, layer turkey, cheese, radicchio leaves, tomatoes, pepperoncini and onion; sprinkle evenly with oil mixture. Top with remaining bread half. Cut sandwich into 4 equal pieces.

Each serving provides: $^1/_2$ Fat, $1^3/_4$ Vegetables, $1^1/_2$ Proteins, 2 Breads

Per serving: 287 Calories, 9 g Total Fat, 5 g Saturated Fat, 28 mg Cholesterol, 991 mg Sodium, 37 g Total Carbohydrate, 3 g Dietary Fiber, 15 g Protein, 152 mg Calcium

ZUCCHINI–MINT SALAD

Makes 4 servings

1 tablespoon + 1 teaspoon olive oil
4 cups thinly sliced zucchini
3 tablespoons minced fresh mint

1 garlic clove, crushed
$^1/_2$ teaspoon salt
$^1/_4$ teaspoon freshly ground black pepper

1. In large nonstick skillet, heat 2 teaspoons of the oil; add 2 cups of the zucchini. Cook over medium-high heat, stirring frequently, 4–5 minutes, until zucchini is golden brown. With slotted spoon, transfer zucchini to medium bowl.
2. In same skillet, cook remaining 2 cups zucchini, stirring frequently, 4–5 minutes, until golden brown; transfer to bowl with cooked zucchini. Add mint, garlic, salt, pepper and remaining 2 teaspoons oil; toss to combine. Refrigerate, covered, until chilled.

Each serving ($^3/_4$ cup) provides: 1 Fat, 2 Vegetables

Per serving: 60 Calories, 5 g Total Fat, 1 g Saturated Fat, 0 mg Cholesterol, 278 mg Sodium, 4 g Total Carbohydrate, 1 g Dietary Fiber, 2 g Protein, 25 mg Calcium

PINK SANGRIA

Makes 4 servings

1 cup whole strawberries, halved	2 teaspoons granulated sugar
1 small navel orange, cut in half and sliced	12 fluid ounces (1$^1/_2$ cups) nonalcoholic
4 fluid ounces ($^1/_2$ cup) sweet red	dry white wine
vermouth	Plain seltzer
$^1/_2$ lemon, sliced	

1. In 1-quart pitcher, combine strawberries, orange, vermouth, lemon and sugar, slightly crushing fruit with back of mixing spoon. Stir in wine; refrigerate, covered, until chilled.
2. Just before serving, fill 4 wine glasses with ice. Pour wine mixture into glasses, dividing liquid and fruit evenly; add enough seltzer to fill glasses.

Each serving provides: $^1/_2$ Fruit, 90 Optional Calories

Per serving: 105 Calories, 1 g Total Fat, 0 g Saturated Fat, 0 mg Cholesterol, 2 mg Sodium, 18 g Total Carbohydrate, 2 g Dietary Fiber, 1 g Protein, 29 mg Calcium

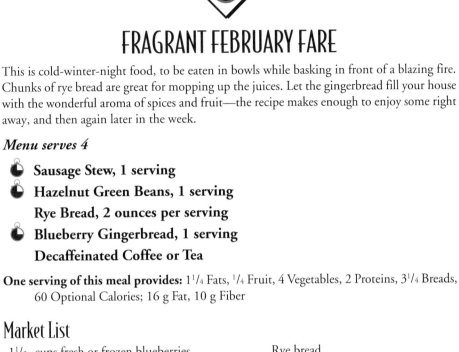

FRAGRANT FEBRUARY FARE

This is cold-winter-night food, to be eaten in bowls while basking in front of a blazing fire. Chunks of rye bread are great for mopping up the juices. Let the gingerbread fill your house with the wonderful aroma of spices and fruit—the recipe makes enough to enjoy some right away, and then again later in the week.

Menu serves 4

- **Sausage Stew, 1 serving**
- **Hazelnut Green Beans, 1 serving**
- **Rye Bread, 2 ounces per serving**
- **Blueberry Gingerbread, 1 serving**
- **Decaffeinated Coffee or Tea**

One serving of this meal provides: $1^1/_4$ Fats, $^1/_4$ Fruit, 4 Vegetables, 2 Proteins, $3^1/_4$ Breads, 60 Optional Calories; 16 g Fat, 10 g Fiber

Market List

$1^1/_2$ cups fresh or frozen blueberries
  1 large yellow or white turnip
 10 ounces red potatoes
  1 small head green cabbage
Fresh flat-leaf parsley
 10 ounces lean (10% or less fat)
     turkey sausages

Rye bread
Corn oil
Shelled hazelnuts
Molasses
One 10-ounce package frozen
    French-style green beans

Special Equipment

Large, deep skillet with cover

Preparation Schedule

Note: For maximum efficiency, assemble all ingredients and equipment before starting preparation.

1. Prepare Blueberry Gingerbread; bake.
2. While gingerbread is baking, cook sausages and vegetables. Add potatoes, broth, seasonings and cabbage; cook 15 minutes.
3. While sausage mixture is cooking, cook green beans; drain.
4. Complete Sausage Stew.
5. Complete Hazelnut Green Beans.
6. Prepare coffeemaker or heat water for tea.

SAUSAGE STEW

Makes 4 servings

1 teaspoon corn oil	¹/₂ teaspoon dried thyme leaves
10 ounces lean (10% or less fat) turkey sausages	¹/₄ teaspoon dried sage leaves
	¹/₄ teaspoon freshly ground black pepper
1 cup chopped onions	¹/₂ small head green cabbage, cut into 4 wedges
1 cup diced yellow or white turnip	
¹/₂ cup diced carrot	1 teaspoon all-purpose flour, dissolved in 1 tablespoon cold water
¹/₂ cup diced celery	
10 ounces red potatoes, cut into 1" chunks	¹/₄ cup minced fresh flat-leaf parsley
1 cup low-sodium chicken broth	2 teaspoons cider vinegar
1 bay leaf	

1. In large, deep skillet, heat oil; add sausages, onions, turnip, carrot and celery. Cook over medium-high heat, stirring frequently, 5 minutes, until onions are golden brown.
2. Add potatoes, broth, bay leaf, thyme, sage and pepper to onion mixture; bring liquid to a boil. Reduce heat to medium; top with cabbage wedges. Cook, covered, 15 minutes, until potatoes and cabbage are tender. With slotted spoon, transfer cabbage to large decorative platter; keep warm.
3. Stir dissolved flour into potato mixture; reduce heat to low. Simmer, stirring frequently, 5 minutes, until liquid is slightly thickened.
4. With slotted spoon, transfer sausages and vegetables to platter with cabbage; remove and discard bay leaf. Stir parsley and vinegar into liquid remaining in skillet; pour over sausages and vegetables.

Each serving (1¹/₂ cups) provides: ¹/₄ Fat, 3 Vegetables, 2 Proteins, ¹/₂ Bread, 10 Optional Calories

Per serving: 237 Calories, 9 g Total Fat, 3 g Saturated Fat, 43 mg Cholesterol, 504 mg Sodium, 24 g Total Carbohydrate, 4 g Dietary Fiber, 16 g Protein, 69 mg Calcium

Hazelnut Green Beans

Makes 4 servings

One 10-ounce package frozen French-style
green beans (2 cups)
2 teaspoons stick margarine

$^1/_2$ ounce shelled hazelnuts, finely chopped
Pinch salt

1. In medium saucepan, cook green beans in $^1/_2$ cup water until tender; drain.
2. Meanwhile, in small skillet, melt margarine; add hazelnuts. Cook over low heat, stirring constantly, 2–3 minutes, until hazelnuts are lightly browned; remove skillet from heat. Add green beans and salt; toss to combine.

Each serving ($^1/_2$ cup) provides: 1 Fat, 1 Vegetable

Per serving: 63 Calories, 4 g Total Fat, 1 g Saturated Fat, 0 mg Cholesterol, 57 mg Sodium, 6 g Total Carbohydrate, 2 g Dietary Fiber, 2 g Protein, 37 mg Calcium

Blueberry Gingerbread

Makes 8 servings

1 cup + 2 tablespoons all-purpose flour
$^1/_4$ cup firmly packed dark brown sugar
1 teaspoon ground ginger
$^1/_2$ teaspoon cinnamon
$^1/_2$ teaspoon double-acting baking powder

$^1/_2$ teaspoon baking soda
$^1/_4$ teaspoon salt
$^1/_4$ cup plain nonfat yogurt
$^1/_4$ cup molasses
$1^1/_2$ cups fresh or frozen blueberries

1. Preheat oven to 350° F. Spray an 8" round cake pan with nonstick cooking spray.
2. In medium bowl, combine flour, sugar, ginger, cinnamon, baking powder, baking soda and salt.
3. In small bowl, combine yogurt and molasses. Add yogurt mixture and $^1/_2$ cup boiling water to flour mixture; with wire whisk, blend just until combined. Transfer mixture to prepared cake pan; sprinkle evenly with blueberries. Bake 20–25 minutes, until toothpick inserted in center comes out clean.

Each serving provides: $^1/_4$ Fruit, $^3/_4$ Bread, 50 Optional Calories

Per serving: 139 Calories, 0 g Total Fat, 0 g Saturated Fat, 0 mg Cholesterol, 190 mg Sodium, 32 g Total Carbohydrate, 1 g Dietary Fiber, 2 g Protein, 65 mg Calcium

FIESTA NIGHT

People of all ages will love this fun dinner. The taco salad is served in tortilla cups, just as in many Mexican restaurants, but our version is not laden with fat! And who could pass by a creamy sundae of frozen yogurt topped with a rich-tasting chocolate–peanut butter sauce?

Menu serves 4

Mexican Taco Salad, 1 serving

Steamed Whole Green Beans, 1 cup per serving

Frozen Yogurt with Nutty Chocolate Sauce, 1 serving

Decaffeinated Coffee or Tea

One serving of this meal provides: $^1/_4$ Milk, $1^1/_4$ Fats, $4^1/_2$ Vegetables, 3 Proteins, 2 Breads, 100 Optional Calories; 19 g Fat, 7 g Fiber

Market List

1 medium avocado
1 pound whole green beans
1 medium tomato
1 head iceberg lettuce
8 ounces cooked ground turkey breast
$1^1/_2$ ounces reduced-fat Monterey Jack cheese
Low-fat (1.5%) buttermilk
Canned mild green chilies

Corn tortillas (6" diameter)
Chopped walnuts
Semisweet chocolate chips
Smooth peanut butter
16 fluid ounces chocolate, vanilla or coffee nonfat sugar-free frozen yogurt

Special Equipment

Microwave oven
Microwave-safe plate
2-cup microwave-safe bowl

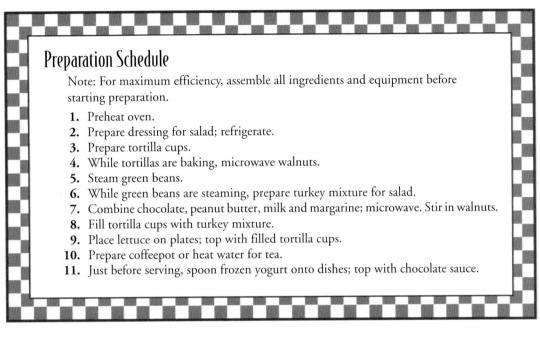

Preparation Schedule

Note: For maximum efficiency, assemble all ingredients and equipment before starting preparation.

1. Preheat oven.
2. Prepare dressing for salad; refrigerate.
3. Prepare tortilla cups.
4. While tortillas are baking, microwave walnuts.
5. Steam green beans.
6. While green beans are steaming, prepare turkey mixture for salad.
7. Combine chocolate, peanut butter, milk and margarine; microwave. Stir in walnuts.
8. Fill tortilla cups with turkey mixture.
9. Place lettuce on plates; top with filled tortilla cups.
10. Prepare coffeepot or heat water for tea.
11. Just before serving, spoon frozen yogurt onto dishes; top with chocolate sauce.

MEXICAN TACO SALAD

Makes 4 servings

$^1/_2$ cup low-fat (1.5%) buttermilk
$^1/_8$ medium avocado, peeled, pitted and coarsely chopped
$^1/_4$ medium onion, cut into chunks
1 tablespoon chopped drained canned mild green chilies
$^1/_8$ teaspoon salt
Dash hot pepper sauce

8 corn tortillas (6" diameter)
8 ounces cooked ground turkey breast, crumbled
$^1/_2$ cup blanched, peeled, seeded and chopped tomato
$^1/_4$ cup sliced scallions (white and green parts)
$1^1/_2$ ounces shredded reduced-fat Monterey Jack cheese
4 cups shredded iceberg lettuce

1. Preheat oven to 400° F.
2. To prepare dressing, in blender or food processor, combine buttermilk, avocado, onion, chilies, salt and hot pepper sauce; purée until smooth. Set aside.
3. To prepare tortilla cups, line eight 8-ounce custard cups with 1 tortilla each, folding to fit. Bake 5 minutes; let cool. Remove tortillas from cups.
4. In medium bowl, combine turkey, tomato, scallions and cheese; divide turkey mixture evenly among tortilla cups. Top each portion of turkey mixture with $^1/_4$ of the dressing.
5. Divide lettuce among 4 plates; top each portion of lettuce with 2 filled tortilla cups.

Each serving (2 filled tortilla cups + 1 cup lettuce) provides: $^1/_4$ Fat, $2^1/_2$ Vegetables, $2^1/_2$ Proteins, 2 Breads, 10 Optional Calories

Per serving: 359 Calories, 18 g Total Fat, 7 g Saturated Fat, 62 mg Cholesterol, 302 mg Sodium, 30 g Total Carbohydrate, 4 g Dietary Fiber, 21 g Protein, 255 mg Calcium

Frozen Yogurt with Nutty Chocolate Sauce

Makes 4 servings

1 ounce coarsely chopped walnuts	1 teaspoon stick margarine
1 ounce semisweet chocolate chips	16 fluid ounces chocolate, vanilla or coffee
1 tablespoon smooth peanut butter	nonfat sugar-free frozen yogurt
1 tablespoon skim milk	

1. Line microwave-safe plate with paper towel. Place walnuts in a single layer on prepared plate. Microwave on High (100% power) 1–2 minutes, until fragrant (do not burn).
2. In 2-cup microwave-safe bowl, combine chocolate, peanut butter, milk and margarine; microwave on Medium (50% power) 1–2 minutes, stirring once, until chocolate is melted and mixture is smooth. Stir in walnuts.
3. Just before serving, divide frozen yogurt evenly among 4 dessert dishes; top each portion with an equal amount of chocolate sauce.

Each serving provides: $^1/_4$ Milk, 1 Fat, $^1/_2$ Protein, 90 Optional Calories

Per serving: 192 Calories, 9 g Total Fat, 2 g Saturated Fat, 0 mg Cholesterol, 98 mg Sodium, 28 g Total Carbohydrate, 1 g Dietary Fiber, 7 g Protein, 165 mg Calcium

2

Fish & Seafood

DINNER FROM SOUTHERN FRANCE

This menu from southern France features the sun-blessed produce of the region, its herbs, garlic and olives. These traditional lighter dishes, rather than those coated with the heavy cream sauces of northern France, make a perfect meal.

Menu serves 4

- **Garlic-Pesto Bread, 1 serving**
- **Salade Niçoise, 1 serving**
- **Strawberries Balsamico, 1 serving**
  Pouilly-Fuissé, 4 fluid ounces per serving

One serving of this meal provides: $1^1/_4$ Fats, 1 Fruit, $2^1/_2$ Vegetables, $1^1/_4$ Proteins, 2 Breads, 125 Optional Calories; 12 g Fat, 9 g Fiber

Market List

4 cups whole strawberries	$^1/_4$ cup part-skim ricotta cheese
2 cups whole green beans	1 loaf French bread
1 medium red onion	Roasted red peppers
2 medium tomatoes	Anchovy fillets
Fresh basil	Extra-virgin olive oil
Fresh thyme	Niçoise olives, small
10 ounces boneless tuna steak or two	Pouilly-Fuissé
$6^1/_2$-ounce cans water-packed tuna	

Dinner from Southern France

Preparation Schedule

Note: For maximum efficiency, assemble all ingredients and equipment before starting preparation.

1. Chill wine.
2. Cook tuna steak if using; chill.
3. Preheat oven.
4. Steam potatoes.
5. While potatoes are steaming, prepare Strawberries Balsamico; let stand.
6. While strawberries are standing, line baking sheet; bake bread.
7. Steam green beans.
8. Purée ricotta cheese mixture; spread on bread.
9. Bake Garlic-Pesto Bread.
10. Complete Salade Niçoise.

GARLIC-PESTO BREAD

Makes 4 servings

6 ounces French bread, split lengthwise	1 garlic clove, pressed
¹/₂ cup packed fresh basil leaves	¹/₂ teaspoon freshly ground pepper
¹/₄ cup part-skim ricotta cheese	

1. Preheat oven to 400° F. Line baking sheet with foil.
2. Place bread halves cut side up on prepared baking sheet; bake 5 minutes, until slightly crisp. Leave oven on.
3. In food processor or blender, combine basil, ricotta cheese, garlic and pepper; purée until smooth. Spread half of the ricotta cheese mixture on each bread half; bake 15 minutes, until hot and very crispy.

Each serving provides: ¹/₄ Protein, 1¹/₂ Breads

Per serving: 145 Calories, 3 g Total Fat, 1 g Saturated Fat, 5 mg Cholesterol, 279 mg Sodium, 25 g Total Carbohydrate, 1 g Dietary Fiber, 6 g Protein, 124 mg Calcium

SALADE NIÇOISE

Makes 4 servings

10 ounces potatoes, pared and cut into $^1/_4$" slices

2 cups trimmed whole green beans

8 ounces boneless cooked tuna steak, chilled, or drained canned water-packed tuna

2 medium tomatoes, cut into wedges

$^1/_2$ cup drained roasted red peppers, chopped

$^1/_4$ cup red wine vinegar

1 tablespoon extra-virgin olive oil

4 anchovy fillets, rinsed and chopped

2 teaspoons chopped fresh thyme leaves

1 garlic clove, minced

20 small Niçoise olives *

$^1/_4$ cup thinly sliced red onion

1. Fill medium saucepan with 1" water; set steamer rack in saucepan. Place potatoes on rack. Bring water to a boil; reduce heat to low. Steam potatoes over simmering water, covered, 12 minutes, until tender. Remove saucepan from heat; divide potatoes evenly among 4 plates.
2. Place green beans on steamer rack in saucepan; return saucepan to heat. Steam over simmering water, covered, 4 minutes, until tender. Transfer beans to colander or medium sieve. Rinse under cold running water; pat dry. Divide beans evenly among plates with potatoes.
3. Place one-fourth of the tuna and tomato wedges on each plate with potatoes and green beans.
4. In small bowl, with wire whisk, combine roasted peppers, vinegar, oil, anchovies, thyme and garlic; drizzle evenly over salads. Top each salad with 5 olives and 1 tablespoon onion.

Each serving provides: $1^1/_4$ Fats, $2^1/_2$ Vegetables, 1 Protein, $^1/_2$ Bread, 10 Optional Calories

Per serving: 258 Calories, 9 g Total Fat, 2 g Saturated Fat, 29 mg Cholesterol, 314 mg Sodium, 24 g Total Carbohydrate, 4 g Dietary Fiber, 21 g Protein, 60 mg Calcium

* If Niçoise olives are not available, substitute small black olives.

STRAWBERRIES BALSAMICO

Makes 4 servings

1 tablespoon + 1 teaspoon granulated sugar

1 tablespoon balsamic vinegar

4 cups whole strawberries, quartered

1. In medium bowl, combine vinegar and sugar, stirring until sugar is dissolved. Add strawberries; toss to coat. Let stand 20 minutes, tossing occasionally.

Each serving provides: 1 Fruit, 15 Optional Calories

Per serving: 62 Calories, 1 g Total Fat, 0 g Saturated Fat, 0 mg Cholesterol, 2 mg Sodium, 15 g Total Carbohydrate, 4 g Dietary Fiber, 1 g Protein, 21 mg Calcium

AN EAST-MEETS-WEST DINNER

Globe-trot from course to course with this menu, where some of the best flavors of Asia and Europe meet. Then travel to the islands of Hawaii and far-off New Zealand for a fun way to enjoy fruit salad!

Menu serves 4

- **Broccoli Bisque, 1 serving**
- **Swordfish Steaks with Ginger-Mustard Marinade, 1 serving**
- **Risotto with Peas and Scallions, 1 serving**
- **Pineapple and Kiwi Kabobs, 1 serving**
  Iced Herbal Tea

One serving of this meal provides: $^1/_4$ Milk, $1^1/_2$ Fats, 1 Fruit, $4^1/_4$ Vegetables, 2 Proteins, $2^1/_4$ Breads, 80 Optional Calories; 17 g Fat, 9 g Fiber

Market List

1 medium pineapple	Four 5-ounce boneless swordfish steaks
2 medium kiwifruits	Coarse-grain country-style mustard
2 bunches broccoli	Arborio or other short-grain rice
1 bunch scallions	One 10-ounce package frozen small
Fresh ginger root	green peas

Preparation Schedule

Note: For maximum efficiency, assemble all ingredients and equipment before starting preparation.

1. Prepare iced tea; refrigerate.
2. Prepare Pineapple and Kiwi Kabobs; refrigerate.
3. Preheat broiler.
4. Prepare marinade for fish. Add fish; let stand.
5. While fish is standing, combine broccoli mixture; cook.
6. While broccoli mixture is cooking, prepare Risotto with Peas and Scallions.
7. Broil fish.
8. While fish is broiling, complete Broccoli Bisque, but do not ladle into bowls.
9. Just before serving, ladle soup into bowls; garnish.
10. Just before serving, transfer fish to platter. Top with pan juices; garnish.
11. Just before serving, sprinkle risotto with scallions.

Broccoli Bisque

Makes 4 servings

6 cups chopped broccoli	1 large garlic clove, minced
2 cups low-sodium chicken broth	Freshly ground black pepper to taste
1 medium onion, chopped	1 cup skim milk
2 tablespoons fresh lemon juice	Small broccoli florets to garnish (optional)

1. In large saucepan, combine chopped broccoli, broth, onion, lemon juice, garlic, pepper and 1 cup water; bring to a boil. Reduce heat to medium; cook, covered, 12–15 minutes, until broccoli is tender, adding more water, 1 tablespoon at a time, if liquid begins to evaporate.
2. Transfer broccoli mixture to food processor; purée until smooth.
3. Return broccoli mixture to saucepan; stir in milk. Cook over low heat, stirring frequently, until hot (do not boil).
4. Just before serving, ladle soup evenly into 4 soup bowls; garnish each portion with broccoli florets if desired.

Each serving (1^1/$_2$ cups) provides: ^{1}/$_4$ Milk, 3^1/$_2$ Vegetables, 10 Optional Calories

Per serving: 85 Calories, 1 g Total Fat, 0 g Saturated Fat, 1 mg Cholesterol, 95 mg Sodium, 13 g Total Carbohydrate, 4 g Dietary Fiber, 7 g Protein, 146 mg Calcium

Swordfish Steaks with Ginger–Mustard Marinade

Makes 4 servings

2 tablespoons fresh lemon juice	2 teaspoons vegetable oil
2 tablespoons reduced-sodium soy sauce	1^1/$_2$ teaspoons grated pared fresh ginger root
2 tablespoons coarse-grain country-style mustard	Four 5-ounce boneless swordfish steaks
4 garlic cloves, lightly crushed	4 whole scallions to garnish (optional)

1. Preheat broiler. Spray broiler pan with nonstick cooking spray.
2. To prepare marinade, in shallow medium bowl, with wire whisk, combine lemon juice, soy sauce, mustard, garlic, oil and ginger. Add swordfish to marinade; turn to coat. Let stand 10 minutes; turn again.
3. Transfer fish to prepared broiler pan; brush with half the marinade. Broil 4" from heat 3–4 minutes, until golden brown. Turn; brush with remaining marinade. Broil 3–4 minutes longer, until golden brown and cooked through.
4. Transfer fish to large decorative platter; top with any remaining pan juices. Serve garnished with scallions if desired.

Each serving (1 swordfish steak) provides: ^{1}/$_2$ Fat, 2 Proteins

Per serving: 213 Calories, 9 g Total Fat, 2 g Saturated Fat, 55 mg Cholesterol, 503 mg Sodium, 3 g Total Carbohydrate, 0 g Dietary Fiber, 29 g Protein, 13 mg Calcium

Risotto with Peas and Scallions

Makes 4 servings

3¹/₂ cups low-sodium chicken broth
  1 tablespoon + 1 teaspoon vegetable oil
  1 medium onion, finely chopped
  7 ounces arborio or other short-grain rice
  8 fluid ounces (1 cup) dry white wine

  1 cup frozen small green peas
³/₄ cup sliced scallions (white and
     green parts)
Freshly ground black pepper to taste

1. In medium saucepan, bring broth to a boil. Reduce heat to low; let simmer until ready to use.
2. In separate medium saucepan, heat oil; add onion. Cook over medium heat, stirring frequently, 1 minute. Add rice; stir to coat. Continuing to stir, cook 1 minute longer. Add wine and 1 cup of the simmering broth; cook, stirring frequently, until most of the liquid is absorbed.
3. Stir in 1 cup of the remaining simmering broth, the peas and ¹/₂ cup of the scallions; cook, stirring constantly, until liquid is absorbed. Add remaining broth; cook, stirring constantly, until absorbed and mixture is creamy; stir in pepper. Serve sprinkled with remaining scallions.

Each serving (1 cup) provides: 1 Fat, ³/₄ Vegetable, 2¹/₄ Breads, 70 Optional Calories

Per serving: 326 Calories, 6 g Total Fat, 1 g Saturated Fat, 0 mg Cholesterol, 94 mg Sodium, 49 g Total Carbohydrate, 3 g Dietary Fiber, 8 g Protein, 32 mg Calcium

Pineapple and Kiwi Kabobs

For each serving, cut *3 ounces fresh pineapple* and *¹/₂ medium kiwifruit, pared,* into 1" chunks; thread onto a 6" bamboo skewer.

Each serving provides: 1 Fruit

Per serving: 71 Calories, 1 g Total Fat, 0 g Saturated Fat, 0 mg Cholesterol, 3 mg Sodium, 18 g Total Carbohydrate, 3 g Dietary Fiber, 1 g Protein, 19 mg Calcium

UNIQUE TUNA SALAD DINNER

Lightly cooked cucumbers make an unexpected side dish in this lightning-fast dinner. The Candied Oranges are luscious and beautiful; they can be served at a dressy dinner without apology.

Menu serves 4

- **Warm Tuna Salad, 1 serving**
- **Braised Cucumbers, 1 serving**
- **Candied Oranges, 1 serving**
  Sparkling Mineral Water

One serving of this meal provides: 1 Fruit, $3^3/_4$ Vegetables, $^3/_4$ Protein, 2 Breads, 65 Optional Calories; 1 g Fat, 6 g Fiber

Market List

1 bunch scallions
1 bunch watercress
3 medium cucumbers

Fresh or dried dill
Fresh flat-leaf parsley
Orange-flavored liqueur

Preparation Schedule

Note: For maximum efficiency, assemble all ingredients and equipment before starting preparation.

1. Chill mineral water.
2. Cook rice.
3. While rice is cooking, prepare sugar syrup for Candied Oranges.
4. While syrup is cooking, remove zest from orange. Add to sugar syrup; cook.
5. Cook cucumbers.
6. While cucumbers are cooking, slice oranges; arrange on plates.
7. Add liqueur to sugar syrup; pour over oranges.
8. Add tuna salad ingredients to rice; stir.
9. Add dill to cucumbers.
10. Line platter with watercress; top with rice mixture.

WARM TUNA SALAD

Makes 4 servings

8 ounces converted rice	$^1/_4$ cup minced fresh flat-leaf parsley
6 ounces drained canned water-packed tuna, flaked	2 tablespoons fresh lemon juice
$^3/_4$ cup sliced scallions (white portion with some green)	$^1/_4$ teaspoon salt
	$^1/_4$ teaspoon coarsely ground black pepper
$^1/_2$ cup minced celery	3 cups watercress leaves

1. In medium saucepan, bring 2 cups water to a boil; add rice. Reduce heat to low; cook, covered, 20 minutes, until all water is absorbed. Remove from heat.
2. Add tuna, scallions, celery, parsley, lemon juice, salt and pepper to cooked rice; stir gently to combine.
3. Arrange watercress on large decorative platter; top with warm rice mixture.

Each serving provides: $2^1/_4$ Vegetables, $^3/_4$ Protein, 2 Breads

Per serving: 281 Calories, 1 g Total Fat, 0 g Saturated Fat, 18 mg Cholesterol, 317 mg Sodium, 50 g Total Carbohydrate, 2 g Dietary Fiber, 18 g Protein, 96 mg Calcium

BRAISED CUCUMBERS

Makes 4 servings

3 medium cucumbers, pared, seeded and cut into 2" × $^1/_2$" sticks	2 teaspoons chopped fresh dill or $^1/_2$ teaspoon dried
$^1/_2$ cup low-sodium chicken broth or vegetable broth	$^1/_2$ teaspoon salt

In medium skillet, combine cucumbers and broth; cook over medium heat, stirring frequently, 12 minutes, just until tender. Add dill and salt; stir to combine.

Each serving (1 cup) provides: $1^1/_2$ Vegetables, 5 Optional Calories

Per serving: 14 Calories, 0 g Total Fat, 0 g Saturated Fat, 0 mg Cholesterol, 285 mg Sodium, 3 g Total Carbohydrate, 0 g Dietary Fiber, 1 g Protein, 16 mg Calcium

Unique Tuna Salad Dinner

CANDIED ORANGES

Makes 4 servings

3 tablespoons granulated sugar
4 small navel oranges

1 fluid ounce (2 tablespoons) orange-flavored liqueur

1. In small saucepan, combine sugar and $^1/_2$ cup water; cook over medium heat, without stirring, 5 minutes.
2. Meanwhile, with zester or vegetable peeler, remove zest* from 1 orange, forming long strips; cut into slivers. Stir zest into sugar syrup; reduce heat to low. Cook, without stirring, 5 minutes longer.
3. Meanwhile, peel oranges; cut into $^1/_4$" slices. Divide orange slices evenly among 4 plates.
4. Add liqueur to sugar mixture; pour evenly over orange slices.

Each serving provides: 1 Fruit, 60 Optional Calories

Per serving: 116 Calories, 0 g Total Fat, 0 g Saturated Fat, 0 mg Cholesterol, 0 mg Sodium, 27 g Total Carbohydrate, 3 g Dietary Fiber, 1 g Protein, 57 mg Calcium

 * *The zest of the orange is the peel without any of the pith (white membrane). To remove zest from orange, use a zester or fine side of a vegetable grater.*

ELEGANT COMPANY DINNER

This beautiful meal is perfect for entertaining. Your guests will love the distinctive flavors of ginger, lemon and vanilla in these elegant yet simple dishes.

Menu serves 4

- 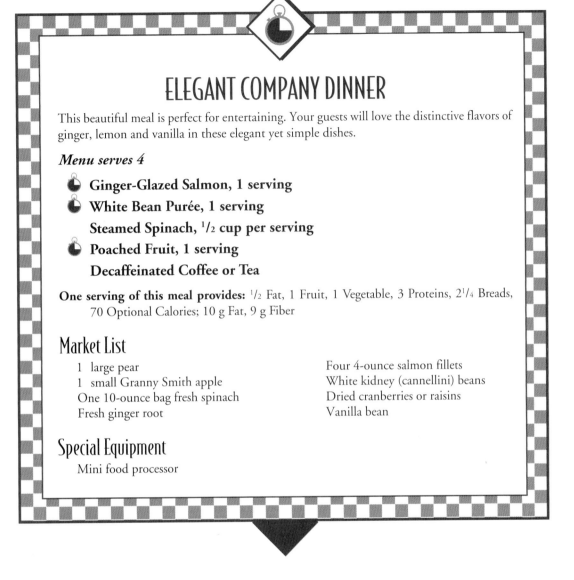 **Ginger-Glazed Salmon, 1 serving**
- **White Bean Purée, 1 serving**
- **Steamed Spinach, $^1/_2$ cup per serving**
- **Poached Fruit, 1 serving**
- **Decaffeinated Coffee or Tea**

One serving of this meal provides: $^1/_2$ Fat, 1 Fruit, 1 Vegetable, 3 Proteins, $2^1/_4$ Breads, 70 Optional Calories; 10 g Fat, 9 g Fiber

Market List

1 large pear
1 small Granny Smith apple
One 10-ounce bag fresh spinach
Fresh ginger root

Four 4-ounce salmon fillets
White kidney (cannellini) beans
Dried cranberries or raisins
Vanilla bean

Special Equipment

Mini food processor

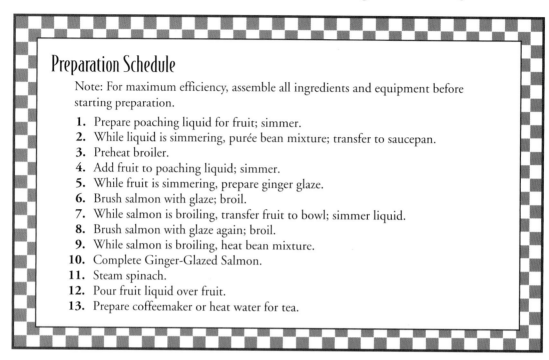

Preparation Schedule

Note: For maximum efficiency, assemble all ingredients and equipment before starting preparation.

1. Prepare poaching liquid for fruit; simmer.
2. While liquid is simmering, purée bean mixture; transfer to saucepan.
3. Preheat broiler.
4. Add fruit to poaching liquid; simmer.
5. While fruit is simmering, prepare ginger glaze.
6. Brush salmon with glaze; broil.
7. While salmon is broiling, transfer fruit to bowl; simmer liquid.
8. Brush salmon with glaze again; broil.
9. While salmon is broiling, heat bean mixture.
10. Complete Ginger-Glazed Salmon.
11. Steam spinach.
12. Pour fruit liquid over fruit.
13. Prepare coffeemaker or heat water for tea.

GINGER-GLAZED SALMON

Makes 4 servings

¹/₄ cup coarsely chopped pared fresh ginger root

2 tablespoons firmly packed light brown sugar

2 tablespoons fresh lemon juice

1 teaspoon low-sodium soy sauce

Four 4-ounce salmon fillets

1. Preheat broiler. Line broiler pan with foil.
2. To prepare glaze, in mini food processor or blender, combine ginger, sugar, lemon juice and soy sauce; purée until smooth.
3. Place salmon fillets on prepared broiler pan; brush fillets evenly with glaze, reserving remaining glaze. Broil 4" from heat, 5 minutes.
4. Brush fillets evenly with some of the remaining glaze; broil 5 minutes longer, until fish flakes easily when tested with fork.
5. Remove fillets from broiler; brush evenly with remaining glaze.

Each serving provides: 3 Proteins, 25 Optional Calories

Per serving: 194 Calories, 7 g Total Fat, 1 g Saturated Fat, 62 mg Cholesterol, 104 mg Sodium, 8 g Total Carbohydrate, 0 g Dietary Fiber, 23 g Protein, 21 mg Calcium

WHITE BEAN PURÉE

Makes 4 servings

1 pound 2 ounces drained cooked white
 kidney (cannellini) beans
1/3 cup fresh lemon juice
1 tablespoon + 1 teaspoon reduced-calorie
 tub margarine

1 tablespoon grated lemon zest *
1 teaspoon salt
1/2 teaspoon freshly ground black pepper

1. In food processor, combine beans, lemon juice, margarine, lemon zest, salt and pepper; purée until smooth.
2. Transfer bean mixture to small saucepan. Place over medium heat; cook, stirring constantly, 2–3 minutes, until heated through.

Each serving provides: 1/2 Fat, 2 1/4 Breads

Per serving: 186 Calories, 3 g Total Fat, 0 g Saturated Fat, 0 mg Cholesterol, 590 mg Sodium, 31 g Total Carbohydrate, 5 g Dietary Fiber, 11 g Protein, 44 mg Calcium

  * The zest of the lemon is the peel without any of the pith (white membrane). To remove zest from lemon, use a zester or fine side of a vegetable grater.

POACHED FRUIT

Makes 4 servings

1 lemon
1/4 cup granulated sugar
One 2" vanilla bean, split
1 large pear, pared, cored and
 cut into wedges

1 small Granny Smith apple, pared, cored
 and cut into wedges
2 tablespoons dried cranberries or raisins

1. With zester or vegetable peeler, remove the zest * from the lemon, forming long strips; place in medium saucepan. Cut lemon in half; squeeze juice into same saucepan.
2. Add 1 cup water, the sugar and vanilla bean to zest-juice mixture; bring to a boil. Reduce heat to low; simmer 5 minutes.
3. Add pear, apple and cranberries to lemon mixture; simmer 10 minutes longer, until fruit is tender. Remove and discard vanilla bean.
4. With slotted spoon, transfer fruit to medium bowl. Simmer liquid, stirring occasionally, 5 minutes, until syrupy; pour over fruit mixture.

Each serving provides: 1 Fruit, 45 Optional Calories

Per serving: 125 Calories, 0 g Total Fat, 0 g Saturated Fat, 0 mg Cholesterol, 0 mg Sodium, 32 g Total Carbohydrate, 2 g Dietary Fiber, 0 g Protein, 12 mg Calcium

  * The zest of the lemon is the peel without any of the pith (white membrane). To remove zest from lemon, use a zester or fine side of a vegetable grater.

QUICK AND ELEGANT ITALIAN SEAFOOD SUPPER

Quick to make, this lavish meal is a feast for seafood lovers; remember to provide a bowl for discarding the mussel shells. As an elegant touch, serve this meal with a glass of crisp dry white wine.

Menu serves 8

- **Bouillabaisse, 1 serving**
- **Garlic Toast, 1 serving**
- **Crudités, 1 cup per serving**
- **Zabaglione with Berries, 1 serving**
- **Dry White Wine, 4 fluid ounces per serving**

One serving of this meal provides: 1 Fat, 1 Fruit, $2^1/_2$ Vegetables, 3 Proteins, $1^1/_2$ Breads, 145 Optional Calories; 14 g Fat, 8 g Fiber

Market List

2 cups blackberries
2 cups blueberries
2 cups raspberries
Vegetables for crudités
Fresh flat-leaf parsley
24 medium mussels
10 ounces turbot fillets
10 ounces boneless tuna steak
8 ounces cooked shelled lump
    crabmeat

1 loaf French bread
Bottled clam juice
2 cups egg substitute, frozen or
    refrigerated
Dried chervil leaves
Ground saffron
Dry marsala wine

Special Equipment

8 fluted champagne or parfait glasses

Quick and Elegant Italian Seafood Supper

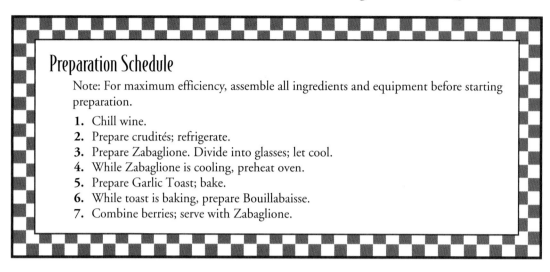

BOUILLABAISSE

Makes 8 servings

2 teaspoons olive oil	1 cup chopped canned plum tomatoes
1 cup chopped onions	2" × ¹/₂" strip orange zest *
4 garlic cloves, pressed	¹/₂ teaspoon dried thyme leaves
24 medium mussels, scrubbed and debearded	¹/₂ teaspoon dried chervil leaves
10 ounces turbot fillets, cut into chunks	1 bay leaf
10 ounces boneless tuna steak, cut into chunks	Pinch ground saffron†
1¹/₂ cups clam juice	8 ounces cooked shelled lump crabmeat
	2 tablespoons chopped fresh flat-leaf parsley

1. In large nonstick saucepan, heat oil; add onions and garlic. Cook over medium-high heat, stirring frequently, 2–3 minutes, until garlic is golden. Add mussels, turbot, tuna, clam juice, tomatoes, orange zest, thyme, chervil, bay leaf and saffron; bring liquid to a boil. Cook, covered, 5 minutes, until mussels open and fish flakes easily when tested with a fork.
2. Add crabmeat and parsley to fish mixture; stir to combine. Remove and discard orange zest and bay leaf before serving.

Each serving (1¹/₂ cups) provides: ¹/₄ Fat, ¹/₂ Vegetable, 2 Proteins

Per serving: 191 Calories, 9 g Total Fat, 2 g Saturated Fat, 64 mg Cholesterol, 282 mg Sodium, 4 g Total Carbohydrate, 1 g Dietary Fiber, 22 g Protein, 55 mg Calcium

* The zest of the orange is the peel without any of the pith (white membrane). To remove zest from orange, use a zester or vegetable grater; wrap orange in plastic wrap and refrigerate for use at another time.

† If saffron is not available, substitute ground turmeric; flavor will not be the same.

Garlic Toast

Makes 8 servings

2 tablespoons olive oil
2 tablespoons low-sodium chicken broth
2 garlic cloves, pressed

12 ounces French bread, cut diagonally
    into 16 slices

1. Preheat oven to 350° F. Line baking sheet with foil.
2. In small bowl, combine oil, broth and garlic. With pastry brush, brush one side of each bread slice with oil mixture; place on prepared baking sheet, spread side up.
3. Bake 10–13 minutes, until lightly browned.

Each serving (2 slices) provides: ³/₄ Fat, 1¹/₂ Breads

Per serving: 148 Calories, 5 g Total Fat, 1 g Saturated Fat, 0 mg Cholesterol, 260 mg Sodium, 22 g Total Carbohydrate, 1 g Dietary Fiber, 4 g Protein, 33 mg Calcium

Zabaglione with Berries

Makes 8 servings

1 cup skim milk
2 tablespoons + 2 teaspoons granulated
    sugar
1 tablespoon + 1 teaspoon cornstarch
2 cups egg substitute

4 fluid ounces (¹/₂ cup) dry marsala wine
2 cups blackberries
2 cups blueberries
2 cups raspberries

1. In large saucepan, with wire whisk, combine milk, sugar and cornstarch, stirring until cornstarch is dissolved. Continuing to stir, bring mixture to a simmer over medium heat; cook, stirring constantly with whisk, 4 minutes, until thickened.
2. Pour egg substitute into large bowl; with wire whisk, slowly stir in hot milk mixture. Return mixture to large saucepan; cook over low heat, stirring with wire whisk, 5–7 minutes, until hot, thick and fluffy (do not boil). With whisk, slowly stir in marsala; cook, stirring constantly, 1 minute longer.
3. Divide mixture evenly among 8 fluted champagne or parfait glasses. In medium bowl combine blackberries, blueberries and raspberries; serve each portion of zabaglione with ³/₄ cup mixed berries.

Each serving (¹/₂ cup zabaglione + ³/₄ cup berries) provides: 1 Fruit, 1 Protein, 45 Optional Calories

Per serving: 134 Calories, 0 g Total Fat, 0 g Saturated Fat, 1 mg Cholesterol, 100 mg Sodium, 23 g Total Carbohydrate, 4 g Dietary Fiber, 7 g Protein, 80 mg Calcium

SPRINGTIME SALMON SUPPER

The smoky flavor of chipotle peppers is especially good with salmon. Serve these lovely packets of flavor with a medley of bright vegetables and pasta shells, red, ripe tomatoes and a divine peach dessert made with the ripest and most fragrant peaches you can find.

Menu serves 4

- Salmon in Foil Packets, 1 serving
- Spring Shells, 1 serving
  Tomato Slices, $^1/_2$ cup per serving
- Peaches in Honey and Almond Cream, 1 serving
  Sparkling Mineral Water with Lime Twist

One serving of this meal provides: 1 Fat, 1 Fruit, $3^1/_2$ Vegetables, $3^1/_4$ Proteins, 2 Breads, 70 Optional Calories; 15 g Fat, 7 g Fiber

Market List

4 medium peaches	Small pasta shells
2 medium tomatoes	Low-sodium chicken broth or
1 medium head iceberg lettuce	vegetable broth
4 small plum tomatoes	Almond extract
1 medium red bell pepper	Slivered almonds
1 medium zucchini	8 fluid ounces vanilla nonfat
1 medium yellow squash	sugar-free frozen yogurt
Fresh cilantro	One 10-ounce package frozen
Fresh basil	green peas
Four 4-ounce salmon fillets	
Canned chipotle peppers in	
adobo sauce	

Special Equipment

Microwave oven
1-quart shallow microwave-safe dish

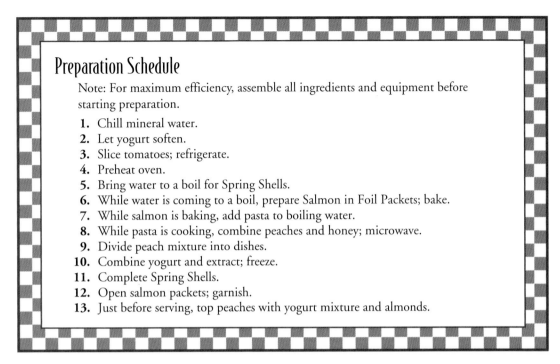

Preparation Schedule

Note: For maximum efficiency, assemble all ingredients and equipment before starting preparation.

1. Chill mineral water.
2. Let yogurt soften.
3. Slice tomatoes; refrigerate.
4. Preheat oven.
5. Bring water to a boil for Spring Shells.
6. While water is coming to a boil, prepare Salmon in Foil Packets; bake.
7. While salmon is baking, add pasta to boiling water.
8. While pasta is cooking, combine peaches and honey; microwave.
9. Divide peach mixture into dishes.
10. Combine yogurt and extract; freeze.
11. Complete Spring Shells.
12. Open salmon packets; garnish.
13. Just before serving, top peaches with yogurt mixture and almonds.

SALMON IN FOIL PACKETS

Makes 4 servings

One 7-ounce can chipotle peppers in
   adobo sauce
4 small plum tomatoes, blanched,
   peeled, seeded and chopped
1 tablespoon minced fresh cilantro

2 garlic cloves, pressed
2 teaspoons fresh lime juice
2 cups finely shredded iceberg lettuce
Four 4-ounce salmon fillets
Lime slices to garnish (optional)

1. Preheat oven to 400° F. Line baking sheet with foil.
2. In food processor or blender, purée chipotle peppers with sauce until smooth. Transfer 2 teaspoons pureed mixture to medium bowl; refrigerate remaining mixture, covered, for use at another time.
3. Stir tomatoes, cilantro, garlic and lime juice into pureed peppers; set aside.
4. Onto each of four 12 × 12" pieces of foil, place ½ cup of the lettuce; top each with 1 salmon fillet, then one-fourth of the tomato mixture.
5. Bring 2 opposite sides of foil together; fold over to seal. Fold remaining 2 sides to seal. Place packets seam side up on prepared baking sheet; bake 20 minutes (salmon should flake easily when tested with fork).
6. Open packets carefully, allowing steam to escape; garnish with lime slices if desired.

Each serving provides: 1½ Vegetables, 3 Proteins

Per serving: 179 Calories, 8 g Total Fat, 1 g Saturated Fat, 63 mg Cholesterol, 92 mg Sodium, 4 g Total Carbohydrate, 1 g Dietary Fiber, 23 g Protein, 38 mg Calcium

SPRING SHELLS

Makes 4 servings

$5^1/_4$ ounces small pasta shells
$^1/_2$ cup diced carrot ($^1/_2$" dice)
$^1/_2$ cup diced red bell pepper ($^1/_2$" dice)
$^1/_2$ cup diced zucchini ($^1/_2$" dice)
$^1/_2$ cup diced yellow squash ($^1/_2$" dice)
$^1/_2$ cup frozen green peas
$^1/_2$ cup low-sodium chicken broth or
    vegetable broth

$^1/_4$ cup packed fresh basil leaves, slivered
2 teaspoons olive oil
1 tablespoon fresh lemon juice
$^1/_2$ teaspoon salt
Freshly ground black pepper to taste

1. In large pot of boiling water, cook shells 3 minutes. Add carrot; cook 5 minutes longer.
2. Add red pepper, zucchini and squash to pasta mixture; cook 3 minutes longer.
3. Add peas to pasta mixture; cook 2 minutes longer. Drain; transfer to large bowl. Add broth, basil, oil, lemon juice, salt and black pepper; toss to combine.

Each serving ($1^1/_2$ cups) provides: $^1/_2$ Fat, 1 Vegetable, 2 Breads, 5 Optional Calories

Per serving: 195 Calories, 3 g Total Fat, 0 g Saturated Fat, 0 mg Cholesterol, 309 mg Sodium, 35 g Total Carbohydrate, 2 g Dietary Fiber, 7 g Protein, 59 mg Calcium

PEACHES IN HONEY AND ALMOND CREAM

Makes 4 servings

4 medium peaches, blanched, peeled,
    pitted and sliced
2 tablespoons honey
8 fluid ounces vanilla nonfat sugar-free
    frozen yogurt, softened

$^1/_4$ teaspoon almond extract
1 ounce slivered almonds

1. In a 1-quart shallow microwave-safe dish, combine peaches and honey. Cover with vented plastic wrap; microwave on High (100% power) 1 minute. Remove cover carefully; toss mixture to coat evenly. Divide peach mixture evenly among 4 dessert dishes.
2. In small bowl, with wire whisk, combine yogurt and extract. Top each portion of peach mixture with one-fourth of the yogurt mixture; sprinkle evenly with almonds.

Each serving provides: $^1/_2$ Fat, 1 Fruit, $^1/_4$ Protein, 65 Optional Calories

Per serving: 170 Calories, 4 g Total Fat, 0 g Saturated Fat, 0 mg Cholesterol, 34 mg Sodium, 35 g Total Carbohydrate, 3 g Dietary Fiber, 4 g Protein, 101 mg Calcium

A CELEBRATION DINNER

When nothing but the very best will do, here is a menu to help you celebrate in style. It's so easy and elegant that you'll have no trouble thinking of things to celebrate!

Menu serves 2

- **Oysters on the Half Shell, 1 serving**
- **Smoked Salmon Canapés, 1 serving**
- **Stuffed New Potatoes, 1 serving**
- **Strawberries in Champagne, 1 serving**

One serving of this meal provides: $^1/_2$ Fruit, $^1/_4$ Vegetable, $2^1/_4$ Proteins, 2 Breads, 125 Optional Calories; 6 g Fat, 6 g Fiber

Market List

2   cups whole strawberries
15 ounces tiny new potatoes
Fresh dill
Fresh flat-leaf parsley (optional)
12 medium oysters, shucked and left on the half shell
2   ounces very thinly sliced smoked Nova Scotia salmon

Nonfat sour cream
Nonfat cream cheese
Black caviar
Cocktail (party-style) rye bread, sliced
Raspberry vinegar
Bottled capers
Champagne

Special Equipment

Oyster forks (optional)
Small teaspoon or demitasse spoon
Microwave oven

Microwave-safe dish
Fluted champagne or parfait glasses

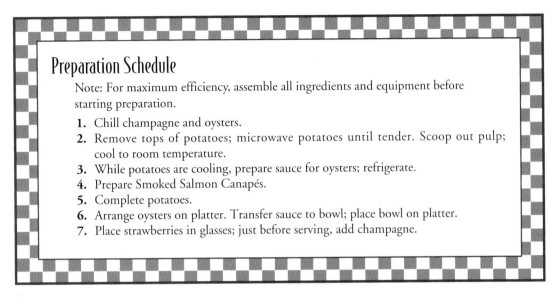

Preparation Schedule

Note: For maximum efficiency, assemble all ingredients and equipment before starting preparation.

1. Chill champagne and oysters.
2. Remove tops of potatoes; microwave potatoes until tender. Scoop out pulp; cool to room temperature.
3. While potatoes are cooling, prepare sauce for oysters; refrigerate.
4. Prepare Smoked Salmon Canapés.
5. Complete potatoes.
6. Arrange oysters on platter. Transfer sauce to bowl; place bowl on platter.
7. Place strawberries in glasses; just before serving, add champagne.

OYSTERS ON THE HALF SHELL

Makes 2 servings

12 medium oysters, shucked and left
    on the half shell
¹/₄ cup minced shallots
2 tablespoons red wine vinegar

1 tablespoon raspberry vinegar
Pinch salt
Freshly ground black pepper to taste

1. Place oysters in large bowl filled with crushed ice; refrigerate, covered, until ready to serve.
2. To prepare sauce, in small bowl, with wire whisk, blend together shallots, red wine vinegar, raspberry vinegar, salt and pepper; refrigerate, covered.
3. Just before serving, arrange oysters in a circle on large decorative platter. Transfer sauce to small decorative bowl; place bowl in center of platter. Serve with toothpicks or oyster forks for dipping or small teaspoon or demitasse spoon to spoon sauce onto oysters.

Each serving provides: ¹/₄ Vegetable, 1 Protein

Per serving: 76 Calories, 2 g Total Fat, 1 g Saturated Fat, 47 mg Cholesterol, 164 mg Sodium, 7 g Total Carbohydrate, 0 g Dietary Fiber, 7 g Protein, 46 mg Calcium

SMOKED SALMON CANAPÉS

Makes 2 servings

6 slices (2 ounces) cocktail (party-style) rye bread, halved diagonally to form 12 triangles	1 tablespoon drained capers, rinsed
2 tablespoons nonfat cream cheese	12 small dill sprigs
2 ounces very thinly sliced smoked Nova Scotia salmon, cut into 12 equal pieces	1 lemon, cut into wedges
	Additional dill sprigs to garnish (optional)

1. Spread each bread triangle with $1/2$ teaspoon cream cheese; top each with 1 piece of salmon, a few capers and 1 dill sprig.
2. Arrange canapés on medium decorative platter; surround with lemon wedges to be used to squeeze onto canapés before eating. Serve at room temperature, garnished with additional dill sprigs if desired.

Each serving (6 canapés) provides: 1 Protein, 1 Bread, 15 Optional Calories

Per serving: 135 Calories, 2 g Total Fat, 0 g Saturated Fat, 9 mg Cholesterol, 623 mg Sodium, 21 g Total Carbohydrate, 2 g Dietary Fiber, 11 g Protein, 175 mg Calcium

STUFFED NEW POTATOES

Makes 2 servings

15 ounces tiny new potatoes	Fresh flat-leaf parsley sprigs to garnish (optional)
2 tablespoons nonfat sour cream	
$1/2$ ounce black caviar	

1. To prepare potato shells, remove a $1/4$" slice from top of each potato; place potatoes on microwave-safe dish. Microwave potatoes on High (100% power) 3 minutes, until tender but not mushy. With small teaspoon or melon baller, scoop out about 1 teaspoon pulp from top of each potato; reserve pulp for use at another time. Potato shells should weigh a total of 8 ounces; cool to room temperature.
2. Fill each potato shell with an equal amount of sour cream; top with an equal amount of caviar. Arrange stuffed potatoes on medium decorative platter; serve garnished with parsley if desired.

Each serving (5 stuffed potatoes) provides: $1/4$ Protein, 1 Bread, 10 Optional Calories

Per serving: 142 Calories, 2 g Total Fat, 0 g Saturated Fat, 42 mg Cholesterol, 127 mg Sodium, 27 g Total Carbohydrate, 2 g Dietary Fiber, 5 g Protein, 19 mg Calcium

Strawberries in Champagne

For each serving, place *¹/₂ cup whole strawberries* in a fluted champagne or parfait glass; top with *4 fluid ounces (¹/₂ cup) chilled champagne.*

Each serving provides: ¹/₂ Fruit, 100 Optional Calories

Per serving: 103 Calories, 0 g Total Fat, 0 g Saturated Fat, 0 mg Cholesterol, 7 mg Sodium, 6 g Total Carbohydrate, 2 g Dietary Fiber, 1 g Protein, 21 mg Calcium

SENSATIONAL SCALLOP DINNER

For an even easier and quicker meal, try serving this creamy seafood entrée on crisp toast points instead of noodles. The accompanying artichoke hearts are simply elegant, so you can get all the compliments without much work. Add a glass of chilled white wine and a wedge of ripe melon for dessert and your meal is complete!

Menu serves 4

- **Scallops in Tarragon Cream, 1 serving**
- **Pink Noodles, 1 serving**
- **Artichoke Hearts with Pine Nuts, 1 serving**
- **Honeydew Melon, 2" wedge per serving**
- **Dry White Wine, 4 fluid ounces per serving**

One serving of this meal provides: $1^{1}/_{2}$ Fats, 1 Fruit, $2^{1}/_{4}$ Vegetables, 2 Proteins, $1^{1}/_{2}$ Breads, 140 Optional Calories; 10 g Fat, 6 g Fiber

Market List

1 medium honeydew melon
Fresh flat-leaf parsley
Fresh tarragon
1 pound 4 ounces bay or sea scallops
Nonfat sour cream
Bottled clam juice
Thin noodles

Sun-dried tomato halves
   (not packed in oil)
Tomato juice
Pignolias (pine nuts)
One 10-ounce package frozen
   artichoke hearts
Anisette (anise-flavored liqueur)

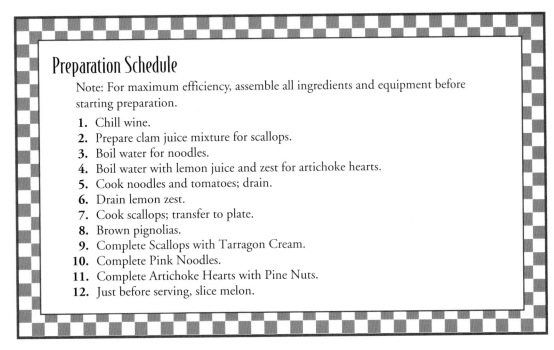

Preparation Schedule

Note: For maximum efficiency, assemble all ingredients and equipment before starting preparation.

1. Chill wine.
2. Prepare clam juice mixture for scallops.
3. Boil water for noodles.
4. Boil water with lemon juice and zest for artichoke hearts.
5. Cook noodles and tomatoes; drain.
6. Drain lemon zest.
7. Cook scallops; transfer to plate.
8. Brown pignolias.
9. Complete Scallops with Tarragon Cream.
10. Complete Pink Noodles.
11. Complete Artichoke Hearts with Pine Nuts.
12. Just before serving, slice melon.

SCALLOPS IN TARRAGON CREAM

Makes 4 servings

$^1/_2$ cup clam juice
 2 fluid ounces ($^1/_4$ cup) dry white wine
 1 teaspoon anisette (anise-flavored liqueur)
$^1/_2$ teaspoon cornstarch
 2 teaspoons vegetable oil
 1 pound 4 ounces bay or sea scallops
 2 tablespoons minced shallots

$^1/_4$ cup nonfat sour cream
 2 tablespoons minced fresh flat-leaf parsley
 2 tablespoons minced fresh tarragon
 2 teaspoons fresh lemon juice
Fresh tarragon sprigs to garnish (optional)

1. In small bowl, with wire whisk, combine clam juice, wine, anisette and cornstarch, blending until cornstarch is dissolved; set aside.
2. In large nonstick skillet, heat oil; add scallops. Cook over medium-high heat, stirring constantly, 1 minute, just until opaque. With slotted spoon, transfer scallops to plate; set aside.
3. In same skillet, cook shallots over medium-high heat, stirring constantly, 1 minute, until softened. Add clam juice mixture; cook, stirring constantly, 3 minutes, until slightly thickened.
4. Return scallops to skillet; add sour cream, parsley, minced tarragon and lemon juice; cook, stirring frequently, just until heated (do not boil). Garnish with tarragon sprigs if desired.

Each serving provides: $^1/_2$ Fat, 2 Proteins, 30 Optional Calories

Per serving: 177 Calories, 3 g Total Fat, 0 g Saturated Fat, 47 mg Cholesterol, 305 mg Sodium, 7 g Total Carbohydrate, 0 g Dietary Fiber, 25 g Protein, 69 mg Calcium

PINK NOODLES

Makes 4 servings

4¹/₂ ounces thin noodles
  8 sun-dried tomato halves
        (not packed in oil), slivered
¹/₂ cup tomato juice

  1 teaspoon stick margarine
Pinch freshly ground black pepper
Pinch cinnamon

1. In medium saucepan of boiling water, cook noodles and tomatoes 2–3 minutes, until barely tender; drain and set aside.
2. Meanwhile, in separate medium saucepan, combine tomato juice, margarine, pepper and cinnamon; cook over low heat, stirring frequently, until margarine is melted and mixture is heated. Remove from heat.
3. Add cooked noodles and tomatoes to tomato juice mixture; stir to combine.

Each serving provides: ¹/₄ Fat, 1¹/₄ Vegetables, 1¹/₂ Breads

Per serving: 152 Calories, 2 g Total Fat, 0 g Saturated Fat, 30 mg Cholesterol, 135 mg Sodium, 28 g Total Carbohydrate, 2 g Dietary Fiber, 5 g Protein, 20 mg Calcium

ARTICHOKE HEARTS WITH PINE NUTS

Makes 4 servings

3 tablespoons fresh lemon juice
1 teaspoon slivered lemon zest *
2 teaspoons olive oil
1 tablespoon + 1 teaspoon pignolias
      (pine nuts)

Pinch freshly ground black pepper
2 cups cooked frozen artichoke hearts

1. In medium saucepan, combine 2 cups water, 1 tablespoon of the lemon juice and the lemon zest; bring liquid to a boil. Cook over high heat 5–7 minutes, until lemon zest is tender. Drain; set zest aside.
2. In medium skillet, heat oil; add pignolias. Toast over medium heat, stirring constantly, 2 minutes, until lightly golden; remove from heat.
3. Stir remaining 2 tablespoons lemon juice and the pepper into pignolias. Add artichoke hearts and cooked lemon zest; stir gently to combine.

Each serving (¹/₂ cup) provides: ³/₄ Fat, 1 Vegetable, 10 Optional Calories

Per serving: 71 Calories, 4 g Total Fat, 1 g Saturated Fat, 0 mg Cholesterol, 40 mg Sodium, 8 g Total Carbohydrate, 3 g Dietary Fiber, 3 g Protein, 19 mg Calcium

  * *The zest of the lemon is the peel without any of the pith (white membrane). To remove zest from lemon, use a zester or fine side of a vegetable grater.*

FABULOUS PHILIPPINE FISH FEAST

This entrée was inspired by a popular Philippine dish made with calamondins, a tiny citrus fruit with a unique flavor, approximated by this combination of orange, lemon and lime. Lettuce cooked with peas is a classic; try different kinds of lettuce, such as Boston or red leaf.

Menu serves 4

- **Citrus Red Snapper, 1 serving**
- **Green Rice, 1 serving**
- **Braised Lettuce and Peas, 1 serving**
- **Mandarin Orange Sections, $^1/_2$ cup per serving**
- **Club Soda with Lime Wedge**

One serving of this meal provides: 1 Fat, 1 Fruit, 5 Vegetables, 3 Proteins, 2 Breads, 20 Optional Calories; 7 g Fat, 3 g Fiber

Market List

Orange juice
1 bunch scallions
1 medium yellow bell pepper
1 head Romaine lettuce
Fresh flat-leaf parsley
Four 8-ounce red snapper fillets
Peanut oil
Canned Mandarin orange sections (no sugar added)

Club soda
One 10-ounce package frozen chopped spinach
One 10-ounce package frozen green peas
Ground coriander

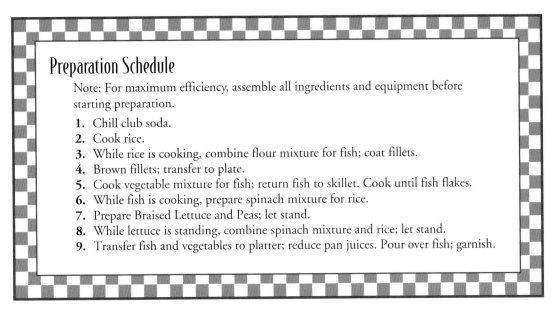

Preparation Schedule

Note: For maximum efficiency, assemble all ingredients and equipment before starting preparation.

1. Chill club soda.
2. Cook rice.
3. While rice is cooking, combine flour mixture for fish; coat fillets.
4. Brown fillets; transfer to plate.
5. Cook vegetable mixture for fish; return fish to skillet. Cook until fish flakes.
6. While fish is cooking, prepare spinach mixture for rice.
7. Prepare Braised Lettuce and Peas; let stand.
8. While lettuce is standing, combine spinach mixture and rice; let stand.
9. Transfer fish and vegetables to platter; reduce pan juices. Pour over fish; garnish.

Fabulous Philippine Fish Feast

CITRUS RED SNAPPER

Makes 4 servings

2 tablespoons all-purpose flour
³/₄ teaspoon ground coriander
³/₄ teaspoon ground ginger
¹/₄ teaspoon ground red pepper
Four 8-ounce red snapper fillets
2 teaspoons peanut oil
1 cup sliced yellow bell pepper

¹/₄ cup sliced scallions (white and green parts)
¹/₄ cup low-sodium chicken broth
2 tablespoons orange juice
1 tablespoon fresh lemon juice
1 tablespoon fresh lime juice
Lemon and lime slices to garnish (optional)

1. On paper plate or sheet of wax paper, combine flour, coriander, ginger and red pepper. Coat one side of each fish fillet with flour mixture; set aside.
2. In large nonstick skillet, heat oil; add fish fillets, floured side down. Cook over medium-high heat until browned on bottom. With spatula, transfer fish to plate; set aside.
3. Add yellow pepper, scallions, broth and orange, lemon and lime juice to skillet; stir to combine. Return fish to skillet, browned side up; reduce heat to low. Cook, covered, 3–5 minutes, until fish flakes easily when tested with fork and vegetables are tender; with slotted spatula, transfer fish and vegetables to large decorative platter.
4. Cook pan juices until reduced in volume to about ¹/₄ cup; pour over fish. Garnish with lemon and lime slices if desired.

Each serving provides: ¹/₂ Fat, ³/₄ Vegetables, 3 Proteins, 20 Optional Calories

Per serving: 279 Calories, 5 g Total Fat, 1 g Saturated Fat, 84 mg Cholesterol, 150 mg Sodium, 7 g Total Carbohydrate, 1 g Dietary Fiber, 48 g Protein, 83 mg Calcium

GREEN RICE

Makes 4 servings

6 ounces converted rice
1 teaspoon vegetable oil
¹/₄ cup minced celery
1 garlic clove, minced
2 cups well-drained thawed frozen chopped spinach

2 tablespoons minced fresh flat-leaf parsley
¹/₄ teaspoon dried thyme leaves

1. In medium saucepan, bring 1³/₄ cups water to a boil; add rice. Reduce heat to low; cook, covered, 15 minutes, just until all water is absorbed. Remove from heat.
2. Meanwhile, in medium skillet, heat oil; add celery and garlic. Cook over medium heat, stirring frequently, 1 minute, until just softened. Add spinach, parsley and thyme; cook, stirring constantly, 2 minutes, until heated through.
3. Add spinach mixture to cooked rice; stir to combine.

Each serving provides: $^1/_4$ Fat, $1^1/_4$ Vegetables, $1^1/_2$ Breads

Per serving: 197 Calories, 2 g Total Fat, 0 g Saturated Fat, 0 mg Cholesterol, 89 mg Sodium, 40 g Total Carbohydrate, 3 g Dietary Fiber, 6 g Protein, 153 mg Calcium

BRAISED LETTUCE AND PEAS

Makes 4 servings

1 teaspoon vegetable oil	Pinch salt
6 cups shredded Romaine lettuce	Pinch freshly ground black pepper
1 cup frozen green peas	

In large nonstick skillet, heat oil; add lettuce and peas. Cook over medium heat, tossing constantly, 1 minute, until lettuce is wilted. Remove from heat; let stand, covered, 5 minutes, until peas are tender. Sprinkle with salt and pepper.

Each serving provides: $^1/_4$ Fat, 3 Vegetables, $^1/_2$ Bread

Per serving: 51 Calories, 1 g Total Fat, 0 g Saturated Fat, 0 mg Cholesterol, 80 mg Sodium, 7 g Total Carbohydrate, 3 g Dietary Fiber, 3 g Protein, 39 mg Calcium

HERB-LOVERS' DELIGHT

The secret of low-fat cooking is to replace fat with flavor. This menu takes advantage of what are, perhaps, the best of flavors—fresh herbs and garlic. The results are rich-tasting dishes that are quick to prepare and easy on the waistline.

Menu serves 4

- 🕐 **White Bean Soup, 1 serving**
- 🕐 **Scallops with Herb Sauce, 1 serving**
- 🕐 **Garlic-Roasted Carrots, 1 serving**
- 🕐 **Potatoes with Parsley, 1 serving**
- **Dry White Wine, 4 fluid ounces per serving**

One serving of this meal provides: $2^{1}/_{4}$ Fats, $1^{1}/_{2}$ Vegetables, 3 Proteins, 1 Bread, 105 Optional Calories; 12 g Fat, 8 g Fiber

Market List

Fresh flat-leaf parsley	15 ounces sea scallops
Fresh basil	Extra-virgin olive oil
Fresh thyme	Great northern beans
Fresh rosemary	

Preparation Schedule

Note: For maximum efficiency, assemble all ingredients and equipment before starting preparation.

1. Chill wine.
2. Preheat oven.
3. Pare and boil potatoes.
4. While potatoes are boiling, bring soup ingredients to a simmer.
5. While soup is simmering, prepare Garlic-Roasted Carrots; bake, covered.
6. While carrots are baking, cool soup.
7. While soup is cooling, purée herb mixture for scallops.
8. Cook scallops; let cool.
9. While scallops are cooling, roast carrots.
10. While carrots are roasting, purée soup.
11. Complete Scallops with Herb Sauce.
12. Complete Potatoes with Parsley.
13. Ladle soup; sprinkle with lemon zest and seasonings.

White Bean Soup

Makes 4 servings

1 teaspoon extra-virgin olive oil	2 tablespoons chopped fresh rosemary
1 garlic clove, minced	$^3/_4$ teaspoon freshly ground black pepper
12 ounces drained cooked great	1 cup low-sodium chicken broth
northern beans	1 teaspoon grated lemon zest *

1. In medium saucepan, heat oil; add garlic. Cook over medium heat, stirring constantly, 1 minute, until tender but not browned. Add beans, 1 tablespoon of the rosemary and $^1/_2$ teaspoon of the pepper; stir to coat. Stir in broth; bring liquid to a boil. Reduce heat to low; simmer 10 minutes. Cool slightly.
2. Transfer bean mixture to food processor; purée until smooth. Return mixture to saucepan; cook over low heat until heated.
3. Just before serving, ladle soup equally into 4 soup bowls; sprinkle each portion with one-fourth of the lemon zest, remaining rosemary and remaining pepper.

Each serving provides: $^1/_4$ Fat, $1^1/_2$ Proteins, 5 Optional Calories

Per serving: 122 Calories, 2 g Total Fat, 0 g Saturated Fat, 0 mg Cholesterol, 16 mg Sodium, 19 g Total Carbohydrate, 3 g Dietary Fiber, 8 g Protein, 67 mg Calcium

   * *The zest of the lemon is the peel without any of the pith (white membrane). To remove zest from lemon, use a zester or fine side of a vegetable grater; wrap lemon in plastic wrap and refrigerate for use at another time.*

Scallops with Herb Sauce

Makes 4 servings

$^1/_2$ cup packed fresh flat-leaf parsley leaves	1 tablespoon vegetable oil
$^1/_2$ cup packed fresh basil leaves	$^1/_2$ garlic clove, minced
3 tablespoons low-sodium chicken broth	$^1/_4$ teaspoon salt
2 tablespoons fresh thyme leaves	$^1/_4$ teaspoon freshly ground black pepper
1 tablespoon fresh lemon juice	15 ounces sea scallops

1. In food processor or blender, combine parsley, basil, broth, thyme, lemon juice, oil, garlic, salt and pepper; purée until smooth. Set aside.
2. Spray large nonstick skillet with nonstick cooking spray; place over medium heat. Add scallops; cook, turning once, 2–3 minutes on each side, until golden brown and heated through. Remove from heat; transfer scallops to medium bowl. Let skillet cool slightly.
3. Pour reserved herb mixture into cooled skillet; cook over medium heat, stirring constantly, 1–2 minutes, until heated. Pour over scallops; toss to combine.

Each serving provides: $^3/_4$ Fat, $1^1/_2$ Proteins

Per serving: 138 Calories, 5 g Total Fat, 1 g Saturated Fat, 35 mg Cholesterol, 313 mg Sodium, 5 g Total Carbohydrate, 0 g Dietary Fiber, 18 g Protein, 95 mg Calcium

GARLIC-ROASTED CARROTS

Makes 4 servings

3 medium carrots, cut into
   ¹/₄" diagonal slices

1 teaspoon olive oil
2 garlic cloves, quartered

1. Preheat oven to 400° F.
2. In a 1-quart shallow baking dish, combine carrots, 1 tablespoon water, the oil and garlic; bake, covered, 10 minutes. Remove cover; roast 10 minutes, until carrots and garlic are tender.

Each serving provides: ¹/₄ Fat, 1¹/₂ Vegetables

Per serving: 45 Calories, 1 g Total Fat, 0 g Saturated Fat, 0 mg Cholesterol, 27 mg Sodium, 8 g Total Carbohydrate, 2 g Dietary Fiber, 1 g Protein, 23 mg Calcium

POTATOES WITH PARSLEY

For each serving, pare *5 ounces potato*, cut into chunks. Boil in lightly salted water to cover until tender; drain. Toss with *1 teaspoon stick margarine* and *2 teaspoons chopped fresh flat-leaf parsley.*

Each serving provides: 1 Fat, 1 Bread

Per serving: 147 Calories, 4 g Total Fat, 1 g Saturated Fat, 0 mg Cholesterol, 186 mg Sodium, 26 g Total Carbohydrate, 2 g Dietary Fiber, 3 g Protein, 15 mg Calcium

A MEDITERRANEAN FISH DINNER

All the flavors of the Mediterranean come together in this menu with its classic combination of herbs, vegetables and seafood.

Menu serves 4

- **Fresh Cod Niçoise, 1 serving**
- **Mashed Potato–Garlic Galette, 1 serving**
- **Ratatouille, 1 serving**
  Grapes, 12 large or 20 small per serving
  Chardonnay, 4 fluid ounces per serving

One serving of this meal provides: $2^1/_4$ Fats, 1 Fruit, $6^1/_2$ Vegetables, 2 Proteins, $1^1/_2$ Breads, 115 Optional Calories; 14 g Fat, 10 g Fiber

Market List

2 large bunches grapes	Fresh oregano
1 medium eggplant	Fresh flat-leaf parsley (optional)
1 medium yellow bell pepper	Four 4-ounce cod fillets
1 medium zucchini	12 medium mussels
6 large plum tomatoes	Pitted black olives, large
Fresh basil	Vegetable broth
Fresh thyme	Chardonnay

Special Equipment

9" ceramic pie plate
Mini food processor

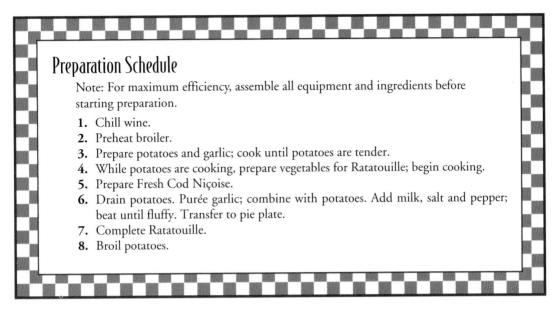

Preparation Schedule

Note: For maximum efficiency, assemble all equipment and ingredients before starting preparation.

1. Chill wine.
2. Preheat broiler.
3. Prepare potatoes and garlic; cook until potatoes are tender.
4. While potatoes are cooking, prepare vegetables for Ratatouille; begin cooking.
5. Prepare Fresh Cod Niçoise.
6. Drain potatoes. Purée garlic; combine with potatoes. Add milk, salt and pepper; beat until fluffy. Transfer to pie plate.
7. Complete Ratatouille.
8. Broil potatoes.

A Mediterranean Fish Dinner

FRESH COD NIÇOISE

Makes 4 servings

1 tablespoon + 1 teaspoon olive oil	1 bay leaf
3 cups canned plum tomatoes, well drained and chopped	$^1/_2$ teaspoon cumin Pinch salt
$^1/_4$ cup finely chopped shallots	Pinch freshly ground black pepper
6 large pitted black olives, sliced	Four 4-ounce cod fillets
2 tablespoons grated lemon zest *	12 medium mussels, scrubbed and
1 tablespoon chopped fresh oregano leaves or $^1/_2$ teaspoon dried	debearded
1 garlic clove, minced	Fresh flat-leaf parsley sprigs to garnish (optional)

1. In large nonstick skillet, heat oil; add tomatoes, shallots, olives, lemon zest, oregano, garlic, bay leaf, cumin, salt and pepper. Cook over medium heat, stirring frequently, until mixture comes to a boil.
2. Place cod fillets over tomato mixture; spoon some tomato mixture over fillets. Cook 10 minutes; turn fish over. Add mussels; cook 5 minutes longer, until mussels open and cod flakes easily when tested with fork. Remove and discard bay leaf. Serve garnished with parsley if desired.

Each serving (6 ounces) provides: $1^1/_4$ Fats, $1^3/_4$ Vegetables, 2 Proteins

Per serving: 214 Calories, 7 g Total Fat, 1 g Saturated Fat, 57 mg Cholesterol, 532 mg Sodium, 12 g Total Carbohydrate, 2 g Dietary Fiber, 26 g Protein, 95 mg Calcium

  * *The zest of the lemon is the peel without any of the pith (white membrane). To remove zest from lemon, use a zester or fine side of a vegetable grater; wrap lemon in plastic wrap and refrigerate for use at another time.*

MASHED POTATO–GARLIC GALETTE

Makes 4 servings

1 pound 14 ounces pared potatoes, cut into $1^1/_2$" cubes	$^1/_4$ cup skim milk Pinch salt
4 whole garlic cloves *	Freshly ground black pepper to taste

1. Preheat broiler. Spray 9" ceramic pie plate with nonstick cooking spray.
2. In medium saucepan of cold salted water, combine potatoes and garlic; cook over medium-high heat, covered, 15 minutes, until potatoes are tender. Drain; transfer garlic to mini food processor or blender.* Return potatoes to saucepan; cover and keep warm.
3. Purée garlic, then return garlic to saucepan with potatoes. Add milk, salt and pepper; with potato masher or fork, then wire whisk or electric mixer, beat potato mixture until fluffy.
4. Transfer potato mixture to prepared pie plate; spread evenly. Broil 4" from heat 5 minutes, until top is golden brown.

Each serving (4 ounces) provides: 1¹/₂ Breads, 5 Optional Calories

Per serving: 180 Calories, 0 g Total Fat, 0 g Saturated Fat, 0 mg Cholesterol, 54 mg Sodium, 40 g Total Carbohydrate, 3 g Dietary Fiber, 5 g Protein, 39 mg Calcium

* To make removing the garlic cloves easier, spear each one with a toothpick before cooking; remove toothpicks before placing garlic in food processor or blender.

RATATOUILLE

Makes 4 servings

- 4 cups cubed eggplant (¹/₂" cubes)
- 6 large plum tomatoes, blanched, peeled, seeded and coarsely chopped
- 2 cups vegetable broth *
- 1 medium zucchini, cut into ¹/₂" cubes
- 1 medium yellow bell pepper, cored, seeded and cut into ¹/₂" pieces
- 1 medium onion, chopped
- 2 tablespoons chopped fresh basil leaves or 1 teaspoon dried

- 1 tablespoon + 1 teaspoon olive oil
- 1 tablespoon chopped fresh thyme leaves or ¹/₂ teaspoon dried
- 1 garlic clove, minced
- Pinch salt
- Freshly ground black pepper to taste
- Fresh basil, oregano or flat-leaf parsley sprigs to garnish (optional)

1. In large nonstick skillet, combine eggplant, tomatoes, 1 cup of the broth, the zucchini, yellow pepper, onion, basil, oil, thyme, garlic, salt and black pepper; cook over medium heat, covered, stirring frequently, 15–20 minutes, just until vegetables are tender and liquid is evaporated.
2. Stir remaining broth into vegetable mixture; cook over medium-high heat, uncovered, until thickened. Transfer mixture to large decorative bowl; serve garnished with fresh herbs if desired.

Each serving (1¹/₂ cups) provides: 1 Fat, 4³/₄ Vegetables, 10 Optional Calories

Per serving with vegetable broth: 111 Calories, 6 g Total Fat, 1 g Saturated Fat, 0 mg Cholesterol, 552 mg Sodium, 15 g Total Carbohydrate, 3 g Dietary Fiber, 3 g Protein, 59 mg Calcium

* If vegetable broth is not available, substitute 2 cups water. Omit Optional Calories in Selection Information.

Per serving with water: 101 Calories, 6 g Total Fat, 1 g Saturated Fat, 0 mg Cholesterol, 52 mg Sodium, 14 g Total Carbohydrate, 3 g Dietary Fiber, 3 g Protein, 59 mg Calcium

PERFECT PARTY REPAST

This entrée is a loose adaptation of the classic Homard Americaine; it *is* expensive, but it makes a gorgeous dish for a special dinner—the lovely rice ring is flecked with specks of color. Be sure not to increase the amount of saffron since too much will give it a medicinal flavor.

Menu serves 4

- **Party Lobster, 1 serving**
- **Saffron Rice Ring, 1 serving**
- **Wilted Arugula Salad, 1 serving**
- **Fruit Parfait, 1 serving**
- **Sparkling Mineral Water with Lemon Wedge**

One serving of this meal provides: $1^1/_4$ Fats, $1^1/_4$ Fruits, 4 Vegetables, 2 Proteins, 2 Breads, 55 Optional Calories; 5 g Fat, 8 g Fiber

Market List

1 medium kiwifruit	Bottled clam juice
1 cup whole strawberries	Pitted black olives, large or small
1 small mango	Walnut oil
1 medium red bell pepper	Tomato purée
1 bunch scallions	Canned pineapple chunks (no sugar
3 bunches arugula	added)
Fresh tarragon or dried chervil leaves	Ground saffron
Fresh flat-leaf parsley	Anisette (anise-flavored liqueur)
1 pound cooked shelled lobster	Dark rum
Tomato sauce	

Special Equipment

1 4-cup ring mold
4 wine or parfait glasses

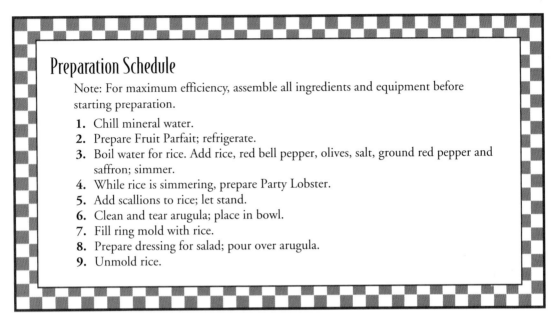

Preparation Schedule

Note: For maximum efficiency, assemble all ingredients and equipment before starting preparation.

1. Chill mineral water.
2. Prepare Fruit Parfait; refrigerate.
3. Boil water for rice. Add rice, red bell pepper, olives, salt, ground red pepper and saffron; simmer.
4. While rice is simmering, prepare Party Lobster.
5. Add scallions to rice; let stand.
6. Clean and tear arugula; place in bowl.
7. Fill ring mold with rice.
8. Prepare dressing for salad; pour over arugula.
9. Unmold rice.

PARTY LOBSTER

Makes 4 servings

2 teaspoons olive oil	1 pound diced cooked shelled lobster
$^1/_2$ cup minced onion	2 tablespoons minced fresh tarragon leaves
$^1/_4$ cup minced carrot	or 1 teaspoon dried chervil leaves
$^1/_4$ cup minced celery	2 tablespoons minced fresh flat-leaf
2 garlic cloves, minced	parsley
1 cup tomato sauce	$^1/_4$ fluid ounce ($1^1/_2$ teaspoons) anisette
2 fluid ounces ($^1/_4$ cup) dry white wine	(anise-flavored liqueur)
$^1/_4$ cup clam juice	$^1/_4$ teaspoon freshly ground black pepper
1 teaspoon cornstarch	Pinch salt
2 tablespoons tomato purée	

1. In medium skillet, heat oil; add onion, carrot, celery and garlic. Cook over medium-high heat, stirring constantly, 3–4 minutes, until garlic is golden brown. Add tomato sauce; cook, covered, 5 minutes.
2. In small bowl, combine wine, clam juice and cornstarch, stirring until cornstarch is dissolved; stir into vegetable mixture. Add tomato purée; stir to combine. Cook over medium heat 2–3 minutes, until mixture is slightly thickened. Stir in lobster, tarragon, parsley, anisette, pepper and salt; cook, stirring frequently, 5 minutes, until heated and flavors are blended.

Each serving ($1^1/_4$ cups) provides: $^1/_2$ Fat, $1^3/_4$ Vegetables, 2 Proteins, 20 Optional Calories

Per serving: 187 Calories, 3 g Total Fat, 0 g Saturated Fat, 82 mg Cholesterol, 909 mg Sodium, 11 g Total Carbohydrate, 2 g Dietary Fiber, 25 g Protein, 102 mg Calcium

SAFFRON RICE RING

Makes 4 servings

   8 ounces regular long-grain rice
      (*not* converted)
 ¹/₂ cup minced red bell pepper
   6 large or 10 small pitted black olives,
      chopped

   1 teaspoon salt
¹/₈ teaspoon ground red pepper
Pinch ground saffron *
¹/₄ cup chopped scallions (white portion
      with some green)

1. In medium saucepan, bring 2 cups water to a boil; add rice, red bell pepper, olives, salt, ground red pepper and saffron. Reduce heat to low; simmer, covered, 15 minutes, until liquid is absorbed. Remove saucepan from heat.
2. Stir scallions into rice mixture; let stand, covered, 5 minutes.
3. Spray a 4-cup ring mold with nonstick cooking spray; spoon hot rice mixture into mold, pressing down with back of spoon. Let stand, covered, about 10 minutes or until mixture holds together.
4. Just before serving, invert mold onto medium decorative platter; lift off mold.

Each serving provides: ¹/₄ Fat, ¹/₂ Vegetable, 2 Breads

Per serving: 222 Calories, 1 g Total Fat, 0 g Saturated Fat, 0 mg Cholesterol, 616 mg Sodium, 47 g Total Carbohydrate, 1 g Dietary Fiber, 4 g Protein, 31 mg Calcium

Serving Suggestions

1. Fill this elegant rice ring with Party Lobster (see recipe).
2. Omit ring mold. Spoon rice around edge of large decorative platter; fill center with Party Lobster (see recipe).

  * *If saffron is not available, substitute ground turmeric; flavor will not be the same.*

Wilted Arugula Salad

Makes 4 servings

3 cups torn arugula
2 teaspoons walnut oil
¹/₂ cup minced onion

2 tablespoons balsamic vinegar
¹/₂ teaspoon granulated sugar
¹/₄ teaspoon salt

1. Place arugula in large salad bowl; set aside.
2. In small skillet, heat oil; add onion. Cook over medium heat, stirring frequently, 2–3 minutes, until lightly golden. Add vinegar, sugar and salt; stir to combine.
3. Pour hot onion mixture over arugula; toss until arugula is coated and slightly wilted.

Each serving (³/₄ cup) provides: ¹/₂ Fat, 1³/₄ Vegetables

Per serving: 34 Calories, 2 g Total Fat, 0 g Saturated Fat, 0 mg Cholesterol, 147 mg Sodium, 3 g Total Carbohydrate, 1 g Dietary Fiber, 1 g Protein, 35 mg Calcium

Fruit Parfait

Makes 4 servings

1 cup whole strawberries, halved
1 medium kiwifruit, pared and sliced
¹/₂ cup drained canned pineapple chunks (no sugar added)
1 small mango, pared, pitted and cut into chunks

1 fluid ounce (2 tablespoons) dark rum
1 tablespoon fresh lime juice
1 tablespoon honey

1. In 4 wine or parfait glasses, layer strawberries, kiwifruit and pineapple.
2. In food processor or blender, combine mango, rum, lime juice and honey; purée until smooth.
3. Spoon an equal amount of mango mixture over each portion of fruit.

Each serving provides: 1¹/₄ Fruits, 35 Optional Calories

Per serving: 104 Calories, 0 g Total Fat, 0 g Saturated Fat, 0 mg Cholesterol, 3 mg Sodium, 23 g Total Carbohydrate, 2 g Dietary Fiber, 1 g Protein, 21 mg Calcium

FISHERMAN'S DELIGHT

Whether you yearn to sink your hook into the water or prefer to snag your catch at the local fish market, this unusual halibut dinner is sure to please even the most finicky fish eaters. Fresh steamed vegetables and a crunchy salad laced with the aroma of citrus fruit are perfect accompaniments.

Menu serves 6

- **Crunchy Garlic-Broiled Halibut, 1 serving**
  Steamed Cauliflower and Broccoli Florets, 1 cup per serving
- **Radish-Orange Salad, 1 serving**
- **Watermelon Slush, 1 serving**

One serving of this meal provides: $1^1/_2$ Fats, $1^1/_4$ Fruits, 3 Vegetables, 2 Proteins, $^1/_4$ Bread; 11 g Fat, 7 g Fiber

Market List

$^1/_4$ medium watermelon (about $3^1/_2$ pounds)	Fresh flat-leaf parsley
1 head cauliflower	Fresh mint
1 bunch broccoli	Six 6-ounce halibut steaks
1 bunch radishes	Peanut oil
	Ground coriander

Special Equipment

Mini food processor

Preparation Schedule

Note: For maximum efficiency, assemble all ingredients and equipment before starting preparation.

1. Preheat broiler.
2. Prepare Radish-Orange Salad; refrigerate.
3. Prepare parsley mixture for fish.
4. Steam cauliflower and broccoli.
5. While vegetables are steaming, complete Crunchy Garlic-Broiled Halibut.
6. Just before serving, prepare Watermelon Slush.

Fisherman's Delight

CRUNCHY GARLIC-BROILED HALIBUT

Makes 6 servings

$^1/_3$ cup chopped fresh flat-leaf parsley	Six 6-ounce halibut steaks
2 tablespoons olive oil	$^1/_4$ cup + 1$^1/_2$ teaspoons plain dried
3 garlic cloves	bread crumbs

1. Preheat broiler. Line baking sheet with foil.
2. In mini food processor, combine parsley, oil, garlic and 1 tablespoon + 1$^1/_2$ teaspoons water; process until finely chopped. Transfer mixture to small bowl.
3. Place fish on prepared baking sheet; spread each fish steak with a thin layer of parsley mixture. Broil fish 4" from heat, 3 minutes. Remove fish from broiler; leave broiler on.
4. Add bread crumbs to remaining parsley mixture; stir to combine. Pat an equal amount of bread crumb mixture onto each fish steak; broil 3 minutes longer, until fish flakes easily when tested with a fork.

Each serving (1 halibut steak) provides: 1 Fat, 2 Proteins, $^1/_4$ Bread

Per serving: 222 Calories, 8 g Total Fat, 1 g Saturated Fat, 46 mg Cholesterol, 123 mg Sodium, 4 g Total Carbohydrate, 0 g Dietary Fiber, 31 g Protein, 87 mg Calcium

RADISH-ORANGE SALAD

Makes 6 servings

3 small oranges, peeled	Freshly ground black pepper to taste
$^1/_4$ cup fresh lime juice	1$^1/_2$ cups thinly sliced radishes
1 tablespoon peanut oil	6 medium celery ribs, thinly sliced
$^1/_2$ teaspoon ground coriander	

1. Cut oranges horizontally into 1" slices; stack slices and cut in half.
2. In medium bowl, with wire whisk, combine lime juice, oil, coriander and pepper. Add oranges, radishes and celery; toss gently to combine.

Each serving (1 cup) provides: $^1/_2$ Fat, $^1/_2$ Fruit, 1 Vegetable

Per serving: 61 Calories, 3 g Total Fat, 0 g Saturated Fat, 0 mg Cholesterol, 33 mg Sodium, 10 g Total Carbohydrate, 3 g Dietary Fiber, 1 g Protein, 46 mg Calcium

WATERMELON SLUSH

Makes 6 servings

4¹/₂ cups cubed seeded watermelon
  2 tablespoons fresh lemon juice
  1 tablespoon chopped fresh mint leaves

2–3 ice cubes
Fresh mint leaves to garnish (optional)

1. In blender, combine watermelon, lemon juice, mint and ice cubes; process until smooth.
2. Divide watermelon mixture among 6 tall glasses; garnish with mint leaves if desired.

Each serving (1 cup) provides: ³/₄ Fruit

Per serving: 40 Calories, 1 g Total Fat, 0 g Saturated Fat, 0 mg Cholesterol, 2 mg Sodium, 9 g Total Carbohydrate, 0 g Dietary Fiber, 1 g Protein, 10 mg Calcium

LIGHT AND ELEGANT LUNCH

This elegant lunch or light supper with its delicate herbs will remind you of the finest meals in the very best restaurants. It's a surefire way to show off your talents. Nobody has to know how easy it is to prepare!

Menu serves 4

- 🕐 **Minted Green Pea Soup, 1 serving**
- 🕐 **Lobster and Roasted Red Pepper Salad, 1 serving**
- 🕐 **Parmesan-Garlic Toasts, 1 serving**
- **Fresh Raspberries, ³/₄ cup per serving**
- **Iced Herbal Tea**

One serving of this meal provides: 1 Fat, 1 Fruit, 2³/₄ Vegetables, 1¹/₄ Proteins, 2 Breads; 8 g Fat, 10 g Fiber

Market List

3 cups raspberries	Grated Parmesan cheese
Assorted salad greens	Roasted red peppers
Fresh mint	Extra-virgin olive oil
Fresh thyme	Two 10-ounce packages frozen
8 ounces shelled cooked lobster	green peas
1 loaf French bread	

Preparation Schedule

Note: For maximum efficiency, assemble all ingredients and equipment before starting preparation.

1. Prepare iced tea; refrigerate.
2. Tear salad greens; refrigerate.
3. Preheat oven.
4. Prepare garlic spread; spread on toast. Arrange on baking sheet; sprinkle with cheese.
5. Cook peas.
6. While peas are cooking, prepare lobster mixture.
7. Bake Parmesan-Garlic Toasts.
8. While toasts are baking, purée soup.
9. Toss lobster mixture with greens.

Minted Green Pea Soup

Makes 4 servings

3 cups frozen green peas
1 tablespoon + 1 teaspoon chopped fresh mint leaves

$^1/_2$ teaspoon salt
Pinch freshly ground black pepper

1. In medium saucepan, combine peas and $1^1/_2$ cups water; bring to a boil. Reduce heat to low; simmer 6–7 minutes, until tender. Remove from heat; cool slightly.
2. Transfer peas and cooking liquid to food processor. Add mint, salt and pepper; purée until smooth.

Each serving provides: $1^1/_2$ Breads

Per serving: 83 Calories, 0 g Total Fat, 0 g Saturated Fat, 0 mg Cholesterol, 394 mg Sodium, 15 g Total Carbohydrate, 4 g Dietary Fiber, 6 g Protein, 26 mg Calcium

Lobster and Roasted Red Pepper Salad

Makes 4 servings

1 tablespoon + 1 teaspoon fresh lemon juice
2 teaspoons chopped fresh thyme
2 teaspoons extra-virgin olive oil
8 ounces shelled cooked lobster, cut into chunks

$1^1/_2$ cups drained roasted red peppers, slivered
4 cups torn assorted salad greens

1. In large bowl, with wire whisk, combine lemon juice, thyme and oil. Add lobster and roasted peppers; toss to combine.
2. Just before serving, add salad greens; toss gently to combine.

Each serving provides: $^1/_2$ Fat, $2^3/_4$ Vegetables, 1 Protein

Per serving: 101 Calories, 3 g Total Fat, 0 g Saturated Fat, 41 mg Cholesterol, 221 mg Sodium, 6 g Total Carbohydrate, 2 g Dietary Fiber, 13 g Protein, 72 mg Calcium

Parmesan-Garlic Toasts

Makes 4 servings

  6 garlic cloves, chopped
  2 teaspoons olive oil
  2 ounces French bread, cut diagonally
       into 12 thin slices
 3/4 ounce grated Parmesan cheese

1. Preheat oven to 400° F. Line baking sheet with foil.
2. In small saucepan, combine 1/2 cup water, the garlic and oil; bring to a boil. Reduce heat to low; simmer 10 minutes, until thickened and smooth, pressing mixture against side of pan with wooden spoon.
3. Spread an equal amount of garlic mixture onto 1 side of each bread slice; arrange on prepared baking sheet. Sprinkle evenly with Parmesan cheese. Bake 10 minutes, until crisp.

Each serving (3 slices) provides: 1/2 Fat, 1/4 Protein, 1/2 Bread

Per serving: 90 Calories, 4 g Total Fat, 1 g Saturated Fat, 4 mg Cholesterol, 186 mg Sodium, 9 g Total Carbohydrate, 0 g Dietary Fiber, 4 g Protein, 92 mg Calcium

SUNDAY BRUNCH

There is nothing quite as decadent as a lazy Sunday brunch. Let the word out about this delightful meal and you'll probably have everyone offering to help—who knows, maybe this thirty-minute meal will be done in a mere fifteen!

Menu serves 4

- **Lemon-Ricotta Crêpes, 1 serving**
- **Basil-Tomato Shrimp Toasts, 1 serving**
- **Tropical Fruit Salad, 1 serving**
- **Almond Crème Coffee, 1 serving**

One serving of this meal provides: $3/4$ Fat, $1^1/2$ Fruits, $1/2$ Vegetable, $2^1/2$ Proteins, $3/4$ Bread, 110 Optional Calories; 13 g Fat, 4 g Fiber

Market List

2 medium kiwifruits
1 small mango
1 medium papaya
1 medium banana
1 medium tomato
Fresh basil
Fresh ginger root

24 small or 16 medium shrimp
$1^1/4$ cups part-skim ricotta cheese
Liquid almond-flavored nondairy
 creamer
4 prepared crêpes (6" diameter)
1 loaf French bread
Mayonnaise

Special Equipment

Toaster oven

Preparation Schedule

Note: For maximum efficiency, assemble all ingredients and equipment before starting preparation.

1. Prepare Tropical Fruit Salad; refrigerate.
2. Toast bread; cook shrimp.
3. While shrimp are cooking, heat crêpes.
4. Drain shrimp.
5. Prepare shrimp mixture.
6. Prepare ricotta cheese mixture.
7. Fill crêpes.
8. Complete Basil-Tomato Shrimp Toasts.
9. Prepare coffeemaker.

LEMON-RICOTTA CRÊPES

Makes 4 servings

1¹/₄ cups part-skim ricotta cheese
¹/₄ cup fresh lemon juice
2 tablespoons granulated sugar

1 tablespoon grated lemon zest *
4 prepared crêpes (6" diameter), heated

1. In small bowl, combine ricotta cheese, lemon juice, sugar and lemon zest.
2. Spoon one-fourth of the cheese mixture onto center of each crêpe; roll up to enclose.

Each serving provides: 1¹/₂ Proteins, ¹/₄ Bread, 80 Optional Calories

Per serving: 180 Calories, 7 g Total Fat, 4 g Saturated Fat, 28 mg Cholesterol, 176 mg Sodium, 19 g Total Carbohydrate, 0 g Dietary Fiber, 10 g Protein, 212 mg Calcium

* The zest of the lemon is the peel without any of the pith (white membrane). To remove zest from lemon, use a zester or fine side of a vegetable grater.

Sunday Brunch

BASIL-TOMATO SHRIMP TOASTS

Makes 4 servings

  2 ounces French bread, cut diagonally
       into 8 thin slices
 24 small or 16 medium shrimp, peeled
       and deveined
  1 medium tomato, blanched, peeled,
       seeded and chopped

 $^1/_4$ cup chopped fresh basil leaves
  1 tablespoon mayonnaise
  2 teaspoons fresh lemon juice
 $^1/_2$ teaspoon freshly ground black pepper

1. In oven or toaster oven, toast bread until golden brown; remove from oven and set aside to cool.

2. In medium saucepan, combine shrimp and 1 cup water; bring to a boil. Reduce heat to low; simmer until shrimp turn pink; drain. Rinse under cold running water; drain again.

3. Transfer shrimp to medium bowl; stir in tomato, basil, mayonnaise, lemon juice and pepper.

4. Top each slice of toast with an equal amount of shrimp mixture.

Each serving provides: $^3/_4$ Fat, $^1/_2$ Vegetable, 1 Protein, $^1/_2$ Bread

Per serving: 136 Calories, 4 g Total Fat, 1 g Saturated Fat, 88 mg Cholesterol, 194 mg Sodium, 11 g Total Carbohydrate, 1 g Dietary Fiber, 13 g Protein, 68 mg Calcium

TROPICAL FRUIT SALAD

Makes 4 servings

  2 medium kiwifruits, peeled, halved and
       cut into 1/2" slices
  1 small mango, peeled, pitted and cubed
 $^1/_2$ medium papaya, peeled, seeded and
       cubed

 $^1/_2$ medium banana, peeled and sliced
  2 tablespoons fresh lime juice
 $^1/_2$ teaspoon grated, pared fresh ginger root

In large bowl, combine kiwifruits, mango, papaya, banana, lime juice and ginger; refrigerate, covered, until chilled.

Each serving provides: $1^1/_2$ Fruits

Per serving: 85 Calories, 0 g Total Fat, 0 g Saturated Fat, 0 mg Cholesterol, 5 mg Sodium, 22 g Total Carbohydrate, 3 g Dietary Fiber, 1 g Protein, 27 mg Calcium

Almond Crème Coffee

For each serving, in coffee cup, combine *¾ cup hot coffee* and *1 tablespoon liquid almond-flavored nonfat creamer.*

Each serving provides: 30 Optional Calories

Per serving: 20 Calories, 0 g Total Fat, 0 g Saturated Fat, 0 mg Cholesterol, 9 mg Sodium, 8 g Total Carbohydrate, 0 g Dietary Fiber, 0 g Protein, 4 mg Calcium

A MIDSUMMER NIGHT'S DREAMY DINNER

Fresh clams and garden-fresh vegetables, herbs and fruits are the things a midsummer night's dream is made of. This easy, delicious meal can be prepared so quickly, you'll have plenty of time to sit outside listening to the sounds of a summer night.

Menu serves 4

🕐 **Stuffed Clams, 1 serving**

🕐 **Penne Pasta with Salsa Cruda, 1 serving**

🕐 **Tricolor Salad with Gorgonzola Dressing, 1 serving**

🕐 **Macédoine of Summer Fruits, 1 serving**

    Iced Tea with Lemon

One serving of this meal provides: 2 Fats, 2 Fruits, 6 Vegetables, 1 Protein, 2 $^1/_4$ Breads, 25 Optional Calories; 15 g Fat, 6 g Fiber

Market List

2 medium peaches	Fresh oregano
6 medium apricots	Fresh thyme
2 small nectarines	Fresh basil
2 large or 4 small plums	Fresh flat-leaf parsley
1 medium Italian sweet green pepper	12 medium clams
6 large plum tomatoes	1$^1/_2$ ounces Gorgonzola cheese
4 medium whole mushrooms	Grated Parmesan cheese
1 small head radicchio	White wine vinegar
1 bunch arugula	Penne or other medium-size pasta
1 small head Boston or other tender, light green lettuce	

Special Equipment

Mini food processor

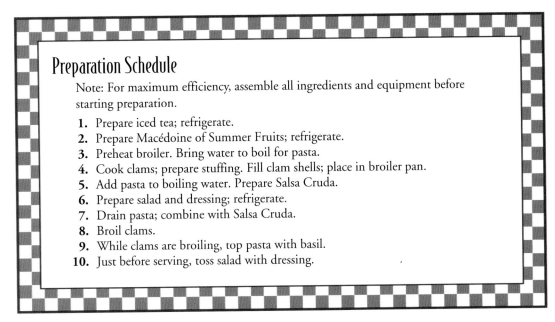

Preparation Schedule

Note: For maximum efficiency, assemble all ingredients and equipment before starting preparation.

1. Prepare iced tea; refrigerate.
2. Prepare Macédoine of Summer Fruits; refrigerate.
3. Preheat broiler. Bring water to boil for pasta.
4. Cook clams; prepare stuffing. Fill clam shells; place in broiler pan.
5. Add pasta to boiling water. Prepare Salsa Cruda.
6. Prepare salad and dressing; refrigerate.
7. Drain pasta; combine with Salsa Cruda.
8. Broil clams.
9. While clams are broiling, top pasta with basil.
10. Just before serving, toss salad with dressing.

STUFFED CLAMS

Makes 4 servings

12 medium clams
2 fluid ounces (¹/₄ cup) dry white wine
¹/₂ medium Italian sweet green pepper, cored, seeded and cut into chunks
4 medium whole mushrooms
³/₄ ounce plain dried bread crumbs
2 tablespoons chopped fresh flat-leaf parsley
1 tablespoon + 1 teaspoon olive oil

1 tablespoon chopped fresh oregano leaves or ¹/₂ teaspoon dried
1 tablespoon chopped fresh thyme leaves or ¹/₂ teaspoon dried
2 garlic cloves, minced
Pinch salt
Freshly ground black pepper to taste
2 teaspoons grated Parmesan cheese
2 lemons, cut into wedges

1. Preheat broiler. Line broiler pan with foil.
2. In large saucepan, combine clams and wine; steam, covered, over medium-high heat 10 minutes, until clams open. Discard any unopened clams. With slotted spoon, remove clams from saucepan; reserve cooking liquid. Remove clams from shells, reserving one half of each clam shell.
3. In food processor, combine green pepper, mushrooms, bread crumbs, parsley, oil, oregano, thyme, garlic, salt, black pepper, clams and ¹/₄ cup cooking liquid; with on-off motion, pulse processor 3–4 times, until mixture is coarsely chopped and ingredients are blended. If mixture is too dry, add additional cooking liquid, 1 teaspoon at a time, until mixture is moist but holds its shape.
4. Divide clam mixture among reserved clam shells, pressing into place; arrange in prepared broiler pan. Sprinkle stuffed clams evenly with Parmesan cheese; broil 4" from heat 5–10 minutes, until tops are golden brown and crisp. Serve with lemon wedges.

Each serving (6 stuffed clams) provides: 1 Fat, ¹/₂ Vegetable, ¹/₂ Protein, ¹/₄ Bread, 20 Optional Calories

Per serving: 127 Calories, 6 g Total Fat, 1 g Saturated Fat, 15 mg Cholesterol, 122 mg Sodium, 13 g Total Carbohydrate, 1 g Dietary Fiber, 8 g Protein, 91 mg Calcium

PENNE PASTA WITH SALSA CRUDA

Makes 4 servings

6 ounces penne or other medium-size pasta
6 large plum tomatoes, blanched, peeled, seeded and finely chopped

1 small garlic clove, minced
Pinch salt
Freshly ground black pepper to taste
¹/₂ cup torn fresh basil leaves

1. In large pot of boiling water, cook penne 9–11 minutes, until tender.
2. Meanwhile, in large bowl, combine tomatoes, garlic, salt and pepper.

3. Drain penne; place in large decorative bowl. Add tomato mixture; toss to coat thoroughly. Let mixture stand at room temperature until ready to serve.

4. Just before serving, sprinkle pasta mixture with basil.

Each serving (2 cups) provides: 1$^1/_2$ Vegetables, 2 Breads

Per serving: 180 Calories, 1 g Total Fat, 0 g Saturated Fat, 0 mg Cholesterol, 44 mg Sodium, 37 g Total Carbohydrate, 2 g Dietary Fiber, 6 g Protein, 60 mg Calcium

Tricolor Salad with Gorgonzola Dressing

Makes 4 servings

1 small head radicchio, leaves separated and torn into bite-size pieces

1 bunch arugula, stems removed and leaves torn into bite-size pieces

$^1/_2$ head Boston or other tender, light green lettuce, leaves torn into bite-size pieces

1$^1/_2$ ounces Gorgonzola cheese, crumbled

2 tablespoons white wine vinegar

1 tablespoon + 1 teaspoon olive oil

$^1/_2$ fluid ounce (1 tablespoon) dry white wine

1 teaspoon prepared yellow mustard

Pinch salt

Freshly ground black pepper to taste

1. To prepare salad, in large salad bowl, combine radicchio, arugula and Boston lettuce; refrigerate, covered, until ready to serve.

2. Meanwhile, to prepare dressing, in mini food processor or blender, combine cheese, vinegar, oil, wine, mustard, salt and pepper; with on-off motion, pulse processor 4–5 times, until mixture is creamy and smooth. Transfer dressing to small bowl; refrigerate, covered, until ready to serve.

3. Just before serving, pour dressing over salad; toss lightly to coat thoroughly.

Each serving provides: 1 Fat, 4 Vegetables, $^1/_2$ Protein, 5 Optional Calories

Per serving: 101 Calories, 8 g Total Fat, 3 g Saturated Fat, 8 mg Cholesterol, 208 mg Sodium, 4 g Total Carbohydrate, 1 g Dietary Fiber, 4 g Protein, 133 mg Calcium

Macédoine of Summer Fruits

For each serving, combine $^1/_4$ *cup each sliced peaches, apricots, nectarines and plums.* Add *2 teaspoons fresh lemon juice*; toss to combine.

Each serving provides: 2 Fruits

Per serving: 79 Calories, 1 g Total Fat, 0 g Saturated Fat, 0 mg Cholesterol, 0 mg Sodium, 19 g Total Carbohydrate, 3 g Dietary Fiber, 2 g Protein, 12 mg Calcium

SEAFOOD STEW SUPPER

Fresh okra is best in this mouthwatering gumbo, as it helps to thicken the stew slightly; if unavailable, frozen okra is a suitable substitute. And if you wish, use clams or mussels in place of the crabmeat. Fresh brandy gives this simple berry dessert a sophisticated flair, but kirsch or any fragrant liqueur would also be wonderful.

Menu serves 4

- **Seafood Gumbo, 1 serving**
- **Corny Rice, 1 serving**
- **Berries Romanoff, 1 serving**
  Lime-Flavored Sparkling Mineral Water

One serving of this meal provides: $3/4$ Fat, 1 Fruit, $3^3/4$ Vegetables, 2 Proteins, 2 Breads, 75 Optional Calories; 9 g Fat, 12 g Fiber

Market List

1 cup blackberries
1 cup blueberries
1 cup raspberries
1 medium green bell pepper
1 medium red bell pepper
8 ounces okra
1 cup corn kernels, fresh or frozen
1 bunch scallions
10 ounces shelled crabmeat

10 ounces shelled and deveined shrimp
Aspartame-sweetened vanilla nonfat yogurt
Bottled clam juice
Frozen light whipped topping (8 calories per tablespoon)
Fruit-flavored brandy

Special Equipment

4 parfait glasses

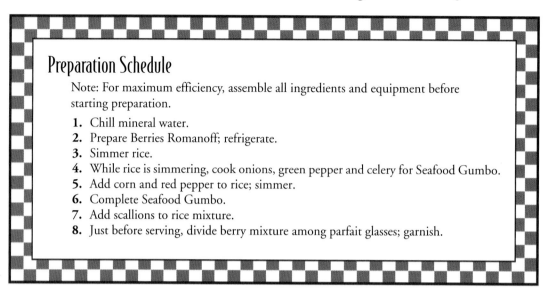

Preparation Schedule

Note: For maximum efficiency, assemble all ingredients and equipment before starting preparation.

1. Chill mineral water.
2. Prepare Berries Romanoff; refrigerate.
3. Simmer rice.
4. While rice is simmering, cook onions, green pepper and celery for Seafood Gumbo.
5. Add corn and red pepper to rice; simmer.
6. Complete Seafood Gumbo.
7. Add scallions to rice mixture.
8. Just before serving, divide berry mixture among parfait glasses; garnish.

Seafood Gumbo

Makes 4 servings

1 tablespoon olive oil	10 ounces shelled crabmeat, cut into bite-size pieces
1^1/$_2$ cups chopped onions	10 ounces shelled and deveined shrimp
1 cup minced green bell pepper	^{1}/$_2$ teaspoon dried thyme leaves
^{1}/$_2$ cup minced celery	^{1}/$_4$ teaspoon freshly ground black pepper
2 cups canned stewed tomatoes	Dash hot pepper sauce
2 cups sliced okra	
1^1/$_2$ cups clam juice	

1. In medium saucepan, heat oil; add onions, green pepper and celery. Cook over medium heat, stirring occasionally, 10 minutes, until onions are golden brown.
2. Add tomatoes, okra and clam juice to onion mixture; bring liquid to a boil. Reduce heat to low; simmer 10 minutes.
3. Add crabmeat, shrimp, thyme, black pepper and hot pepper sauce; simmer 5 minutes longer, until seafood is cooked through and mixture is slightly thickened.

Each serving (2^1/$_4$ cups) provides: ^{3}/$_4$ Fat, 3^1/$_2$ Vegetables, 2 Proteins, 5 Optional Calories

Per serving: 264 Calories, 6 g Total Fat, 1 g Saturated Fat, 179 mg Cholesterol, 841 mg Sodium, 20 g Total Carbohydrate, 6 g Dietary Fiber, 32 g Protein, 229 mg Calcium

CORNY RICE

Makes 4 servings

6 ounces converted rice
$^1/_2$ teaspoon salt
1 cup fresh or frozen corn kernels

$^1/_4$ cup minced red bell pepper
$^1/_4$ cup sliced scallions (white and green parts)

1. In medium saucepan, bring $1^3/_4$ cups water to a boil; add rice and salt. Reduce heat to low; simmer, covered, 10 minutes, until liquid is partially absorbed.
2. Add corn and red pepper to simmering rice; continue to simmer, covered, 10 minutes longer, until all liquid is absorbed. Stir in scallions.

Each serving (1 cup) provides: $^1/_4$ Vegetable, 2 Breads

Per serving: 195 Calories, 1 g Total Fat, 0 g Saturated Fat, 0 mg Cholesterol, 283 mg Sodium, 43 g Total Carbohydrate, 2 g Dietary Fiber, 4 g Protein, 33 mg Calcium

BERRIES ROMANOFF

Makes 4 servings

1 cup blackberries
1 cup blueberries
1 cup raspberries
1 fluid ounce (2 tablespoons) fruit-flavored brandy

2 teaspoons granulated sugar
1 cup thawed frozen light whipped topping (8 calories per tablespoon)
$^1/_2$ cup aspartame-sweetened vanilla nonfat yogurt

1. Set aside 12 berries for garnish; place remaining berries in medium bowl. Add brandy and sugar to berries in bowl; stir to combine, crushing berries slightly.
2. Fold whipped topping and yogurt into berry mixture; refrigerate until well chilled.
3. Just before serving, divide berry mixture evenly among 4 parfait glasses; garnish each portion with 3 reserved berries.

Each serving (1 cup) provides: 1 Fruit, 70 Optional Calories

Per serving: 127 Calories, 2 g Total Fat, 0 g Saturated Fat, 1 mg Cholesterol, 18 mg Sodium, 24 g Total Carbohydrate, 4 g Dietary Fiber, 2 g Protein, 58 mg Calcium

3

Meat

SOOTHING SUPPER

Steak and potatoes! What could be more welcoming than this hearty combination? With the magic of the microwave, cooking time for the potato is cut down to a minimum, and with the quick-to-prepare salad and dessert, you'll have dinner on the table in next to no time.

Menu serves 4

- **Marinated Flank Steak, 1 serving**
- **Crunchy Fennel Salad, 1 serving**
- **Microwave-Baked Potato, 8 ounces per serving**
- **Nonfat Sour Cream, 2 tablespoons per serving**
- **Rhubarb Compote, 1 serving**
- **Decaffeinated Coffee or Tea**

One serving of this meal provides: 4¼ Vegetables, 3 Proteins, 2 Breads, 135 Optional Calories; 11 g Fat, 6 g Fiber

Market List

6 rhubarb stalks
2 medium fennel bulbs
1 medium red onion

15 ounces flank steak
Nonfat sour cream
Rice wine vinegar

Special Equipment

Microwave oven
Microwave-safe baking dish

Preparation Schedule

Note: For maximum efficiency, assemble all ingredients and equipment before starting preparation.

1. Prepare marinade; add steak.
2. Microwave potatoes.
3. While steak is marinating, preheat broiler.
4. Dissolve sugar for Rhubarb Compote. Add rhubarb and zest; simmer.
5. While rhubarb is simmering, broil steak.
6. While steak is broiling, prepare Crunchy Fennel Salad.
7. Slice steak.
8. Prepare coffeemaker or heat water for tea.

Soothing Supper

Rhubarb Compote

Makes 4 servings

$^1/_2$ cup granulated sugar

4 cups diagonally sliced rhubarb (1" pieces)

1 tablespoon grated orange zest *

1. In medium saucepan, combine 1 cup water and the sugar; place over medium heat. Cook, stirring constantly, until sugar is dissolved.
2. Add rhubarb and orange zest to dissolved sugar; bring liquid just to a boil. Reduce heat to low; simmer 10 minutes, until rhubarb is tender.

Each serving provides: 2 Vegetables, 90 Optional Calories

Per serving: 124 Calories, 0 g Total Fat, 0 g Saturated Fat, 0 mg Cholesterol, 5 mg Sodium, 31 g Total Carbohydrate, 0 g Dietary Fiber, 1 g Protein, 108 mg Calcium

* The zest of the orange is the peel without any of the pith (white membrane). To remove zest from orange, use a zester or fine side of a vegetable grater; wrap orange in plastic wrap and refrigerate for use at another time.

STEAK DINNER CAJUN-STYLE

This robust Cajun meal is reminiscent of those you'd enjoy in Louisiana. If you can't find hominy, substitute rice or corn. And make some extra Pepper and Onion Marmalade; it's just as delicious with chicken or pork.

Menu serves 4

- **Cajun Flank Steak, 1 serving**
- **Hominy and Beans, 1 serving**
- **Pepper and Onion Marmalade, 1 serving**
- **Melon Chunks, 1 cup per serving**
- **Iced Tea with Lemon**

One serving of this meal provides: 1 Fat, 1 Fruit, $2^1/_2$ Vegetables, 3 Proteins, $1^1/_2$ Breads, 10 Optional Calories; 14 g Fat, 6 g Fiber

Market List

Melon
3 medium red bell peppers
Fresh flat-leaf parsley
One 15-ounce flank steak

Low-sodium beef broth
Whole hominy
Dry lima beans
Corn oil

Preparation Schedule

Note: For maximum efficiency, assemble all ingredients and equipment before starting preparation.

1. Prepare iced tea; refrigerate.
2. Cut up melon; refrigerate.
3. Preheat broiler; spray rack in broiler pan.
4. Prepare Pepper and Onion Marmalade; cook, covered.
5. While marmalade is cooking, prepare garlic mixture for steak; rub on steak.
6. Prepare Hominy and Beans.
7. Broil steak.
8. While steak is broiling, prepare Worcestershire sauce mixture.
9. Slice steak; add juices to Worcestershire sauce mixture. Arrange steak on platter; top with Worcestershire sauce mixture.

CAJUN FLANK STEAK

Makes 4 servings

1 tablespoon Worcestershire sauce	1 teaspoon dried thyme leaves
1^1/$_2$ teaspoons hot pepper sauce	One 15-ounce flank steak
2 garlic cloves, pressed	2 tablespoons low-sodium beef broth

1. Preheat broiler. Spray rack in broiler pan with nonstick cooking spray.
2. In small bowl, combine 2 teaspoons of the Worcestershire sauce, 1 teaspoon of the hot pepper sauce, the garlic and thyme; rub steak with mixture. Let stand 10 minutes.
3. Place steak on prepared broiler rack; broil 4" from heat 3–5 minutes on each side or until done to taste.
4. Meanwhile, in clean small bowl, combine the remaining 1 teaspoon Worcestershire sauce, the remaining ^{1}/$_2$ teaspoon hot pepper sauce and the broth.
5. Slice steak thinly across the grain; add juices that accumulate while slicing to Worcestershire sauce mixture. Arrange steak on large decorative platter; top with Worcestershire sauce mixture.

Each serving (3 ounces) provides: 3 Proteins

Per serving: 186 Calories, 9 g Total Fat, 4 g Saturated Fat, 57 mg Cholesterol, 162 mg Sodium, 2 g Total Carbohydrate, 0 g Dietary Fiber, 23 g Protein, 16 mg Calcium

HOMINY AND BEANS

Makes 4 servings

1 tablespoon stick margarine	^{1}/$_4$ teaspoon salt
2 cups drained cooked whole hominy	^{1}/$_4$ teaspoon freshly ground black pepper
4 ounces drained cooked dry lima beans	^{1}/$_4$ teaspoon dried sage leaves
2 tablespoons minced fresh flat-leaf parsley	

In medium skillet, melt margarine; add hominy and lima beans. Cook, stirring occasionally, just until mixture is heated through. Sprinkle with parsley, salt, pepper and sage; stir to combine.

Each serving (scant ^{3}/$_4$ cup) provides: ^{3}/$_4$ Fat, 1^1/$_2$ Breads

Per serving: 132 Calories, 3 g Total Fat, 0 g Saturated Fat, 0 mg Cholesterol, 170 mg Sodium, 22 g Total Carbohydrate, 3 g Dietary Fiber, 4 g Protein, 10 mg Calcium

PEPPER AND ONION MARMALADE

Makes 4 servings

1 teaspoon corn oil
3 cups sliced red bell peppers
2 cups sliced onions

1 tablespoon cider vinegar
2 teaspoons granulated sugar

1. In large nonstick skillet, heat oil; add bell peppers and onions. Cook over medium-high heat, stirring frequently, 5–7 minutes, until onions are golden brown.
2. Add vinegar, sugar and $^1/_3$ cup water to vegetable mixture; reduce heat to low. Cook, covered, 20 minutes, until vegetables are very soft. Serve mixture warm or at room temperature.

Each serving ($^1/_2$ cup + 2 tablespoons) provides: $^1/_4$ Fat, $2^1/_2$ Vegetables, 10 Optional Calories

Per serving: 69 Calories, 1 g Total Fat, 0 g Saturated Fat, 0 mg Cholesterol, 4 mg Sodium, 14 g Total Carbohydrate, 2 g Dietary Fiber, 2 g Protein, 23 mg Calcium

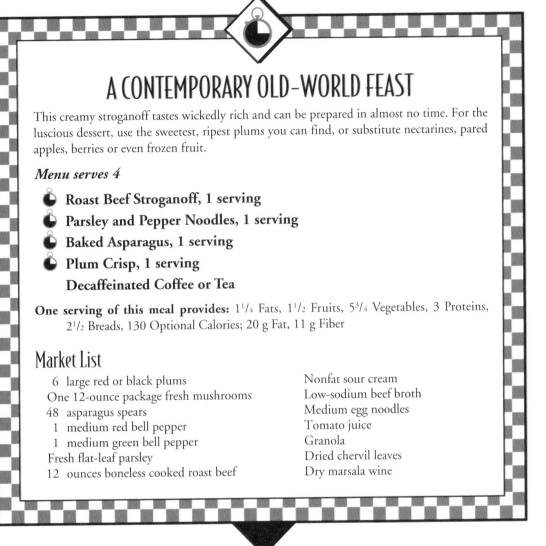

A CONTEMPORARY OLD-WORLD FEAST

This creamy stroganoff tastes wickedly rich and can be prepared in almost no time. For the luscious dessert, use the sweetest, ripest plums you can find, or substitute nectarines, pared apples, berries or even frozen fruit.

Menu serves 4

- **Roast Beef Stroganoff, 1 serving**
- **Parsley and Pepper Noodles, 1 serving**
- **Baked Asparagus, 1 serving**
- **Plum Crisp, 1 serving**
- **Decaffeinated Coffee or Tea**

One serving of this meal provides: $1^1/_4$ Fats, $1^1/_2$ Fruits, $5^3/_4$ Vegetables, 3 Proteins, $2^1/_2$ Breads, 130 Optional Calories; 20 g Fat, 11 g Fiber

Market List

6 large red or black plums
One 12-ounce package fresh mushrooms
48 asparagus spears
1 medium red bell pepper
1 medium green bell pepper
Fresh flat-leaf parsley
12 ounces boneless cooked roast beef

Nonfat sour cream
Low-sodium beef broth
Medium egg noodles
Tomato juice
Granola
Dried chervil leaves
Dry marsala wine

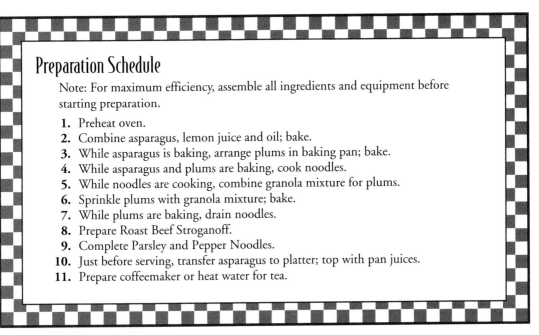

Preparation Schedule

Note: For maximum efficiency, assemble all ingredients and equipment before starting preparation.

1. Preheat oven.
2. Combine asparagus, lemon juice and oil; bake.
3. While asparagus is baking, arrange plums in baking pan; bake.
4. While asparagus and plums are baking, cook noodles.
5. While noodles are cooking, combine granola mixture for plums.
6. Sprinkle plums with granola mixture; bake.
7. While plums are baking, drain noodles.
8. Prepare Roast Beef Stroganoff.
9. Complete Parsley and Pepper Noodles.
10. Just before serving, transfer asparagus to platter; top with pan juices.
11. Prepare coffeemaker or heat water for tea.

ROAST BEEF STROGANOFF

Makes 4 servings

1 teaspoon vegetable oil	$^{1}/_{2}$ teaspoon dried thyme leaves
3 cups sliced mushrooms	12 ounces boneless cooked roast beef,
2 cups sliced onions	cut into thin strips
1 cup low-sodium beef broth	$^{1}/_{2}$ cup nonfat sour cream
2 tablespoons red wine vinegar	$^{1}/_{4}$ teaspoon salt
$1^{1}/_{2}$ teaspoons dried chervil leaves	Freshly ground black pepper to taste

1. In large nonstick skillet, heat oil; add mushrooms and onions. Cook over medium-high heat, stirring occasionally, 5–7 minutes, until mushroom liquid has evaporated and onions are golden brown.
2. Stir broth, vinegar, chervil and thyme into vegetable mixture; Bring liquid to a boil. Reduce heat to low; cook, covered, 5 minutes, until flavors are blended.
3. Stir roast beef, sour cream, salt and pepper into vegetable mixture; cook, stirring constantly just until heated (do not boil).

Each serving (1$^{1}/_{2}$ cups) provides: $^{1}/_{4}$ Fat, 2$^{1}/_{2}$ Vegetables, 3 Proteins, 25 Optional Calories

Per serving: 236 Calories, 7 g Total Fat, 3 g Saturated Fat, 69 mg Cholesterol, 217 mg Sodium, 12 g Total Carbohydrate, 2 g Dietary Fiber, 29 g Protein, 68 mg Calcium

A Contemporary Old-World Feast

Parsley and Pepper Noodles

Makes 4 servings

 1 teaspoon olive oil
 1 cup diced red bell pepper
 1 cup diced green bell pepper
4¹/₂ ounces medium egg noodles, cooked
     and drained

¹/₄ cup tomato juice
¹/₄ cup minced fresh flat-leaf parsley
¹/₄ teaspoon salt
¹/₄ teaspoon freshly ground black pepper

1. In medium skillet, heat oil; add red and green peppers. Cook over medium-high heat, stirring frequently, 5 minutes, until lightly browned.
2. Add noodles, tomato juice, parsley, salt and black pepper to bell pepper mixture; toss to combine.

Each serving (1 cup) provides: ¹/₄ Fat, 1¹/₄ Vegetables, 1¹/₂ Breads

Per serving: 149 Calories, 3 g Total Fat, 0 g Saturated Fat, 30 mg Cholesterol, 199 mg Sodium, 27 g Total Carbohydrate, 2 g Dietary Fiber, 5 g Protein, 22 mg Calcium

Baked Asparagus

Makes 4 servings

48 asparagus spears, trimmed
 1 tablespoon fresh lemon juice

 1 tablespoon olive oil

1. Preheat oven to 425° F.
2. In a 13 × 9" baking pan, combine asparagus, lemon juice and oil, turning to coat. Bake, covered, 15–20 minutes, just until asparagus are tender. Serve warm or at room temperature.
3. Just before serving, transfer to large decorative platter; top with pan juices.

Each serving (12 asparagus spears) provides: ³/₄ Fat, 2 Vegetables

Per serving: 68 Calories, 4 g Total Fat, 1 g Saturated Fat, 0 mg Cholesterol, 3 mg Sodium, 7 g Total Carbohydrate, 2 g Dietary Fiber, 5 g Protein, 38 mg Calcium

PLUM CRISP

Makes 4 servings

6 large red or black plums, pitted and
   sliced

2 fluid ounces (¹/₄ cup) dry marsala wine

3 tablespoons firmly packed light
   brown sugar

4 ounces granola

¹/₄ teaspoon cinnamon

1. Preheat oven to 425° F. Spray an 8" square baking pan with nonstick cooking spray.
2. Arrange plum slices in prepared baking pan. Sprinkle plums with marsala and 1 tablespoon of the sugar; bake, tightly covered, 15 minutes.
3. Meanwhile, in small bowl, combine granola, cinnamon and the remaining 2 tablespoons sugar.
4. Sprinkle granola mixture over baked plums; bake, uncovered, 10 minutes longer, until topping is golden brown and mixture is bubbly.

Each serving provides: 1¹/₂ Fruits, 1 Bread, 105 Optional Calories

Per serving: 287 Calories, 7 g Total Fat, 3 g Saturated Fat, 0 mg Cholesterol, 18 mg Sodium, 51 g Total Carbohydrate, 5 g Dietary Fiber, 5 g Protein, 62 mg Calcium

TUSCAN DINNER PARTY

An elegant appetizer or entrée, carpaccio is a popular cold Italian dish made with paper-thin slices of meat or fish in a flavorful sauce. Here, we've captured its essence by adorning roast beef with capers. Our antipasto, loaded with favorites, is great to serve family-style. And our light peachy dessert/drink will tickle your nose and delight your palate!

Menu serves 4

- **Carpaccio with Caper Sauce, 1 serving**
- **Antipasto Platter, 1 serving**
  Iced Grapes, 20 small or 12 large per serving
- **Bellinis, 1 serving**

One serving of this meal provides: $1\frac{1}{2}$ Fats, 2 Fruits, 1 Vegetable, 3 Proteins, 1 Bread, 40 Optional Calories; 16 g Fat, 6 g Fiber

Market List

2 large bunches grapes
1 medium peach
Fresh flat-leaf parsley
8 ounces cooked roast beef
3 ounces prosciutto or cooked ham
Bottled capers
Chick-peas (garbanzo beans)

Canned hearts of palm
Roasted red peppers
Pitted black olives, large
Breadsticks
Peach nectar
Nonalcoholic sparkling white wine

Preparation Schedule

Note: For maximum efficiency, assemble all ingredients and equipment before starting preparation.

1. Prepare Antipasto Platter; refrigerate.
2. Prepare Carpaccio with Caper sauce.
3. Just before serving, set grapes on ice.
4. Just before serving, prepare Bellinis.

CARPACCIO WITH CAPER SAUCE

Makes 4 servings

1 cup packed fresh flat-leaf parsley leaves
1 tablespoon olive oil
1 tablespoon fresh lemon juice
2 teaspoons drained capers, rinsed
$^1/_8$ teaspoon freshly ground black pepper

$^1/_8$ teaspoon dried red pepper flakes (optional)
Pinch salt
6 ounces cooked roast beef, thinly sliced

1. In food processor, combine parsley, oil, lemon juice, 1 teaspoon of the capers, the black pepper and red pepper flakes and the salt; process until thick and well blended. Stir in remaining capers.
2. Divide roast beef evenly among 4 plates; top each portion with an equal amount of parsley mixture.

Each serving provides: $^3/_4$ Fat, $1^1/_2$ Proteins

Per serving: 116 Calories, 6 g Total Fat, 1 g Saturated Fat, 34 mg Cholesterol, 104 mg Sodium, 2 g Total Carbohydrate, 1 g Dietary Fiber, 13 g Protein, 27 mg Calcium

ANTIPASTO PLATTER

Makes 4 servings

6 ounces drained cooked chick-peas (garbanzo beans)
1 cup drained canned hearts of palm, halved lengthwise
1 cup drained roasted red peppers
6 large pitted black olives, halved
2 teaspoons olive oil

1 tablespoon red wine vinegar
Pinch salt
Freshly ground black pepper to taste
3 ounces breadsticks
3 ounces thinly sliced prosciutto or cooked ham, halved lengthwise

1. On large decorative platter, arrange chick-peas, hearts of palm, roasted peppers and olives; drizzle evenly with oil and vinegar, then sprinkle with salt and pepper.
2. Wrap each breadstick with an equal amount of prosciutto; place on platter.

Each serving provides: $^3/_4$ Fat, 1 Vegetable, $1^1/_2$ Proteins, 1 Bread

Per serving with prosciutto: 253 Calories, 9 g Total Fat, 2 g Saturated Fat, 17 mg Cholesterol, 848 mg Sodium, 31 g Total Carbohydrate, 4 g Dietary Fiber, 14 g Protein, 71 g Calcium

Per serving with ham: 235 Calories, 7 g Total Fat, 1 g Saturated Fat, 11 mg Cholesterol, 711 mg Sodium, 31 g Total Carbohydrate, 4 g Dietary Fiber, 12 g Protein, 73 mg Calcium

BELLINIS

Makes 4 servings

12 fluid ounces (1¹/₂ cups) nonalcoholic   1 cup peach nectar, chilled
    sparkling white wine, chilled   1 medium peach, cut into thin wedges

Just before serving, divide wine and peach nectar among 4 tall glasses; add an equal amount
of peach wedges to each glass.

Each serving provides: 1 Fruit, 40 Optional Calories

Per serving: 67 Calories, 0 g Total Fat, 0 g Saturated Fat, 0 mg Cholesterol, 4 mg Sodium,
17 g Total Carbohydrate, 1 g Dietary Fiber, 0 g Protein, 5 mg Calcium

HEARTY COLD-WEATHER SUPPER

You can find excellent fresh salsa in the dairy case at your local supermarket; it is a versatile fat-free sauce, so keep it on hand for topping everything from these meat loaves to pasta, rice or beans.

Menu serves 4

- **Mini Meat Loaves with Salsa, 1 serving**
- **Carrot-Potato Purée, 1 serving**
- **Cabbage with Cider, 1 serving**
- **Reduced-Calorie Vanilla Pudding (made with skim milk), $^1/_2$ cup per serving**
- **Warm Apple Cider, $^1/_2$ cup per serving**

One serving of this meal provides: $^3/_4$ Milk, 1 Fat, $1^1/_4$ Fruits, $5^1/_4$ Vegetables, $3^1/_4$ Proteins, $1^1/_4$ Breads, 45 Optional Calories; 16 g Fat, 9 g Fiber

Market List

Apple cider
1 medium jalapeño pepper
1 medium head green cabbage
1 medium head red cabbage
1 pound 4 ounces russet potatoes
Fresh cilantro or dried oregano leaves
15 ounces lean ground beef (10% or less fat)

Sun-dried tomatoes (not packed in oil)
Canned mild green chile peppers
Salsa, mild or hot
Reduced-calorie vanilla pudding mix
Egg substitute, frozen or refrigerated

Special Equipment

Food mill or potato ricer

Preparation Schedule

Note: For maximum efficiency, assemble all ingredients and equipment before starting preparation.

1. Preheat oven.
2. Combine tomato mixture for meat loaves; let stand.
3. While mixture is standing, cover potatoes and carrots with water; simmer.
4. While vegetables are simmering, combine mixture for meat loaves. Fill muffin cups; bake.
5. While meat loaves are baking, prepare vanilla pudding; refrigerate.
6. Drain potatoes and carrots.
7. Heat milk mixture for Carrot-Potato Purée.
8. While milk mixture is heating, cook onions for Cabbage with Cider.
9. Rice potatoes and carrots into heated milk mixture; mix.
10. Complete Cabbage with Cider.
11. Place meat loaves on platter; top with salsa.
12. Just before serving, warm cider.

Mini Meat Loaves with Salsa

Makes 4 servings

8 sun-dried tomato halves (not packed
   in oil), chopped
3 tablespoons yellow cornmeal
2 garlic cloves, pressed
1/3 cup boiling water
15 ounces lean ground beef (10% or
   less fat)
1/2 cup minced onion
1/2 cup drained canned mild green chile
   peppers, chopped

1 medium jalapeño pepper, seeded and
   minced
1/4 cup egg substitute
2 tablespoons minced fresh cilantro or
   1/2 teaspoon dried oregano leaves
3/4 teaspoon salt
1/4 teaspoon freshly ground black pepper
1/2 cup mild or hot salsa

1. Preheat oven to 375° F. Spray eight 2³/4" muffin cups with nonstick cooking spray.
2. In medium bowl, combine tomatoes, cornmeal, garlic and boiling water; let stand 5 minutes.
3. Add beef, onion, chile peppers, jalapeño pepper, egg substitute, cilantro, salt and black pepper to tomato mixture; mix well.
4. Fill each prepared cup with an equal amount of beef mixture; partially fill remaining muffin cups with water (this will help prevent muffin pan from warping and/or burning). Bake 20–25 minutes, until cooked though. Remove pan from oven and carefully drain off water (remember, it will be boiling hot). Place meat loaves on large decorative platter; top each with 1 tablespoon salsa.

Each serving (2 mini meat loaves) provides: 1³/4 Vegetables, 3¹/4 Proteins, ¹/4 Bread, 10 Optional Calories

Per serving: 256 Calories, 11 g Total Fat, 4 g Saturated Fat, 66 mg Cholesterol, 800 mg Sodium, 15 g Total Carbohydrate, 2 g Dietary Fiber, 25 g Protein, 24 mg Calcium

Carrot-Potato Purée

Makes 4 servings

1 pound 4 ounces diced pared russet potatoes	1 tablespoon stick margarine
2 cups diced carrots	1 teaspoon salt
$^1/_2$ cup evaporated skimmed milk	$^1/_4$ teaspoon freshly ground black pepper
	Pinch nutmeg

1. In large saucepan, combine potatoes and carrots; cover with water. Bring water to a boil; reduce heat to low. Simmer 10 minutes, until vegetables are tender; drain and set aside.
2. In same saucepan, combine milk, margarine, salt, pepper and nutmeg. Place milk mixture over low heat; cook 5 minutes, just until mixture is hot and margarine is melted (do not boil).
3. With food mill or potato ricer, rice potatoes and carrots into hot milk mixture; with fork, mix just until combined.

Each serving (1$^1/_4$ cups) provides: $^1/_4$ Milk, $^3/_4$ Fat, 1 Vegetable, 1 Bread

Per serving: 189 Calories, 3 g Total Fat, 1 g Saturated Fat, 1 mg Cholesterol, 650 mg Sodium, 35 g Total Carbohydrate, 4 g Dietary Fiber, 0 g Protein, 8 mg Calcium

Cabbage with Cider

Makes 4 servings

1 teaspoon vegetable oil	$^1/_2$ cup apple cider
1 cup sliced onions	1 tablespoon cider vinegar
2 cups shredded green cabbage	1 teaspoon granulated sugar
2 cups shredded red cabbage	

1. In large skillet, heat oil; add onions. Cook over medium-high heat, stirring occasionally, 3–4 minutes, until golden brown.
2. Add green and red cabbage, cider, vinegar and sugar; toss to combine. Reduce heat to low; cook, covered, stirring occasionally, 7–10 minutes, until cabbage is tender.

Each serving (1 cup) provides: $^1/_4$ Fat, $^1/_4$ Fruit, 2$^1/_2$ Vegetables, 5 Optional Calories

Per serving: 62 Calories, 1 g Total Fat, 0 g Saturated Fat, 0 mg Cholesterol, 12 mg Sodium, 12 g Total Carbohydrate, 2 g Dietary Fiber, 1 g Protein, 45 mg Calcium

FLAVOR-PACKED QUICK DINNER

Picadillo can be quickly put together, and it is always delicious; for a delightful change, try using ground chicken or turkey instead of beef. Yes, there *is* hot pepper sauce in the dessert, but don't shy away! You'll be surprised at how delicious a mixture it is: cold, hot, sweet and creamy all at once.

Menu serves 4

Picadillo, 1 serving

    Cooked Long-Grain Rice, 1 cup per serving

    or

    Warm Corn Tortillas (6" diameter), 2 per serving

Pepper and Radish Salad, 1 serving

Mango Bango, 1 serving

    Unsweetened Black Cherry–Flavored Seltzer

One serving of this meal provides: 1 Fat, 2 Fruits, 4¼ Vegetables, 2 Proteins, 2 Breads, 40 Optional Calories; 14 g Fat, 10 g Fiber

Market List

3 small mangoes
1 medium head iceberg lettuce
1 medium red bell pepper
1 medium green bell pepper
1 bunch radishes
Fresh cilantro
10 ounces lean ground beef (10% or less fat)
Long-grain rice or corn tortillas (6" diameter)

Unsweetened black cherry–flavored seltzer
Low-sodium beef broth
Pimiento-stuffed green olives, large or small
8 fluid ounces vanilla nonfat sugar-free frozen yogurt

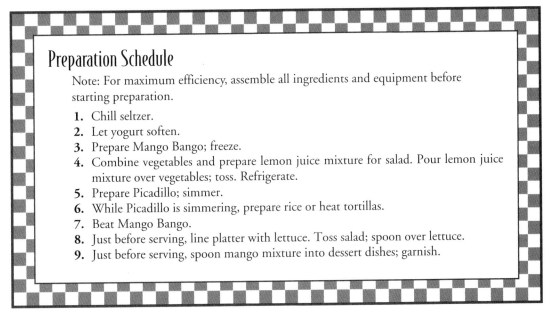

Preparation Schedule

Note: For maximum efficiency, assemble all ingredients and equipment before starting preparation.

1. Chill seltzer.
2. Let yogurt soften.
3. Prepare Mango Bango; freeze.
4. Combine vegetables and prepare lemon juice mixture for salad. Pour lemon juice mixture over vegetables; toss. Refrigerate.
5. Prepare Picadillo; simmer.
6. While Picadillo is simmering, prepare rice or heat tortillas.
7. Beat Mango Bango.
8. Just before serving, line platter with lettuce. Toss salad; spoon over lettuce.
9. Just before serving, spoon mango mixture into dessert dishes; garnish.

PICADILLO

Makes 4 servings

 1 teaspoon vegetable oil
10 ounces lean ground beef (10% or less fat)
 2 cups chopped onions
 1 cup canned stewed tomatoes
 $^1/_2$ cup low-sodium beef broth
 $^1/_4$ cup raisins
 6 large or 10 small pimiento-stuffed green olives, sliced

 2 teaspoons mild or hot chili powder
 $^1/_2$ teaspoon ground cumin
 $^1/_2$ teaspoon dried oregano leaves
 $^1/_8$ teaspoon cinnamon
Pinch salt
Pinch freshly ground black pepper

1. In medium nonstick skillet, heat oil; add beef and onions. Cook over medium-high heat, stirring to break up meat, 4–5 minutes, until beef is no longer pink.
2. Stir tomatoes, broth, raisins, olives, chili powder, cumin, oregano, cinnamon, salt and pepper into beef mixture; bring liquid to a boil. Reduce heat to low; simmer, stirring occasionally, 10 minutes, until mixture is slightly thickened and flavors are blended.

Each serving ($^3/_4$ cup) provides: $^1/_2$ Fat, $^1/_2$ Fruit, $1^1/_2$ Vegetables, 2 Proteins, 5 Optional Calories

Per serving: 221 Calories, 10 g Total Fat, 3 g Saturated Fat, 44 mg Cholesterol, 433 mg Sodium, 19 g Total Carbohydrate, 4 g Dietary Fiber, 17 g Protein, 56 mg Calcium

PEPPER AND RADISH SALAD

Makes 4 servings

1 cup diced red bell pepper ($^1/_4$" dice)
1 cup diced green bell pepper ($^1/_4$" dice)
1 cup sliced radishes
$^1/_4$ cup sliced scallions
2 tablespoons fresh lemon or lime juice

1 tablespoon minced fresh cilantro
2 teaspoons olive oil
$^1/_4$ teaspoon salt
2 cups shredded iceberg lettuce

1. In medium bowl, combine red and green peppers, radishes and scallions.
2. In small bowl, with wire whisk, combine lemon juice, cilantro, oil and salt. Pour lemon juice mixture over vegetables; toss to coat. Refrigerate, covered, until chilled.
3. Just before serving, line medium decorative platter with lettuce. Toss bell pepper mixture again, then spoon over lettuce.

Each serving ($1^1/_4$ cups) provides: $^1/_2$ Fat, $2^3/_4$ Vegetables

Per serving: 47 Calories, 3 g Total Fat, 0 g Saturated Fat, 0 mg Cholesterol, 147 mg Sodium, 6 g Total Carbohydrate, 2 g Dietary Fiber, 1 g Protein, 36 mg Calcium

MANGO BANGO (SPICY MANGO CREAM)

Makes 4 servings

3 small mangoes, peeled, pitted and diced
1 tablespoon fresh lime juice
1 teaspoon hot pepper sauce

8 fluid ounces vanilla nonfat sugar-free
    frozen yogurt, softened
Lime slices to garnish (optional)

1. In food processor or blender, combine mangoes, lime juice and hot pepper sauce; purée until smooth. Add yogurt; purée again until smooth.
2. Transfer mixture to medium metal mixing bowl; freeze, covered, until ready to serve, occasionally beating with fork to keep ice crystals from forming.
3. Just before serving, divide mango mixture evenly among 4 dessert dishes; serve garnished with lime slices if desired.

Each serving ($^3/_4$ cup) provides: $1^1/_2$ Fruits, 35 Optional Calories

Per serving: 118 Calories, 0 g Total Fat, 0 g Saturated Fat, 0 mg Cholesterol, 68 mg Sodium, 31 g Total Carbohydrate, 1 g Dietary Fiber, 3 g Protein, 87 mg Calcium

QUICK AND COLORFUL VEAL DINNER

Everybody will love this meal! The classic entrée is as delicious with chicken cutlets as it is with veal. The pasta side dish is pretty and satisfying; when served with a salad and some extra cheese, it makes a good main course as well. An unusual and fun soup, this blueberry-laced delight is also great made with strawberries.

Menu serves 4

- **Veal with Lemon and Capers, 1 serving**
- **Vegetable Linguine, 1 serving**
- **Blueberry Soup, 1 serving**
- **White Wine Spritzer, 1 serving**

One serving of this meal provides: 1 Fat, $1^1/_4$ Fruits, 3 Vegetables, $3^1/_4$ Proteins, 2 Breads, 120 Optional Calories; 10 g Fat, 8 g Fiber

Market List

$3^3/_4$ cups blueberries
1 medium zucchini
1 medium yellow squash
Fresh flat-leaf parsley
Fresh basil
Fresh mint (optional)
15 ounces veal scallops

Aspartame-sweetened vanilla nonfat
yogurt
Bottled capers
Linguine
Grated Parmesan cheese
Club soda
Berry-flavored brandy

Preparation Schedule

Note: For maximum efficiency, assemble all ingredients and equipment before starting preparation.

1. Purée blueberry mixture for soup; refrigerate.
2. Bring water for linguine to a boil.
3. While water is coming to a boil, combine flour mixture for veal.
4. Complete Vegetable Linguine.
5. Complete Veal with Lemon and Capers.
6. Just before serving, divide soup into bowls. Top soup with yogurt; garnish.
7. Just before serving, prepare White Wine Spritzer.

VEAL WITH LEMON AND CAPERS

Makes 4 servings

  1 tablespoon all-purpose flour
 1/4 teaspoon salt
 1/4 teaspoon freshly ground black pepper
 15 ounces veal scallops
  2 teaspoons olive oil
 1/2 cup low-sodium chicken broth

  2 tablespoons fresh lemon juice
  1 tablespoon chopped fresh flat-leaf
     parsley
  1 tablespoon drained capers, rinsed
     Lemon slices to garnish (optional)

1. On paper plate or sheet of wax paper, combine flour, salt and pepper. Coat one side of each veal scallop with flour mixture; set aside.
2. In medium nonstick skillet, heat oil; add veal, floured-side down. Cook over medium-high heat 1 minute on each side, until lightly browned and cooked through. Remove veal from skillet; set aside.
3. In same skillet, combine broth, lemon juice, parsley and capers; bring to a boil over high heat. Cook 2 minutes, until liquid is reduced in volume to about 1/3 cup.
4. Return veal and any accumulated juices to skillet; cook, turning as needed, just until heated. Serve garnished with lemon slices if desired.

Each serving provides: 1/2 Fat, 3 Proteins, 10 Optional Calories

Per serving: 147 Calories, 4 g Total Fat, 1 g Saturated Fat, 83 mg Cholesterol, 265 mg Sodium, 2 g Total Carbohydrate, 0 g Dietary Fiber, 23 g Protein, 9 mg Calcium

Quick and Colorful Veal Dinner

Vegetable Linguine

Makes 4 servings

6 ounces linguine	2 tablespoons packed fresh basil leaves
4 medium carrots	or $^1/_2$ teaspoon dried
1 medium zucchini	2 teaspoons olive oil
1 medium yellow squash	1 small garlic clove
$^1/_2$ cup packed fresh flat-leaf parsley sprigs	$^3/_4$ ounce grated Parmesan cheese
$^1/_2$ cup low-sodium chicken broth	Freshly ground black pepper to taste

1. In large pot of boiling water, cook linguine 7–8 minutes, until barely tender.
2. Meanwhile, with vegetable peeler, slice carrots thinly down to the core, forming long strands.
3. With vegetable peeler, slice zucchini and yellow squash thinly down to the seeds, forming long strands.
4. Add carrot strands to cooking linguine; cook 2 minutes.
5. Meanwhile, in food processor, combine parsley, broth, basil, oil and garlic; purée until smooth.
6. Add zucchini and yellow squash strands to linguine-carrot mixture; drain immediately. Transfer mixture to large bowl. Add parsley mixture; toss to combine. Sprinkle with Parmesan cheese and pepper.

Each serving ($2^1/_2$ cups) provides: $^1/_2$ Fat, 3 Vegetables, $^1/_4$ Protein, 2 Breads, 5 Optional Calories

Per serving: 265 Calories, 5 g Total Fat, 2 g Saturated Fat, 4 mg Cholesterol, 150 mg Sodium, 46 g Total Carbohydrate, 5 g Dietary Fiber, 10 g Protein, 138 mg Calcium

Blueberry Soup

Makes 4 servings

$3^3/_4$ cups blueberries	1 teaspoon fresh lemon juice
$1^1/_2$ fluid ounces (3 tablespoons) berry-flavored brandy	$^1/_2$ cup aspartame-sweetened vanilla nonfat yogurt *
1 tablespoon + 1 teaspoon granulated sugar	Mint leaves to garnish (optional)

1. In food processor or blender, combine blueberries, brandy, sugar and lemon juice; purée until smooth. Refrigerate, covered, until chilled.
2. Just before serving, divide blueberry mixture evenly among 4 soup bowls; top each portion with 2 tablespoons yogurt. Serve garnished with mint if desired.

Each serving ($^1/_2$ cup soup + 2 tablespoons yogurt) provides: $1^1/_4$ Fruits, 55 Optional Calories

Per serving: 136 Calories, 1 g Total Fat, 0 g Saturated Fat, 1 mg Cholesterol, 24 mg Sodium, 29 g Total Carbohydrate, 3 g Dietary Fiber, 2 g Protein, 46 mg Calcium

* *If desired, substitute 4 fluid ounces vanilla nonfat sugar-free frozen yogurt for the aspartame-sweetened yogurt.*

Each serving (¹/₂ cup soup + 2 tablespoons nonfat sugar-free frozen yogurt) provides: 1¹/₄ Fruits, 65 Optional Calories

Per serving: 143 Calories, 1 g Total Fat, 0 g Saturated Fat, 0 mg Cholesterol, 24 mg Sodium, 32 g Total Carbohydrate, 3 g Dietary Fiber, 2 g Protein, 46 mg Calcium

WHITE WINE SPRITZER

For each serving, in tall glass, combine *2 fluid ounces (¹/₄ cup) dry white wine* and enough *club soda* and *ice cubes* to fill glass.

Each serving provides: 50 Optional Calories

Per serving: 40 Calories, 0 g Total Fat, 0 g Saturated Fat, 0 mg Cholesterol, 15 mg Sodium, 0 g Total Carbohydrate, 0 g Dietary Fiber, 0 g Protein, 8 mg Calcium

ELEGANT VEAL DINNER

Sherry adds a subtle elegance to the smooth taste of this sumptuous entrée; try it with chicken cutlets instead of the veal if you prefer. And to bring out its best flavor, be sure the wine is well chilled when you serve it.

Menu serves 4

- **Creamy Veal with Mushrooms, 1 serving**
- **Noodles with Peas, 1 serving**
- **Pan-Roasted Tomatoes and Watercress, 1 serving**
- **Dry White Wine, 4 fluid ounces per serving**

One serving of this meal provides: $^1/_2$ Milk, 1 Fat, $4^1/_4$ Vegetables, 2 Proteins, $2^1/_4$ Breads, 120 Optional Calories; 9 g Fat, 4 g Fiber

Market List

One 12-ounce package fresh mushrooms
 3 large plum tomatoes
 1 bunch watercress
10 ounces veal scallops
Broad egg noodles

One 10-ounce package frozen
   green peas
Dried savory leaves
Dry sherry

Preparation Schedule

Note: For maximum efficiency, assemble all ingredients and equipment before starting preparation.

1. Chill wine.
2. Cook tomatoes; transfer to bowl.
3. Cook garlic; stir in vinegar. Add to tomatoes; season with salt and pepper.
4. Bring water to a boil for noodles.
5. While water is coming to a boil, bring broth to a boil for peas.
6. Add noodles to boiling water.
7. While noodles are cooking, cook veal, mushrooms and onions.
8. While veal is cooking, combine broth mixture for veal.
9. Drain noodles; place in bowl.
10. Add peas, savory and pepper to boiling broth.
11. Add broth mixture to veal mixture; simmer.
12. While veal is simmering, pour pea mixture over noodles; toss.
13. Just before serving, add watercress to tomato mixture; toss.

CREAMY VEAL WITH MUSHROOMS

Makes 4 servings

1 teaspoon vegetable oil	1 fluid ounce (2 tablespoons) dry sherry
10 ounces veal scallops	2 teaspoons cornstarch
3 cups sliced mushrooms	$^1/_2$ teaspoon dried rosemary leaves
1 cup chopped onions	$^1/_2$ teaspoon salt
1 cup low-sodium chicken broth	$^1/_4$ teaspoon dried thyme leaves
1 cup evaporated skimmed milk	$^1/_4$ teaspoon freshly ground black pepper

1. In large nonstick skillet, heat oil; add veal, mushrooms and onions. Cook over medium-high heat, stirring occasionally, 10 minutes, until liquid is evaporated and veal and onions are golden brown.
2. Meanwhile, in small bowl, with wire whisk, combine broth, milk, sherry, cornstarch, rosemary, salt, thyme and pepper, blending until cornstarch is dissolved.
3. Stir broth mixture into veal mixture; continuing to stir, bring liquid to a boil. Reduce heat to low; simmer, stirring occasionally, 3 minutes, until veal is cooked through and tender and liquid has thickened.

Each serving (1$^1/_4$ cups) provides: $^1/_2$ Milk, $^1/_4$ Fat, 2 Vegetables, 2 Proteins, 15 Optional Calories

Per serving: 189 Calories, 3 g Total Fat, 1 g Saturated Fat, 58 mg Cholesterol, 410 mg Sodium, 16 g Total Carbohydrate, 1 g Dietary Fiber, 22 g Protein, 206 mg Calcium

NOODLES WITH PEAS

Makes 4 servings

6 ounces broad egg noodles	$^1/_2$ teaspoon dried savory leaves
$^1/_2$ cup low-sodium chicken broth	Freshly ground black pepper to taste
$^1/_2$ cup frozen green peas	

1. In large pot of boiling water, cook noodles 5–6 minutes, until tender. Drain and place in medium decorative bowl; keep warm.
2. Meanwhile, in small skillet, bring broth to a boil; cook until liquid is reduced in volume by about half. Add peas, savory and pepper; reduce heat to low. Cook, covered, 2 minutes, until peas are cooked.
3. Pour pea mixture over noodles; toss to combine.

Each serving (1 cup) provides: 2$^1/_4$ Breads, 5 Optional Calories

Per serving: 180 Calories, 2 g Total Fat, 0 g Saturated Fat, 40 mg Cholesterol, 36 mg Sodium, 33 g Total Carbohydrate, 2 g Dietary Fiber, 7 g Protein, 21 mg Calcium

PAN-ROASTED TOMATOES AND WATERCRESS

Makes 4 servings

1 tablespoon olive oil
3 large plum tomatoes, cut into $^1/_2$" slices
1 large garlic clove, pressed
2 tablespoons balsamic vinegar

Pinch salt
Pinch freshly ground black pepper
3 cups watercress leaves

1. In medium nonstick skillet, heat oil; add tomatoes. Cook over medium-high heat, turning once, until browned on both sides; transfer to large salad bowl.
2. To same skillet, add garlic; cook, stirring constantly, 15–20 seconds, just until golden brown (do not burn). Remove skillet from heat; stir in vinegar. Scrape mixture into bowl with tomatoes; toss to combine. Add salt and pepper; toss again.
3. Just before serving, add watercress to tomato mixture; toss to combine.

Each serving ($^3/_4$ cup) provides: $^3/_4$ Fat, $2^1/_4$ Vegetables

Per serving: 43 Calories, 4 g Total Fat, 0 g Saturated Fat, 0 mg Cholesterol, 47 mg Sodium, 3 g Total Carbohydrate, 1 g Dietary Fiber, 1 g Protein, 35 mg Calcium

TRADITIONAL EASTERN EUROPEAN DINNER

In this rich meal, pork medallions are braised in cider and served with a crisp cider vinegar sauce. Turnips are transformed into a mellow purée made with potatoes and buttermilk. And brilliant red cabbage, baked with onion and raisins, is as exciting to the eye as it is to the palate.

Menu serves 4

- Cider-Braised Pork Medallions, 1 serving
- Potato-Turnip Purée, 1 serving
- Baked Red Cabbage with Raisins, 1 serving
- Cinnamon Baked Apple, 1 serving
  Decaffeinated Coffee or Tea

One serving of this meal provides: $^1/_2$ Fat, $1^3/_4$ Fruits, $2^3/_4$ Vegetables, 3 Proteins, $^3/_4$ Bread, 55 Optional Calories; 9 g Fat, 4 g Fiber

Market List

4 small apples	1 medium red onion
Apple cider	15 ounces boneless pork tenderloin
12 ounces turnips	Low-fat (1.5%) buttermilk
1 medium head red cabbage	Raisins

Preparation Schedule

Note: For maximum efficiency, assemble all ingredients and equipment before starting preparation.

1. Preheat oven.
2. Prepare Baked Red Cabbage with Raisins; place in oven.
3. While cabbage is baking, prepare Cinnamon Baked Apple; place in oven with cabbage.
4. Coat and brown pork; add cider and let simmer.
5. While pork is simmering, cook turnips and potatoes.
6. Complete Cider-Braised Pork Medallions.
7. Complete Potato-Turnip Purée.
8. Prepare coffeemaker or heat water for tea.

CIDER-BRAISED PORK MEDALLIONS

Makes 4 servings

3   tablespoons all-purpose flour
Freshly ground black pepper
¼   teaspoon salt
15 ounces boneless pork tenderloin, cut
      into twelve 1" medallions

2   teaspoons vegetable oil
½   cup apple cider
1   tablespoon cider vinegar
1   teaspoon grated lemon zest *

1. In gallon-size sealable plastic bag, combine flour, ½ teaspoon pepper and the salt; add 2 or 3 pork medallions. Seal bag; shake to coat. Transfer pork to plate; repeat with remaining medallions.
2. In large nonstick skillet, heat oil; add pork. Cook over high heat, turning once, 1–2 minutes on each side, until lightly browned. Reduce heat to low; add cider. Simmer, covered, 20 minutes, until pork is cooked through and tender. With slotted spoon, transfer pork to large decorative platter; set aside and keep warm.
3. Add vinegar and lemon zest to cider. Increase heat to high; bring liquid to a boil. Cook, stirring occasionally, 5 minutes, until slightly thickened; season with pepper to taste.
4. Just before serving, pour cider mixture over pork.

Each serving provides: ½ Fat, ¼ Fruit, 3 Proteins, ¼ Bread

Per serving: 201 Calories, 8 g Total Fat, 2 g Saturated Fat, 70 mg Cholesterol, 188 mg Sodium, 8 g Total Carbohydrate, 0 g Dietary Fiber, 22 g Protein, 10 mg Calcium

* *The zest of the lemon is the peel without any of the pith (white membrane). To remove zest from lemon, use a zester or fine side of a vegetable grater; wrap lemon in plastic wrap and refrigerate for use at another time.*

POTATO-TURNIP PURÉE

Makes 4 servings

10 ounces potatoes, pared and cut
      into 2" pieces
2   cups cubed pared turnips (2" cubes)
3   tablespoons low-fat (1.5%) buttermilk

½   teaspoon salt
½   teaspoon ground white pepper
⅛   teaspoon ground nutmeg

1. In medium saucepan, combine potatoes and turnips; cover with water. Bring water to a boil; reduce heat to low. Simmer 15 minutes, until vegetables are tender; drain.
2. Transfer vegetables to food processor. Add buttermilk, salt, pepper and nutmeg; purée until smooth.

Each serving provides: 1 Vegetable, ½ Bread, 5 Optional Calories

Per serving: 79 Calories, 0 g Total Fat, 0 g Saturated Fat, 0 mg Cholesterol, 333 mg Sodium, 18 g Total Carbohydrate, 2 g Dietary Fiber, 2 g Protein, 40 mg Calcium

BAKED RED CABBAGE WITH RAISINS

Makes 4 servings

- ¹/₄ cup cider vinegar
- 3 tablespoons firmly packed light brown sugar
- 3 cups finely shredded red cabbage
- ¹/₂ cup thinly sliced red onion
- ¹/₄ cup raisins

1. Preheat oven to 450° F.
2. In a 2-quart shallow baking dish, combine vinegar and sugar, stirring until sugar is dissolved. Add cabbage, onion and raisins; toss gently to combine. Bake, covered, 20 minutes, stirring after 10 minutes, until wilted.

Each serving provides: ¹/₂ Fruit, 1³/₄ Vegetables, 35 Optional Calories

Per serving: 90 Calories, 0 g Total Fat, 0 g Saturated Fat, 0 mg Cholesterol, 13 mg Sodium, 23 g Total Carbohydrate, 2 g Dietary Fiber, 1 g Protein, 47 mg Calcium

CINNAMON BAKED APPLE

Preheat oven to 450° F. For each serving, core *1 small apple*; place in baking pan. Sprinkle with *1 teaspoon light brown sugar and a pinch of cinnamon*; bake, covered, 15 minutes, until tender.

Each serving provides: 1 Fruit, 15 Optional Calories

Per serving: 79 Calories, 0 g Total Fat, 0 g Saturated Fat, 0 mg Cholesterol, 2 mg Sodium, 20 g Total Carbohydrate, 2 g Dietary Fiber, 0 g Protein, 13 mg Calcium

GERMAN-STYLE SUPPER

This entrée is hearty winter food; mulled cider goes perfectly with it, as do gingersnap cookies for dessert.

Menu serves 4

- **German Skillet Pork, 1 serving**
- **Scalloped Potatoes, 1 serving**
- **Sauteed Red Cabbage, 1 serving**
- **Gingersnap Cookies, 2 per serving ($^1/_2$ ounce)**
- **Mulled Cider, 1 serving**

One serving of this meal provides: $^1/_4$ Milk, $1^1/_4$ Fats, $1^1/_4$ Fruits, 4 Vegetables, 2 Proteins, 2 Breads, 55 Optional Calories; 12 g Fat, 8 g Fiber

Market List

1 small Granny Smith apple
Apple cider
1 pound 14 ounces red potatoes
1 medium head red cabbage

10 ounces boneless pork loin
Nonfat sour cream
White wine vinegar
Gingersnap cookies

Preparation Schedule

Note: For maximum efficiency, assemble all ingredients and equipment before starting preparation.

1. Adjust oven racks; preheat oven.
2. Prepare Scalloped Potatoes; bake.
3. While potatoes are baking, prepare German Skillet Pork; simmer.
4. While pork is simmering, prepare Sauteed Red Cabbage; cook, covered.
5. While cabbage is cooking, prepare Mulled Cider; strain into mugs.

German-Style Supper

German Skillet Pork

Makes 4 servings

1 teaspoon vegetable oil	2 tablespoons cider vinegar
10 ounces boneless pork loin, diced	1 teaspoon cornstarch
2 cups sliced onions	$^1/_4$ teaspoon dried sage leaves
1 small Granny Smith apple, pared, cored and cut into $^1/_8$" slices	$^1/_4$ teaspoon dried thyme leaves
$^1/_2$ cup low-sodium chicken broth	$^1/_4$ teaspoon freshly ground black pepper
$^1/_4$ cup apple cider	

1. In medium nonstick skillet, heat oil; add pork and onions. Cook over medium-high heat, stirring frequently, 5 minutes, until onions are golden brown.
2. Add apple to pork mixture; stir to combine.
3. In small bowl, with wire whisk, combine broth, cider, vinegar, cornstarch, sage, thyme and pepper, blending until cornstarch is dissolved; stir into pork mixture. Continuing to stir, bring liquid to a boil. Reduce heat to low; simmer, covered, 10 minutes, until pork is cooked through and mixture is slightly thickened.

Each serving ($^3/_4$ cup) provides: $^1/_4$ Fat, $^1/_4$ Fruit, 1 Vegetable, 2 Proteins, 15 Optional Calories

Per serving: 171 Calories, 6 g Total Fat, 2 g Saturated Fat, 42 mg Cholesterol, 47 mg Sodium, 14 g Total Carbohydrate, 2 g Dietary Fiber, 16 g Protein, 33 mg Calcium

Scalloped Potatoes

Makes 4 servings

1 pound 14 ounces red potatoes, cut into $^1/_8$" slices	$^1/_4$ teaspoon freshly ground black pepper
$^1/_2$ cup evaporated skimmed milk	Pinch nutmeg
$^1/_4$ cup nonfat sour cream	1 tablespoon plain dried bread crumbs
$^1/_2$ teaspoon salt	1 tablespoon stick margarine, cut into small pieces

1. Adjust oven racks to divide oven into thirds; preheat oven to 425° F. Spray an 8" square baking pan with nonstick cooking spray.
2. In medium saucepan, cover potatoes with water. Bring water to a boil; cook 5 minutes, just until potatoes are tender. Drain; transfer to prepared baking pan.
3. In small bowl, combine milk, sour cream, salt, pepper and nutmeg. Pour over potatoes; stir to combine.
4. Sprinkle potato mixture evenly with bread crumbs, then dot evenly with margarine; bake in upper third of oven 10–15 minutes, until topping is browned.

Each serving ($1^1/_4$ cups) provides: $^1/_4$ Milk, $^3/_4$ Fat, $1^1/_2$ Breads, 20 Optional Calories

Per serving: 241 Calories, 4 g Total Fat, 1 g Saturated Fat, 1 mg Cholesterol, 385 mg Sodium, 44 g Total Carbohydrate, 4 g Dietary Fiber, 8 g Protein, 119 mg Calcium

SAUTEED RED CABBAGE

Makes 4 servings

1 teaspoon vegetable oil	1 tablespoon white wine vinegar
6 cups shredded red cabbage	1/2 teaspoon caraway seeds
2 garlic cloves, crushed	1/4 teaspoon salt

1. In large skillet, heat oil; add cabbage and garlic. Cook over medium-high heat, tossing constantly, 3 minutes, until cabbage is slightly wilted.
2. Add vinegar, caraway seeds, salt and 1/4 cup water to cabbage mixture. Reduce heat to low; cook, covered, 10 minutes, until cabbage is tender and flavors are blended.

Each serving (1¹/₄ cups) provides: 1/4 Fat, 3 Vegetables

Per serving: 42 Calories, 1 g Total Fat, 0 g Saturated Fat, 0 mg Cholesterol, 147 mg Sodium, 7 g Total Carbohydrate, 2 g Dietary Fiber, 3 g Protein, 59 mg Calcium

MULLED CIDER

Makes 4 servings

2 cups apple cider	4 whole allspice
1 cinnamon stick	2 whole cloves

1. In medium saucepan, combine cider, cinnamon stick, allspice and cloves; bring to a boil. Reduce heat to low; simmer 5 minutes.
2. Dividing evenly, strain cider mixture into 4 mugs.

Each serving provides: 1 Fruit

Per serving: 59 Calories, 0 g Total Fat, 0 g Saturated Fat, 0 mg Cholesterol, 4 mg Sodium, 15 g Total Carbohydrate, 0 g Dietary Fiber, 0 g Protein, 13 mg Calcium

SOPHISTICATED SUPPER

Serve this very special meal when entertaining friends who appreciate fine dining. Or turn a midweek family meal into a refined repast with this ultra-elegant but extra-easy menu.

Menu serves 4

- **Pork Chops with Creamy Red Pepper Sauce, 1 serving**
- **Orzo-Spinach Pilaf, 1 serving**
  Steamed Sugar Snap Peas, ¹/₂ cup per serving
- **Pears with Herbed Roquefort, 1 serving**
  Sparkling Mineral Water with Lime Slice

One serving of this meal provides: 1 Fat, 1 Fruit, 3 Vegetables, 4 Proteins, 1 Bread, 15 Optional Calories; 17 g Fat, 10 g Fiber

Market List

2 large Bosc pears
1 pound sugar snap peas
2 medium red bell peppers
Fresh or dried sage
Four 5-ounce center-cut loin pork chops
1¹/₂ ounces queso blanco or
        Monterey Jack cheese

1¹/₂ ounces Roquefort or blue cheese
Orzo (rice-shaped pasta)
One 10-ounce package frozen
        chopped spinach
Garlic salt

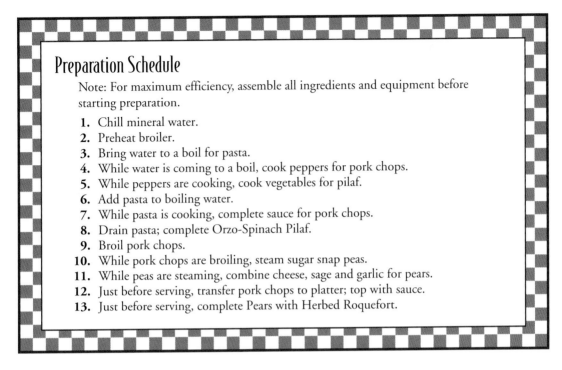

Preparation Schedule

Note: For maximum efficiency, assemble all ingredients and equipment before starting preparation.

1. Chill mineral water.
2. Preheat broiler.
3. Bring water to a boil for pasta.
4. While water is coming to a boil, cook peppers for pork chops.
5. While peppers are cooking, cook vegetables for pilaf.
6. Add pasta to boiling water.
7. While pasta is cooking, complete sauce for pork chops.
8. Drain pasta; complete Orzo-Spinach Pilaf.
9. Broil pork chops.
10. While pork chops are broiling, steam sugar snap peas.
11. While peas are steaming, combine cheese, sage and garlic for pears.
12. Just before serving, transfer pork chops to platter; top with sauce.
13. Just before serving, complete Pears with Herbed Roquefort.

PORK CHOPS WITH CREAMY RED PEPPER SAUCE

Makes 4 servings

1 tablespoon + 1 teaspoon reduced-calorie tub margarine
2 medium red bell peppers, cored, seeded and coarsely chopped
$^1/_2$ cup plain nonfat yogurt
1 tablespoon chopped fresh sage or 1 teaspoon dried

$^1/_4$ teaspoon garlic salt
Four 5-ounce center-cut loin pork chops ($^1/_2$" thick)
Freshly ground black pepper to taste

1. Preheat broiler. Spray rack in broiler pan with nonstick cooking spray.
2. To prepare sauce, in medium skillet, melt margarine; add red peppers. Cook over medium-high heat, stirring occasionally, 8–10 minutes, until tender.
3. Transfer cooked peppers to food processor or blender; purée until smooth.
4. Transfer pureed peppers to medium bowl; stir in yogurt, sage and garlic salt. Set aside.
5. Place pork chops on prepared broiler rack; sprinkle with black pepper. Broil 4" from heat, 7 minutes on each side, until cooked through.
6. Transfer pork chops to large decorative platter; spoon sauce equally over each chop.

Each serving provides: $^1/_2$ Fat, 1 Vegetable, 3 Proteins, 15 Optional Calories

Per serving: 219 Calories, 10 g Total Fat, 3 g Saturated Fat, 70 mg Cholesterol, 199 mg Sodium, 5 g Total Carbohydrate, 1 g Dietary Fiber, 28 g Protein, 90 mg Calcium

Orzo-Spinach Pilaf

Makes 4 servings

3 ounces orzo (rice-shaped pasta)	$^1/_4$ cup low-sodium chicken broth
2 teaspoons olive oil	$1^1/_2$ teaspoons red wine vinegar
$^1/_2$ cup chopped onion	$1^1/_2$ ounces queso blanco* or Monterey Jack
$^1/_2$ cup chopped celery	cheese, shredded
1 garlic clove, minced	Freshly ground black pepper to taste
1 cup well-drained thawed frozen	
chopped spinach	

1. In large pot of boiling water, cook orzo 9–11 minutes, until tender; drain.
2. Meanwhile, in large nonstick skillet, heat oil; add onion, celery and garlic. Cook over medium heat, stirring frequently, 4–5 minutes, until vegetables are tender. Stir in spinach, 2 tablespoons of the broth and the vinegar; cook, stirring frequently, 2–3 minutes longer, until liquid is evaporated.
3. Add orzo, cheese, pepper and remaining 2 tablespoons broth to vegetable mixture; stir just until combined.

Each serving ($^1/_2$ cup) provides: $^1/_2$ Fat, 1 Vegetable, $^1/_2$ Protein, 1 Bread

Per serving: 159 Calories, 6 g Total Fat, 2 g Saturated Fat, 9 mg Cholesterol, 163 mg Sodium, 21 g Total Carbohydrate, 2 g Dietary Fiber, 7 g Protein, 150 mg Calcium

* Queso blanco is a mild white cheese found in Hispanic markets and many supermarkets.

Pears with Herbed Roquefort

Makes 4 servings

$1^1/_2$ ounces Roquefort or blue cheese, crumbled	2 large Bosc pears
$^1/_4$ teaspoon dried sage leaves, crumbled	1 teaspoon fresh lemon juice
$^1/_4$ garlic clove, minced	

1. In small bowl, combine cheese, sage and garlic.
2. Just before serving, halve and core pears; brush cut side of each pear half with lemon juice. Fill each half with an equal amount of cheese mixture.

Each serving (1 filled pear half) provides: 1 Fruit, $^1/_2$ Protein

Per serving: 131 Calories, 4 g Total Fat, 2 g Saturated Fat, 8 mg Cholesterol, 148 mg Sodium, 24 g Total Carbohydrate, 4 g Dietary Fiber, 3 g Protein, 74 mg Calcium

LEFTOVERS IN DISGUISE

Use leftover roast pork or turkey for this mildly spiced casserole. Top off the meal with a citrus fruit salad and a mug of cold beer.

Menu serves 4

⏱ **Chili-Tortilla Pie, 1 serving**
⏱ **Lettuce and Avocado Salad with Thousand Island Dressing, 1 serving**
   Chilled Orange and Grapefruit Sections, $^1/_2$ cup per serving
   Light Beer, 12 fluid ounces per serving

One serving of this meal provides: 1 Fat, 1 Fruit, $4^1/_2$ Vegetables, 3 Proteins, 2 Breads, 125 Optional Calories; 16 g Fat, 8 g Fiber

Market List

1 medium grapefruit	Tomato sauce
1 medium red onion	Corn tortillas (6" diameter)
1 medium head iceberg lettuce	Bottled chili sauce
1 medium avocado	Pickle relish
10 ounces boneless cooked pork or skinless	Corn oil
boneless cooked turkey	Light beer
$1^1/_2$ ounces Monterey Jack cheese	

Preparation Schedule

Note: For maximum efficiency, assemble all ingredients and equipment before starting preparation.

1. Chill beer.
2. Chill orange and grapefruit sections.
3. Preheat oven.
4. Prepare Chili-Tortilla Pie; bake.
5. While pie is baking, prepare dressing for salad; refrigerate.
6. Just before serving, place lettuce and avocado on plates; top with dressing.

CHILI-TORTILLA PIE

Makes 4 servings

2 teaspoons corn oil	2 garlic cloves, pressed
10 ounces boneless cooked pork or skinless boneless cooked turkey, diced	1¹/₂ cups tomato sauce
2 cups chopped onions	1 teaspoon dried oregano leaves
1 tablespoon mild or hot chili powder	8 corn tortillas (6" diameter)
	1¹/₂ ounces shredded Monterey Jack cheese

1. Preheat oven to 375° F. Spray an 8" square baking pan with nonstick cooking spray.
2. In medium nonstick skillet, heat oil; add pork, onions, chili powder and garlic. Cook over medium-high heat, stirring occasionally, 5 minutes, until onions are softened.
3. Add tomato sauce and oregano to pork mixture; bring to a boil. Reduce heat to low; simmer 5 minutes.
4. Line prepared baking pan with 4 of the tortillas; top with pork mixture, then remaining tortillas. Sprinkle with cheese; bake 15 minutes, until lightly browned and bubbly.

Each serving provides: ¹/₂ Fat, 2¹/₂ Vegetables, 3 Proteins, 2 Breads

Per serving with pork: 383 Calories, 13 g Total Fat, 4 g Saturated Fat, 69 mg Cholesterol, 755 mg Sodium, 39 g Total Carbohydrate, 6 g Dietary Fiber, 29 g Protein, 231 mg Calcium

Per serving with turkey: 359 Calories, 11 g Total Fat, 3 g Saturated Fat, 66 mg Cholesterol, 765 mg Sodium, 39 g Total Carbohydrate, 6 g Dietary Fiber, 29 g Protein, 227 mg Calcium

LETTUCE AND AVOCADO SALAD WITH THOUSAND ISLAND DRESSING

Makes 4 servings

¹/₃ cup plain nonfat yogurt	1 teaspoon red wine vinegar
2 tablespoons bottled chili sauce	1 medium head iceberg lettuce, quartered
1 tablespoon minced red onion	¹/₄ medium avocado, peeled and sliced
2 teaspoons pickle relish	

1. In small bowl, combine yogurt, chili sauce, onion, pickle relish and vinegar.
2. Just before serving, divide lettuce wedges and avocado slices evenly among 4 salad plates; top each portion with an equal amount of yogurt mixture.

Each serving provides: ¹/₂ Fat, 2 Vegetables, 25 Optional Calories

Per serving: 57 Calories, 2 g Total Fat, 0 g Saturated Fat, 0 mg Cholesterol, 153 mg Sodium, 8 g Total Carbohydrate, 1 g Dietary Fiber, 2 g Protein, 80 mg Calcium

QUICK CONTINENTAL BRUNCH

Individual timbales, like quiche without the crust, make a fine entrée for a last-minute brunch. Vegetables à la Grecque are great to keep on hand for snacking; once cooked and cooled, they will keep for several days in the refrigerator.

Menu serves 4

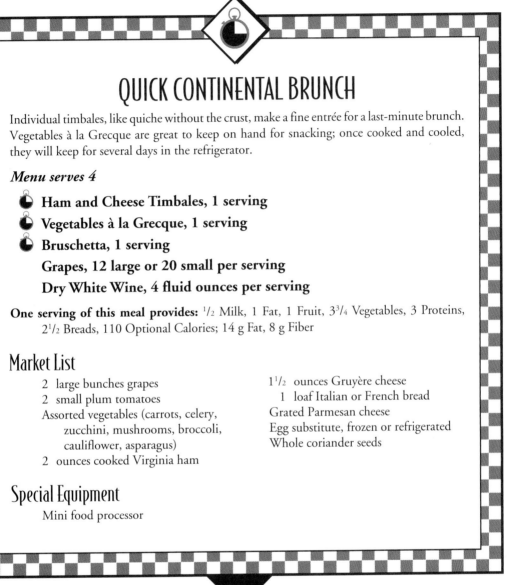

- **Ham and Cheese Timbales, 1 serving**
- **Vegetables à la Grecque, 1 serving**
- **Bruschetta, 1 serving**
- **Grapes, 12 large or 20 small per serving**
- **Dry White Wine, 4 fluid ounces per serving**

One serving of this meal provides: $^1/_2$ Milk, 1 Fat, 1 Fruit, $3^3/_4$ Vegetables, 3 Proteins, $2^1/_2$ Breads, 110 Optional Calories; 14 g Fat, 8 g Fiber

Market List

2 large bunches grapes
2 small plum tomatoes
Assorted vegetables (carrots, celery,
     zucchini, mushrooms, broccoli,
     cauliflower, asparagus)
2 ounces cooked Virginia ham

$1^1/_2$ ounces Gruyère cheese
  1 loaf Italian or French bread
Grated Parmesan cheese
Egg substitute, frozen or refrigerated
Whole coriander seeds

Special Equipment

Mini food processor

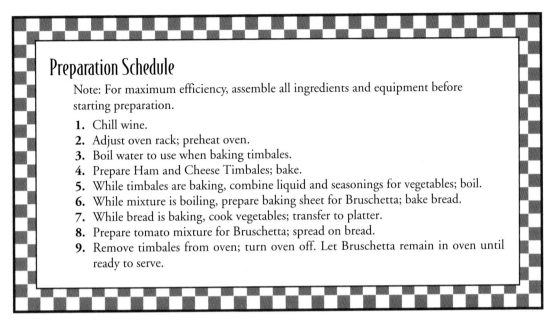

Preparation Schedule

Note: For maximum efficiency, assemble all ingredients and equipment before starting preparation.

1. Chill wine.
2. Adjust oven rack; preheat oven.
3. Boil water to use when baking timbales.
4. Prepare Ham and Cheese Timbales; bake.
5. While timbales are baking, combine liquid and seasonings for vegetables; boil.
6. While mixture is boiling, prepare baking sheet for Bruschetta; bake bread.
7. While bread is baking, cook vegetables; transfer to platter.
8. Prepare tomato mixture for Bruschetta; spread on bread.
9. Remove timbales from oven; turn oven off. Let Bruschetta remain in oven until ready to serve.

Quick Continental Brunch

HAM AND CHEESE TIMBALES

Makes 4 servings

1 teaspoon vegetable oil	2 cups egg substitute
1 cup finely diced onions	1 cup evaporated skimmed milk
2 ounces finely chopped cooked Virginia ham	$^1/_2$ teaspoon salt
	$^1/_4$ teaspoon freshly ground black pepper
1$^1/_2$ ounces shredded Gruyère cheese	Pinch ground red pepper
1 tablespoon grated Parmesan cheese	Pinch nutmeg

1. Adjust oven rack to divide oven in half; preheat oven to 350° F. Spray four 8-ounce custard cups or ramekins with nonstick cooking spray.
2. In small skillet, heat oil; add onions. Cook over medium-high heat, stirring frequently, 3–4 minutes, until golden brown. Stir in ham; remove from heat. Divide mixture evenly among prepared ramekins; sprinkle evenly with Gruyère and Parmesan cheeses.
3. In medium bowl, combine egg substitute, milk, salt, black pepper, red pepper and nutmeg; pour evenly into ramekins.
4. Place large roasting pan on center oven rack; add filled ramekins. Carefully pour boiling water into roasting pan to a depth of about $^1/_2$"; bake 15–25 minutes, until a knife inserted in center of a timbale comes out clean.

Each serving (1 timbale) provides: $^1/_2$ Milk, $^1/_4$ Fat, $^1/_2$ Vegetable, 3 Proteins, 10 Optional Calories

Per serving: 204 Calories, 7 g Total Fat, 3 g Saturated Fat, 24 mg Cholesterol, 780 mg Sodium, 13 g Total Carbohydrate, 1 g Dietary Fiber, 22 g Protein, 361 mg Calcium

VEGETABLES À LA GRECQUE

Makes 4 servings

1$^1/_2$ cups red wine vinegar	1 teaspoon fennel seeds, slightly crushed
4 garlic cloves, slightly crushed	1 teaspoon dried rosemary leaves
3 bay leaves	4 whole cloves
1 teaspoon whole coriander seeds, slightly crushed	$^1/_2$ teaspoon dried red pepper flakes
	6 cups assorted vegetables *

1. In large saucepan, combine vinegar, garlic, bay leaves, coriander, fennel, rosemary, cloves, red pepper flakes and 1$^1/_2$ cups water. Bring liquid to a boil; cook 5 minutes.
2. Add 1 variety of vegetables to vinegar mixture; cook just until tender-crisp. With slotted spoon, transfer vegetable pieces to large decorative platter; repeat with each variety of vegetable, placing them on same platter with contrasting colors adjacent. Discard liquid and seasonings.

Each serving (1¹/₂ cups) provides: 3 Vegetables

Per serving: 49 Calories, 0 g Total Fat, 0 g Saturated Fat, 0 mg Cholesterol, 46 mg Sodium, 10 g Total Carbohydrate, 3 g Dietary Fiber, 3 g Protein, 55 mg Calcium

* *Use any combination of vegetables from the following list: carrot, celery or zucchini sticks; whole or quartered mushrooms; broccoli or cauliflower florets; asparagus spears.*

BRUSCHETTA

Makes 4 servings

10 ounces Italian or French bread, cut into 12 equal slices	2 garlic cloves
	Pinch salt
2 small plum tomatoes, blanched, peeled, seeded and diced	Freshly ground black pepper to taste
1 tablespoon olive oil	

1. Preheat oven to 350° F. Line baking sheet with foil.
2. Place bread slices on prepared baking sheet, cut-side down; bake 10 minutes, until crisp but not brown. Leave oven on.
3. In mini food processor, combine tomatoes, oil, garlic, salt and pepper; process until finely chopped.
4. Spread each slice of bread with an equal amount of tomato mixture; bake 5 minutes. Turn oven off; let bread remain in oven until ready to serve.

Each serving (3 slices) provides: ³/₄ Fat, ¹/₄ Vegetable, 2¹/₂ Breads

Per serving: 227 Calories, 6 g Total Fat, 1 g Saturated Fat, 0 mg Cholesterol, 448 mg Sodium, 37 g Total Carbohydrate, 2 g Dietary Fiber, 6 g Protein, 59 mg Calcium

DINNER À LA MEDITERRANÉE

The tantalizing combination of lamb, feta cheese and mint in this quick-to-prepare entrée was inspired by the sunny Grecian islands. And explore the *pasta-bilities* of using fun pasta shapes, such as wagon wheels or bow ties, when preparing this lemony dill salad.

Menu serves 4

- Broiled Lamb Chops with Feta Cheese, 1 serving
- Spicy Snow Peas, 1 serving
- Dilled Pasta Salad, 1 serving
  Breadsticks, $3/4$ ounce per serving
  Fresh Fruit Salad, $1/2$ cup per serving
  Sparkling Mineral Water with Lemon Twist

One serving of this meal provides: $1/2$ Fat, 1 Fruit, $1 1/2$ Vegetables, $2 1/2$ Proteins, 3 Breads, 5 Optional Calories; 14 g Fat, 5 g Fiber

Market List

Fresh fruit for salad
3 cups snow peas (Chinese pea pods)
Fresh dill
Four 3-ounce boneless lamb chops
$1 1/2$ ounces feta cheese

Breadsticks
Orange marmalade
Bite-size pasta
Dried mint leaves

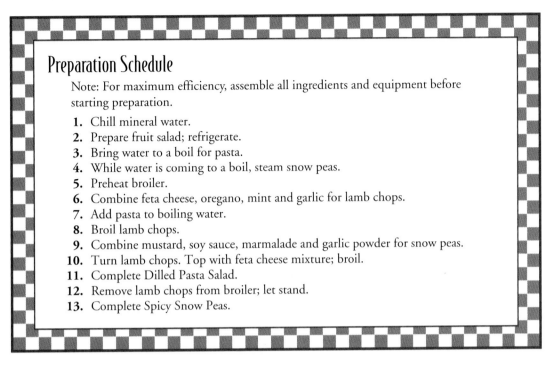

Preparation Schedule

Note: For maximum efficiency, assemble all ingredients and equipment before starting preparation.

1. Chill mineral water.
2. Prepare fruit salad; refrigerate.
3. Bring water to a boil for pasta.
4. While water is coming to a boil, steam snow peas.
5. Preheat broiler.
6. Combine feta cheese, oregano, mint and garlic for lamb chops.
7. Add pasta to boiling water.
8. Broil lamb chops.
9. Combine mustard, soy sauce, marmalade and garlic powder for snow peas.
10. Turn lamb chops. Top with feta cheese mixture; broil.
11. Complete Dilled Pasta Salad.
12. Remove lamb chops from broiler; let stand.
13. Complete Spicy Snow Peas.

BROILED LAMB CHOPS WITH FETA CHEESE

Makes 4 servings

$1^1/_2$ ounces feta cheese, crumbled
$^1/_2$ teaspoon dried oregano leaves
$^1/_2$ teaspoon dried mint leaves, crumbled

$^1/_4$ garlic clove, finely minced
Four 3-ounce boneless lamb chops

1. Preheat broiler. Spray rack in broiler pan with nonstick cooking spray.
2. In small bowl, combine feta cheese, oregano, mint and garlic; set aside.
3. Place lamb on prepared broiler rack; broil 4" from heat 3–4 minutes, until well browned. Turn chops over; spread evenly with feta cheese mixture. Broil 6–8 minutes longer, until lamb is cooked through and cheese mixture is browned. Let stand 5 minutes before serving.

Each serving (1 lamb chop) provides: $2^1/_2$ Proteins

Per serving: 153 Calories, 8 g Total Fat, 4 g Saturated Fat, 0 mg Cholesterol, 166 mg Sodium, 1 g Total Carbohydrate, 0 g Dietary Fiber, 19 g Protein, 66 mg Calcium

Spicy Snow Peas

Makes 4 servings

3 cups snow peas (Chinese pea pods), stem ends and strings removed
1 tablespoon Dijon-style mustard
2 teaspoons reduced-sodium soy sauce

1 teaspoon orange marmalade
1/4 teaspoon garlic powder

1. Fill medium saucepan with 1" water; set steamer rack in saucepan. Place snow peas on rack. Bring water to a boil; reduce heat to low. Steam snow peas over simmering water, covered, 6–8 minutes, until tender-crisp. Transfer snow peas to medium decorative bowl.
2. Meanwhile, in small bowl, combine mustard, soy sauce, marmalade and garlic powder.
3. Drizzle mustard mixture over snow peas; toss to coat.

Each serving (about 3/4 cup) provides: 1 1/2 Vegetables, 5 Optional Calories

Per serving: 56 Calories, 0 g Total Fat, 0 g Saturated Fat, 0 mg Cholesterol, 218 mg Sodium, 10 g Total Carbohydrate, 3 g Dietary Fiber, 3 g Protein, 48 mg Calcium

Dilled Pasta Salad

Makes 4 servings

6 ounces bite-size pasta
2 tablespoons chopped fresh dill
2 teaspoons olive oil
Grated zest of 1 lemon *

2 tablespoons fresh lemon juice
1/4 teaspoon salt
1/4 garlic clove, minced

1. In large pot of boiling water, cook pasta 8–10 minutes, until tender. Drain; rinse.
2. Transfer pasta to large decorative bowl. Add dill, oil, lemon zest, lemon juice, salt and garlic; toss to combine.

Each serving (1 cup) provides: 1/2 Fat, 2 Breads

Per serving: 182 Calories, 3 g Total Fat, 0 g Saturated Fat, 0 mg Cholesterol, 139 mg Sodium, 33 g Total Carbohydrate, 1 g Dietary Fiber, 6 g Protein, 18 mg Calcium

* The zest of the lemon is the peel without any of the pith (white membrane). To remove zest from lemon, use a zester or fine side of a vegetable grater.

SOUTHERN-STYLE LAMB SUPPER

This stew is a fine way to use up the last bits of roast lamb. And our version of Spoon Bread, the old southern staple that's a pleasing halfway point between corn pudding and bread, is quick, easy and delicious.

Menu serves 4

- **Lamb and Lentil Stew, 1 serving**
- **Spoon Bread, 1 serving**
- **Green Beans with Sun-Dried Tomatoes, 1 serving**
- **Blackberries with Citrus Sauce, 1 serving**
- **Planter's Punch, 1 serving**

One serving of this meal provides: $1/4$ Milk, $1\,1/4$ Fats, 1 Fruit, $3\,1/2$ Vegetables, $2\,3/4$ Proteins, 2 Breads, 80 Optional Calories; 13 g Fat, 14 g Fiber

Market List

3 cups blackberries
Fresh flat-leaf parsley
6 ounces boneless cooked lamb
Low-fat (1.5%) buttermilk
Lentils
Sun-dried tomatoes (not packed
    in oil)

Rum extract
Aromatic bitters
One 10-ounce package frozen whole
    or cut green beans

Preparation Schedule

Note: For maximum efficiency, assemble all ingredients and equipment before starting preparation.

1. Preheat oven.
2. Prepare Spoon Bread; bake.
3. While bread is baking, prepare Lamb and Lentil Stew; simmer.
4. While stew is simmering, prepare Green Beans with Sun-Dried Tomatoes.
5. Prepare Blackberries with Citrus Sauce.
6. Just before serving, prepare Planter's Punch.

LAMB AND LENTIL STEW

Makes 4 servings

1 teaspoon olive oil	$^{1}/_{2}$ cup chopped celery
6 ounces boneless cooked lamb, diced	2 tablespoons chopped fresh
1 cup minced onions	flat-leaf parsley
1 cup diced carrot	$^{1}/_{2}$ teaspoon dried marjoram leaves
8 ounces drained cooked lentils	$^{1}/_{2}$ teaspoon dried thyme leaves
1 cup canned stewed tomatoes	Pinch salt
1 cup low-sodium chicken broth	Pinch freshly ground black pepper

1. In medium skillet, heat oil; add lamb, onions and carrot. Cook over medium-high heat, stirring frequently, 4–5 minutes, until onions are golden brown.
2. Stir lentils, tomatoes, broth, celery, parsley, marjoram, thyme, salt and pepper into lamb mixture; bring to a boil. Reduce heat to low; simmer, covered, 20 minutes, until vegetables are tender and flavors are blended.

Each serving (1 cup) provides: $^{1}/_{4}$ Fat, $1^{3}/_{4}$ Vegetables, $2^{1}/_{2}$ Proteins, 5 Optional Calories

Per serving: 217 Calories, 6 g Total Fat, 2 g Saturated Fat, 37 mg Cholesterol, 262 mg Sodium, 23 g Total Carbohydrate, 6 g Dietary Fiber, 18 g Protein, 68 mg Calcium

SPOON BREAD

Makes 4 servings

1 cup yellow cornmeal	1 tablespoon stick margarine, melted
$1^{1}/_{3}$ cups boiling water	1 teaspoon baking soda
1 cup low-fat (1.5%) buttermilk	$^{3}/_{4}$ teaspoon salt
1 egg, beaten	

1. Preheat oven to 375° F. Place an 8" square baking pan in oven.
2. In medium bowl, combine cornmeal and boiling water, stirring to mix well.
3. In small bowl, with wire whisk, combine buttermilk, egg, margarine, baking soda and salt. Pour buttermilk mixture into cornmeal mixture; with wire whisk, blend until smooth.
4. Remove baking pan from oven; spray with nonstick cooking spray.
5. Pour cornmeal mixture into prepared baking pan; bake 20–25 minutes, until golden brown and crusty on top (mixture will be soft inside).

Each serving provides: $^{1}/_{4}$ Milk, $^{3}/_{4}$ Fat, $^{1}/_{4}$ Protein, 2 Breads

Per serving: 195 Calories, 5 g Total Fat, 1 g Saturated Fat, 56 mg Cholesterol, 842 mg Sodium, 30 g Total Carbohydrate, 2 g Dietary Fiber, 7 g Protein, 83 mg Calcium

GREEN BEANS WITH SUN-DRIED TOMATOES

Makes 4 servings

1 teaspoon olive oil
6 sun-dried tomato halves (not packed in oil), slivered or minced, soaked and drained

2 garlic cloves, pressed
2 cups thawed frozen whole or cut green beans
Pinch salt

1. In medium skillet, heat oil; add tomatoes and garlic. Cook over medium heat, stirring frequently, 1–2 minutes, until garlic is golden brown.
2. Stir green beans, 2 tablespoons water and salt into tomato mixture; cook, covered, 2 minutes, until green beans are tender.

Each serving ($^1/_2$ cup) provides: $^1/_4$ Fat, $1^3/_4$ Vegetables

Per serving: 48 Calories, 1 g Total Fat, 0 g Saturated Fat, 0 mg Cholesterol, 41 mg Sodium, 9 g Total Carbohydrate, 2 g Dietary Fiber, 2 g Protein, 37 mg Calcium

BLACKBERRIES WITH CITRUS SAUCE

Makes 4 servings

3 tablespoons fresh orange juice
2 tablespoons granulated sugar
2 tablespoons fresh lemon juice
1 tablespoon fresh lime juice
$1^1/_2$ teaspoons cornstarch

$^1/_2$ teaspoon grated orange zest *
$^1/_2$ teaspoon grated lemon zest *
$^1/_2$ teaspoon grated lime zest *
3 cups blackberries

1. To prepare sauce, in small saucepan, with wire whisk, combine orange juice, sugar, lemon and lime juices, cornstarch, fruit zests and $^1/_3$ cup cold water, blending until cornstarch is dissolved. Cook mixture over medium heat, stirring constantly, 3 minutes, until thickened.
2. Divide berries evenly among 4 dessert dishes; top each portion with one-fourth of the sauce.

Each serving ($^3/_4$ cup berries + 3 tablespoons sauce) provides: 1 Fruit, 30 Optional Calories

Per serving: 93 Calories, 0 g Total Fat, 0 g Saturated Fat, 0 mg Cholesterol, 0 mg Sodium, 23 g Total Carbohydrate, 5 g Dietary Fiber, 1 g Protein, 38 mg Calcium

* *The zest of the fruit is the peel without any of the pith (white membrane). To remove zest, use a zester or fine side of a vegetable grater.*

PLANTER'S PUNCH

Makes 4 servings

¼ cup granulated sugar
¼ cup fresh lemon juice
2 teaspoons rum extract

¼ teaspoon aromatic bitters
Ice cubes

1. In pitcher, combine 2 cups water, the sugar, lemon juice, rum extract and aromatic bitters, stirring until sugar is dissolved.
2. Divide mixture evenly among 4 tall glasses; add enough ice cubes to each serving to fill glasses.

Each serving provides: 65 Optional Calories

Per serving: 65 Calories, 0 g Total Fat, 0 g Saturated Fat, 0 mg Cholesterol, 0 mg Sodium, 14 g Total Carbohydrate, 0 g Dietary Fiber, 0 g Protein, 1 mg Calcium

A CHIC GREEK DINNER

This meal highlights the flavors of the Greek islands. Rather than serving it in courses, try serving everything at once, taverna style.

Menu serves 4

- **Olive and Chick-Pea Combo, 1 serving**
- **Lemon-Marinated Lamb Chops, 1 serving**
- **Tomato-Dill Orzo, 1 serving**
- **Romaine Salad with Feta Dressing, 1 serving**
- **Lemon-Flavored Sparkling Mineral Water**

One serving of this meal provides: $^3/_4$ Fat, $2^3/_4$ Vegetables, $2^1/_2$ Proteins, 2 Breads, 10 Optional Calories; 17 g Fat, 5 g Fiber

Market List

1 head iceberg lettuce
1 head Romaine lettuce
1 medium red onion
1 medium green bell pepper
1 medium tomato
Fresh dill

Fresh flat-leaf parsley
Four 4-ounce loin lamb chops
$2^1/_4$ ounces feta cheese
Chick-peas (garbanzo beans)
Orzo (rice-shaped pasta)
Greek olives, small

Preparation Schedule

Note: For maximum efficiency, assemble all ingredients and equipment before starting preparation.

1. Chill mineral water.
2. Prepare salad and dressing; refrigerate separately. Zest lemon.
3. Cook orzo.
4. While orzo is cooking, prepare marinade for lamb; add lamb.
5. While lamb is marinating, drain orzo.
6. Preheat broiler.
7. Prepare Tomato-Dill Orzo.
8. Broil lamb.
9. While lamb is broiling, prepare parsley mixture for lamb.
10. Just before serving, drizzle dressing over salad.

Olive and Chick-Pea Combo

For each serving, line a small plate with *1 iceberg lettuce leaf,* top with *5 small Greek olives* and *2 ounces drained cooked chick-peas (garbanzo beans).* Refrigerate, covered, until ready to serve.

Each serving provides: $^1/_2$ Fat, $^1/_4$ Vegetable, 1 Bread

Per serving: 142 Calories, 7 g Total Fat, 1 g Saturated Fat, 0 mg Cholesterol, 471 mg Sodium, 17 g Total Carbohydrate, 2 g Dietary Fiber, 5 g Protein, 44 mg Calcium

Lemon-Marinated Lamb Chops

Makes 4 servings

1 tablespoon fresh lemon juice	$^1/_4$ cup fresh flat-leaf parsley leaves
1 teaspoon olive oil	1 teaspoon grated lemon zest *
2 garlic cloves, pressed	$^1/_2$ garlic clove
Freshly ground black pepper	Pinch salt
Four 4-ounce loin lamb chops	

1. To prepare marinade, in gallon-size sealable plastic bag, combine lemon juice, oil, garlic and $^1/_2$ teaspoon pepper; add lamb chops. Seal bag, squeezing out air; turn to coat chops. Let marinate 15 minutes, turning bag occasionally.
2. Meanwhile, preheat broiler.
3. Drain lamb chops, discarding marinade. Place chops on rack in broiler pan; broil 3" from heat, turning once, until browned and cooked to taste.
4. Meanwhile, on cutting board, finely chop together parsley, lemon zest, $^1/_2$ garlic clove, salt and pepper to taste.
5. Just before serving, sprinkle lamb chops with parsley mixture.

Each serving provides: 2 Proteins, 10 Optional Calories

Per serving: 138 Calories, 7 g Total Fat, 2 g Saturated Fat, 54 mg Cholesterol, 82 mg Sodium, 1 g Total Carbohydrate, 0 g Dietary Fiber, 17 g Protein, 20 mg Calcium

* The zest of the lemon is the peel without any of the pith (white membrane). To remove zest from lemon, use a zester or fine side of a vegetable grater.

TOMATO-DILL ORZO

Makes 4 servings

¹/₂ cup canned crushed tomatoes	¹/₄ cup chopped fresh dill
3 ounces orzo (rice-shaped pasta), cooked and drained	2 teaspoons fresh lemon juice
	¹/₄ teaspoon freshly ground black pepper

1. In medium saucepan, cook tomatoes over medium heat, stirring occasionally, 10 minutes.
2. Add orzo and dill; cook, stirring occasionally, 10 minutes longer.
3. Stir in lemon juice and pepper; heat 1 minute, until flavors are blended.

Each serving provides: ¹/₄ Vegetable, 1 Bread

Per serving: 88 Calories, 0 g Total Fat, 0 g Saturated Fat, 0 mg Cholesterol, 52 mg Sodium, 18 g Total Carbohydrate, 1 g Dietary Fiber, 3 g Protein, 26 mg Calcium

ROMAINE SALAD WITH FETA DRESSING

Makes 4 servings

3 cups sliced Romaine lettuce (¹/₂" strips)	1 teaspoon olive oil
1 medium tomato, cut into wedges	1 garlic clove, pressed
¹/₂ cup thinly sliced red onion	¹/₄ teaspoon freshly ground black pepper
¹/₄ cup chopped green bell pepper	1¹/₂ ounces feta cheese, crumbled
2 tablespoons red wine vinegar	

1. To prepare salad, in large bowl, combine lettuce, tomato and onion; set aside.
2. To prepare dressing, in food processor, combine green pepper, vinegar, 2 tablespoons water, the oil, garlic and black pepper; with on-off motion, pulse processor 2–3 times, until bell pepper is finely chopped (do not purée).
3. Just before serving, divide salad evenly among 4 salad plates; drizzle an equal amount of dressing over each portion of salad, then sprinkle each with one-fourth of the cheese.

Each serving provides: ¹/₄ Fat, 2¹/₄ Vegetables, ¹/₂ Protein

Per serving: 65 Calories, 4 g Total Fat, 2 g Saturated Fat, 9 mg Cholesterol, 128 mg Sodium, 6 g Total Carbohydrate, 2 g Dietary Fiber, 3 g Protein, 78 mg Calcium

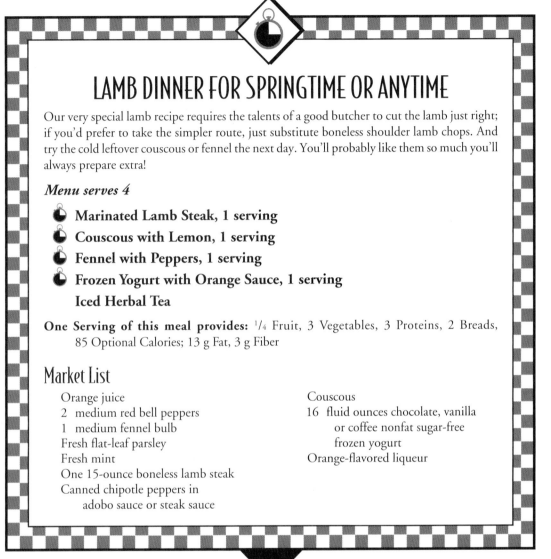

LAMB DINNER FOR SPRINGTIME OR ANYTIME

Our very special lamb recipe requires the talents of a good butcher to cut the lamb just right; if you'd prefer to take the simpler route, just substitute boneless shoulder lamb chops. And try the cold leftover couscous or fennel the next day. You'll probably like them so much you'll always prepare extra!

Menu serves 4

- **Marinated Lamb Steak, 1 serving**
- **Couscous with Lemon, 1 serving**
- **Fennel with Peppers, 1 serving**
- **Frozen Yogurt with Orange Sauce, 1 serving**
- **Iced Herbal Tea**

One Serving of this meal provides: $1/4$ Fruit, 3 Vegetables, 3 Proteins, 2 Breads, 85 Optional Calories; 13 g Fat, 3 g Fiber

Market List

Orange juice
2 medium red bell peppers
1 medium fennel bulb
Fresh flat-leaf parsley
Fresh mint
One 15-ounce boneless lamb steak
Canned chipotle peppers in
    adobo sauce or steak sauce

Couscous
16 fluid ounces chocolate, vanilla
    or coffee nonfat sugar-free
    frozen yogurt
Orange-flavored liqueur

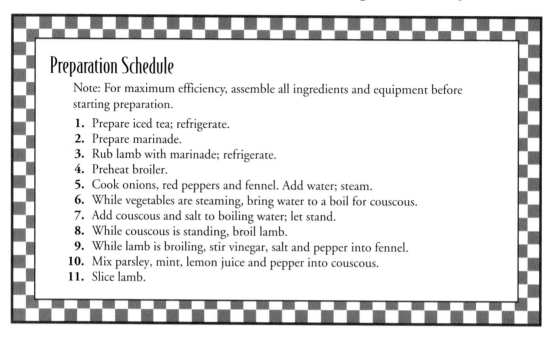

Preparation Schedule

Note: For maximum efficiency, assemble all ingredients and equipment before starting preparation.

1. Prepare iced tea; refrigerate.
2. Prepare marinade.
3. Rub lamb with marinade; refrigerate.
4. Preheat broiler.
5. Cook onions, red peppers and fennel. Add water; steam.
6. While vegetables are steaming, bring water to a boil for couscous.
7. Add couscous and salt to boiling water; let stand.
8. While couscous is standing, broil lamb.
9. While lamb is broiling, stir vinegar, salt and pepper into fennel.
10. Mix parsley, mint, lemon juice and pepper into couscous.
11. Slice lamb.

MARINATED LAMB STEAK

Makes 4 servings

One 15-ounce boneless lamb steak
   (1" thick)
Spicy Marinade or Mild Marinade
   (recipes follow)

1. Rub steak with one of the marinades; refrigerate, covered, until 10 minutes before ready to serve.
2. Preheat broiler. Spray rack in broiler pan with nonstick cooking spray.
3. Place steak on prepared broiler rack; broil 4" from heat, turning once, 3–5 minutes on each side or until done to taste. Thinly slice steak across the grain; serve with juices that accumulate while slicing.

Each serving (3 ounces, including either marinade) provides: 3 Proteins

Per serving with Spicy Marinade: 188 Calories, 9 g Total Fat, 3 g Saturated Fat, 79 mg Cholesterol, 126 mg Sodium, 2 g Total Carbohydrate, 0 g Dietary Fiber, 23 g Protein, 23 mg Calcium

Per serving with Mild Marinade: 183 Calories, 9 g Total Fat, 3 g Saturated Fat, 79 mg Cholesterol, 110 mg Sodium, 1 g Total Carbohydrate, 0 g Dietary Fiber, 23 g Protein, 20 mg Calcium

Spicy Marinade

Makes 4 servings

One 7-ounce can chipotle peppers in   ¹/₂ teaspoon dried oregano leaves
    adobo sauce

1. In food processor or blender, purée chipotle peppers with sauce until smooth. Transfer 1 tablespoon pureed mixture to small bowl; refrigerate remaining mixture, covered, for use at another time.
2. Add oregano to pureed peppers; stir to combine.

Per serving: 8 Calories, 0 g Total Fat, 0 g Saturated Fat, 0 mg Cholesterol, 55 mg Sodium, 2 g Total Carbohydrate, 0 g Dietary Fiber, 0 g Protein, 5 mg Calcium

Mild Marinade

Makes 4 servings

1 teaspoon prepared yellow mustard   1 garlic clove, pressed
1 teaspoon steak sauce

In small bowl, combine mustard, steak sauce and garlic.

Per serving: 3 Calories, 0 g Total Fat, 0 g Saturated Fat, 0 mg Cholesterol, 40 mg Sodium, 1 g Total Carbohydrate, 0 g Dietary Fiber, 0 g Protein, 2 mg Calcium

COUSCOUS WITH LEMON

Makes 4 servings

8 ounces couscous   2 tablespoons minced fresh mint
¹/₂ teaspoon salt   2 tablespoons fresh lemon juice
2 tablespoons minced fresh flat-leaf parsley   Freshly ground black pepper to taste

1. In medium saucepan, bring 1¹/₃ cups water to a boil; add couscous and salt. Remove from heat; let stand, covered, 5 minutes, until liquid is absorbed.
2. With fork, gently mix parsley, mint, lemon juice and pepper into couscous.

Each serving (1 cup) provides: 2 Breads

Per serving: 216 Calories, 0 g Total Fat, 0 g Saturated Fat, 0 mg Cholesterol, 280 mg Sodium, 45 g Total Carbohydrate, 0 g Dietary Fiber, 7 g Protein, 19 mg Calcium

FENNEL WITH PEPPERS

Makes 4 servings

1 tablespoon olive oil	1 teaspoon balsamic vinegar
2 cups thinly sliced onions	$^1/_2$ teaspoon salt
2 cups thinly sliced red bell peppers	$^1/_4$ teaspoon freshly ground black pepper
2 cups thinly sliced fennel	

1. In large nonstick skillet, heat oil; add onions, red bell peppers and fennel. Cook over medium-high heat, stirring frequently, 10 minutes, until onions are deep golden brown.
2. Add $^1/_4$ cup water to vegetable mixture; bring liquid to a boil. Reduce heat to low; steam, covered, 5 minutes.
3. Stir in vinegar, salt and black pepper; serve hot or at room temperature.

Each serving ($^3/_4$ cup) provides: $^3/_4$ Fat, 3 Vegetables

Per serving: 83 Calories, 4 g Total Fat, 0 g Saturated Fat, 0 mg Cholesterol, 331 mg Sodium, 12 g Total Carbohydrate, 3 g Dietary Fiber, 2 g Protein, 49 mg Calcium

FROZEN YOGURT WITH ORANGE SAUCE

Makes 4 servings

$^1/_2$ cup orange juice	$^1/_2$ fluid ounce (1 tablespoon) orange-flavored liqueur
1 tablespoon fresh lemon juice	
1 tablespoon granulated sugar	16 fluid ounces chocolate, vanilla or coffee nonfat sugar-free frozen yogurt
1 teaspoon cornstarch	
$^1/_2$ small navel orange, cut into $^1/_8$" slices	

1. In small saucepan, with wire whisk, combine orange juice, lemon juice, sugar, cornstarch and 2 tablespoons cold water, blending until cornstarch is dissolved. Place over low heat; cook, stirring frequently, 3 minutes, until slightly thickened.
2. Add orange slices to orange juice mixture; cook, stirring frequently, 5 minutes. Remove from heat; stir in liqueur.
3. Divide frozen yogurt evenly among 4 dessert dishes; top each portion with an equal amount of orange mixture.

Each serving (4 fluid ounces yogurt + $^1/_3$ cup sauce) provides: $^1/_4$ Milk, $^1/_4$ Fruit, 85 Optional Calories

Per serving: 127 Calories, 0 g Total Fat, 0 g Saturated Fat, 0 mg Cholesterol, 65 mg Sodium, 31 g Total Carbohydrate, 0 g Dietary Fiber, 4 g Protein, 160 mg Calcium

4

Pasta, Grains & Beans

A NORTHERN ITALIAN SUPPER

With its traditional and contemporary combinations, this elegant meal will take you straight to Milan or Venice. The only thing missing is a sidewalk table overlooking the piazza.

Menu serves 4

- **Prosciutto with Melon, 1 serving**
- **Risotto with Shrimp and Saffron, 1 serving**
- **Fennel, Orange and Red Onion Salad, 1 serving**
- **Tortoni, 1 serving**
  Decaffeinated Espresso with Lemon Twist

One serving of this meal provides: $2^{1}/_{4}$ Fats, $1^{1}/_{4}$ Fruits, $2^{1}/_{2}$ Vegetables, $2^{1}/_{2}$ Proteins, $1^{3}/_{4}$ Breads, 147 Optional Calories; 21 g Fat, 6 g Fiber

Market List

1 medium honeydew melon
Orange juice
Fresh flat-leaf parsley (optional)
2 medium fennel bulbs
1 medium red onion
16 medium shrimp
2 ounces thinly sliced prosciutto
Grated Parmesan cheese
Nonfat mayonnaise
      (10 calories per tablespoon)

Arborio or other short-grain rice
Amaretti cookies (1" diameter)
Decaffeinated espresso beans
8 fluid ounces vanilla nonfat
      sugar-free frozen yogurt
Nonalcoholic white wine
Saffron

Special Equipment

Mini food processor
Espresso maker

A Northern Italian Supper

Preparation Schedule

Note: For maximum efficiency, assemble all ingredients and equipment before starting preparation.

1. Let yogurt soften.
2. Prepare Prosciutto with Melon; chill.
3. Prepare Tortoni; freeze.
4. Heat chicken broth.
5. Prepare salad and dressing; chill separately.
6. Prepare Risotto with Saffron and Shrimp.
7. Just before serving, drizzle dressing over salad; garnish.
8. Prepare espresso.
9. Just before serving, press cookies onto Tortoni.

PROSCIUTTO WITH MELON

For each serving, wrap or drape *one 2" wedge honeydew melon* with *¹/₂ ounce thinly sliced prosciutto;* serve with *1 lime wedge.*

Each serving provides: 1 Fruit, ¹/₂ Protein

Per serving: 72 Calories, 2 g Total Fat, 1 g Saturated Fat, 12 mg Cholesterol, 273 mg Sodium, 10 g Total Carbohydrate, 1 g Dietary Fiber, 5 g Protein, 9 mg Calcium

RISOTTO WITH SAFFRON AND SHRIMP

Makes 4 servings

3¹/₂ cups low-sodium chicken broth
Pinch saffron *
  1 teaspoon olive oil
 ¹/₂ cup finely chopped shallots
  7 ounces arborio or other short-grain rice
  8 fluid ounces (1 cup) nonalcoholic white wine
 16 medium shrimp, peeled, deveined and halved crosswise

  1 tablespoon + 1 teaspoon grated Parmesan cheese
Freshly ground black pepper to taste
Fresh flat-leaf parsley sprigs to garnish (optional)

1. In medium saucepan, bring broth to a boil. Reduce heat to low; let simmer until ready to use.
2. In small bowl, combine ¹/₂ cup warm water and saffron; set aside.

3. In separate medium nonstick saucepan, heat oil; add shallots. Cook over medium heat, stirring frequently, 1 minute. Add rice; stir to coat. Continuing to stir, cook 1 minute longer. Add wine and 1 cup of the simmering broth; cook, stirring frequently, until most of the liquid is absorbed.

4. Stir reserved saffron liquid; add to rice mixture. Stir in $^1/_2$ cup of the remaining simmering broth; cook, stirring frequently, until liquid is absorbed. Add all but $^1/_2$ cup of the remaining broth, $^1/_2$ cup at a time, stirring frequently after each addition until liquid has been absorbed. Add shrimp and remaining $^1/_2$ cup broth; cook, stirring frequently, 3 minutes, until shrimp turn pink and rice mixture is creamy.

5. Remove saucepan from heat; stir in cheese and pepper. Serve garnished with parsley if desired.

Each serving (1 cup) provides: $^1/_4$ Fat, $^1/_4$ Vegetable, 1 Protein, $1^3/_4$ Breads, 30 Optional Calories

Per serving: 330 Calories, 5 g Total Fat, 1 g Saturated Fat, 87 mg Cholesterol, 218 mg Sodium, 54 g Total Carbohydrate, 1 g Dietary Fiber, 19 g Protein, 76 mg Calcium

* If saffron is not available, substitute ground turmeric; flavor will not be the same.

Fennel, Orange and Red Onion Salad

Makes 4 servings

4 cups coarsely chopped fennel (reserve leaves)
1 small navel orange, peeled and cut into $^1/_4$" slices
1 medium red onion, cut into $^1/_8$" slices and separated into rings
2 tablespoons red wine vinegar
2 tablespoons orange juice
2 teaspoons olive oil
2 teaspoons nonfat mayonnaise (10 calories per tablespoon)

Granulated sugar substitute to equal 2 teaspoons sugar
1 teaspoon balsamic vinegar
$^1/_2$ teaspoon prepared yellow mustard
$^1/_2$ teaspoon fennel seeds
Pinch salt
Freshly ground black pepper to taste
Fennel leaves to garnish (optional)

1. Place chopped fennel in large salad bowl.
2. Cut orange slices into quarters; arrange orange quarters and onion rings on fennel. Set salad aside.
3. To prepare dressing, in mini food processor or blender, combine wine vinegar, orange juice, oil, mayonnaise, sugar substitute, balsamic vinegar, mustard, fennel seeds, salt and pepper; purée until thick and creamy.
4. Just before serving, drizzle dressing over salad. Serve garnished with fennel leaves if desired.

Each serving ($1^1/_2$ cups) provides: $^1/_2$ Fat, $^1/_4$ Fruit, $2^1/_4$ Vegetables, 12 Optional Calories

Per serving: 69 Calories, 3 g Total Fat, 0 g Saturated Fat, 0 mg Cholesterol, 169 mg Sodium, 10 g Total Carbohydrate, 2 g Dietary Fiber, 2 g Protein, 77 mg Calcium

TORTONI

Makes 4 servings

8 amaretti cookies (1" diameter)
8 fluid ounces vanilla nonfat sugar-free frozen yogurt, softened

1. Line four 2³/₄" muffin cups with decorative paper or foil baking cups.
2. Place 4 cookies in gallon-size sealable plastic bag; seal, squeezing out air. With meat mallet or heavy skillet, crush cookies; set aside.
3. Divide frozen yogurt evenly among prepared cups; with fork or back of spoon, spread yogurt evenly. Sprinkle each portion with an equal amount of cookie crumbs; freeze until firm.
4. Just before serving, press 1 remaining cookie onto each tortoni.

Each serving provides: 1¹/₂ Fats, 1 Protein, 105 Optional Calories

Per serving: 249 Calories, 11 g Total Fat, 1 g Saturated Fat, 0 mg Cholesterol, 53 mg Sodium, 36 g Total Carbohydrate, 2 g Dietary Fiber, 7 g Protein, 131 mg Calcium

FAMILY-STYLE FRENCH FEAST

This meal features an updated version of a classic French ragoût; it makes enough for eight hearty portions, so if you are serving four, freeze the extra for another quick meal.

Menu serves 4

- **Turkey Ragoût with Pasta, 1 serving**
- **Pepper and Onion Salad, 1 serving**
- **Grape Compote, 1 serving**
- **Dry Red Wine, 4 fluid ounces per serving**

One serving of this meal provides: $3/4$ Fat, $1^1/_2$ Fruits, $2^3/_4$ Vegetables, 1 Protein, 1 Bread, 115 Optional Calories; 8 g Fat, 5 g Fiber

Market List

1 large bunch seedless red grapes
White grape juice
2 medium sweet onions
1 medium red bell pepper
1 medium yellow or green bell pepper

8 ounces ground turkey
2 ounces chicken livers
1 ounce cooked Virginia ham
Spaghetti or fusilli pasta

Preparation Schedule

Note: For maximum efficiency, assemble all ingredients and equipment before starting preparation.

1. Chill wine.
2. Prepare Pepper and Onion Salad; refrigerate.
3. Prepare ragoût; simmer.
4. While ragoût is simmering, cook spaghetti.
5. While spaghetti is cooking, prepare Grape Compote.
6. Drain spaghetti; arrange on platter. Top with ragoût.

Turkey Ragoût with Pasta

Makes 8 servings

1   teaspoon olive oil
$^1/_2$ cup minced onion
$^1/_2$ cup grated carrot
8   ounces ground turkey
2   ounces chicken livers
1   ounce cooked Virginia ham, minced
2   cups canned stewed tomatoes
2   fluid ounces ($^1/_4$ cup) dry red wine
1   tablespoon tomato paste, dissolved in
      2 tablespoons hot water

1   bay leaf
$^1/_2$ teaspoon salt
$^1/_4$ teaspoon freshly ground black pepper
$^1/_4$ teaspoon dried oregano leaves
Pinch ground nutmeg
6   ounces spaghetti or fusilli pasta, cooked
      and drained

1. In medium nonstick skillet, heat oil; add onion and carrot. Cook over medium-high heat, stirring frequently, 3–4 minutes, until golden brown. Add turkey, livers and ham; cook, stirring to break up turkey, 3–4 minutes, until turkey and livers are no longer pink. With fork, mash livers against side of skillet.
2. Add tomatoes, wine, tomato paste, bay leaf, salt, pepper, oregano and nutmeg to turkey mixture; bring to a boil. Reduce heat to low; simmer, stirring occasionally, 20–25 minutes, until mixture is thickened and flavors are blended. Remove and discard bay leaf.
3. Just before serving, place spaghetti on large decorative platter; top with turkey mixture.

Each serving provides: $^3/_4$ Vegetable, 1 Protein, 1 Bread, 10 Optional Calories

Per serving: 170 Calories, 4 g Total Fat, 1 g Saturated Fat, 54 mg Cholesterol, 405 mg Sodium, 22 g Total Carbohydrate, 2 g Dietary Fiber, 11 g Protein, 38 mg Calcium

Pepper and Onion Salad .

Makes 4 servings

1   tablespoon olive oil
1   cup thinly sliced red bell pepper
1   cup thinly sliced yellow or
      green bell pepper
1   large garlic clove, lightly crushed

2   cups thinly sliced sweet onions
1   tablespoon red wine vinegar
$^1/_2$ teaspoon salt
$^1/_2$ teaspoon freshly ground black pepper

1. In large skillet, heat oil; add red and yellow peppers and garlic. Cook over medium heat, stirring frequently, 3–4 minutes, until softened. Add onions, vinegar, salt and black pepper; cook, stirring constantly, 1 minute longer.
2. Transfer mixture to large glass or stainless steel bowl; refrigerate, covered, until chilled.
3. Just before serving, remove and discard garlic from salad; toss salad to combine.

Each serving provides: $^3/_4$ Fat, 2 Vegetables

Per serving: 78 Calories, 4 g Total Fat, 0 g Saturated Fat, 0 mg Cholesterol, 283 mg Sodium, 11 g Total Carbohydrate, 2 g Dietary Fiber, 2 g Protein, 32 mg Calcium

GRAPE COMPOTE

Makes 4 servings

$^1/_3$ cup white grape juice	36 large seedless red grapes
$^1/_4$ cup golden raisins	1 teaspoon granulated sugar

In small saucepan, combine grape juice and raisins; bring liquid to a boil. Add grapes and sugar; remove from heat. Let stand, covered, 10 minutes, until grapes are softened.

Each serving provides: $1^1/_2$ Fruits, 5 Optional Calories

Per serving: 82 Calories, 0 g Total Fat, 0 g Saturated Fat, 0 mg Cholesterol, 4 mg Sodium, 22 g Total Carbohydrate, 0 g Dietary Fiber, 1 g Protein, 13 mg Calcium

A CONTINENTAL PASTA DINNER

Pasta is wonderfully satisfying, and we've enhanced its goodness in this colorful entrée by adding iron-rich spinach, fiber-filled chick-peas and sweet, chewy raisins. The elegant dessert features a creamy topping made with part-skim ricotta cheese, which provides the appropriate flavor and texture without all the fat.

Menu serves 4

- **Linguine à la Grecque, 1 serving**
  French Bread, 1 ounce per serving
- **Romaine-Artichoke Salad, 1 serving**
- **Peaches with Ginger Cream, 1 serving**
  Decaffeinated Espresso

One serving of this meal provides: 1$\frac{1}{2}$ Fats, 1$\frac{1}{2}$ Fruits, 4 Vegetables, 1$\frac{1}{2}$ Proteins, 3 Breads, 25 Optional Calories; 13 g Fat, 12 g Fiber

Market List

1 head Romaine lettuce
$\frac{1}{2}$ cup part-skim ricotta cheese
1 loaf French bread
Linguine
Chick-peas (garbanzo beans)
Anchovy fillets
Confectioners sugar

Canned peach halves
   (no sugar added)
Decaffeinated espresso beans
One 10-ounce package frozen
   chopped spinach
One 10-ounce package frozen
   artichoke hearts

Special Equipment

Espresso maker
Mini food processor

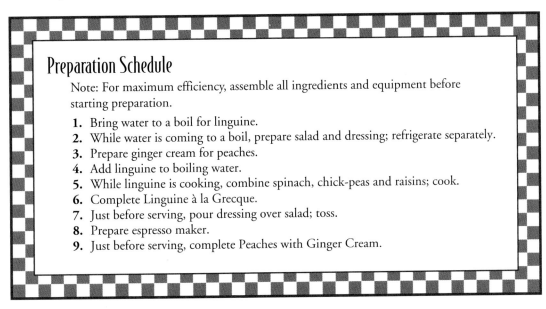

Preparation Schedule

Note: For maximum efficiency, assemble all ingredients and equipment before starting preparation.

1. Bring water to a boil for linguine.
2. While water is coming to a boil, prepare salad and dressing; refrigerate separately.
3. Prepare ginger cream for peaches.
4. Add linguine to boiling water.
5. While linguine is cooking, combine spinach, chick-peas and raisins; cook.
6. Complete Linguine à la Grecque.
7. Just before serving, pour dressing over salad; toss.
8. Prepare espresso maker.
9. Just before serving, complete Peaches with Ginger Cream.

LINGUINE À LA GRECQUE

Makes 4 servings

6 ounces linguine
2 cups well-drained thawed frozen chopped spinach
8 ounces drained cooked chick-peas (garbanzo beans)

$^1/_4$ cup golden raisins
1 tablespoon + 1 teaspoon olive oil
$^1/_2$ teaspoon salt
$^1/_8$ teaspoon dried red pepper flakes

1. In large pot of boiling water, cook linguine 8–10 minutes, until tender; drain.
2. Meanwhile, in medium saucepan, combine spinach, chick-peas and raisins; cook over medium heat, stirring occasionally, until heated.
3. In large bowl, combine linguine and spinach mixture. Drizzle mixture with oil, then sprinkle with salt and red pepper flakes; toss to combine.

Each serving provides: 1 Fat, $^1/_2$ Fruit, 1 Vegetable, 1 Protein, 2 Breads

Per serving: 320 Calories, 7 g Total Fat, 1 g Saturated Fat, 0 mg Cholesterol, 471 mg Sodium, 54 g Total Carbohydrate, 6 g Dietary Fiber, 12 g Protein, 173 mg Calcium

ROMAINE-ARTICHOKE SALAD

Makes 4 servings

2 tablespoons red wine vinegar
4 anchovy fillets, rinsed and mashed
1 tablespoon grated lemon zest *
2 teaspoons olive oil
1 teaspoon Dijon-style mustard

$^1/_2$ teaspoon dried oregano leaves
$^1/_4$ teaspoon freshly ground black pepper
4 cups torn Romaine lettuce leaves
2 cups thawed frozen artichoke hearts

1. To prepare dressing, in small bowl, with wire whisk, combine vinegar, anchovies, lemon zest, oil, mustard, oregano and pepper.
2. In large salad bowl, combine lettuce and artichoke hearts. Pour dressing over salad; toss to combine.

Each serving provides: $^1/_2$ Fat, 3 Vegetables, 10 Optional Calories

Per serving: 74 Calories, 3 g Total Fat, 0 g Saturated Fat, 2 mg Cholesterol, 229 mg Sodium, 9 g Total Carbohydrate, 4 g Dietary Fiber, 4 g Protein, 51 mg Calcium

   * *The zest of the lemon is the peel without any of the pith (white membrane). To remove zest from lemon, use a zester or fine side of a vegetable grater; wrap lemon in plastic wrap and refrigerate for use at another time.*

PEACHES WITH GINGER CREAM

Makes 4 servings

$^1/_2$ cup part-skim ricotta cheese
2 tablespoons skim milk
1 tablespoon confectioners sugar

$^1/_2$ teaspoon ground ginger
8 canned peach halves with $^1/_2$ cup juice (no sugar added)

1. In mini food processor or blender, combine ricotta cheese, milk, sugar and ginger; purée until smooth.
2. Just before serving, divide peach halves and juice evenly among 4 small bowls; top each portion with one-fourth of the ricotta cheese mixture.

Each serving (2 peach halves, 2 tablespoons juice and 2 tablespoons ginger cream) provides: 1 Fruit, $^1/_2$ Protein, 15 Optional Calories

Per serving: 108 Calories, 2 g Total Fat, 2 g Saturated Fat, 10 mg Cholesterol, 47 mg Sodium, 18 g Total Carbohydrate, 1 g Dietary Fiber, 5 g Protein, 101 mg Calcium

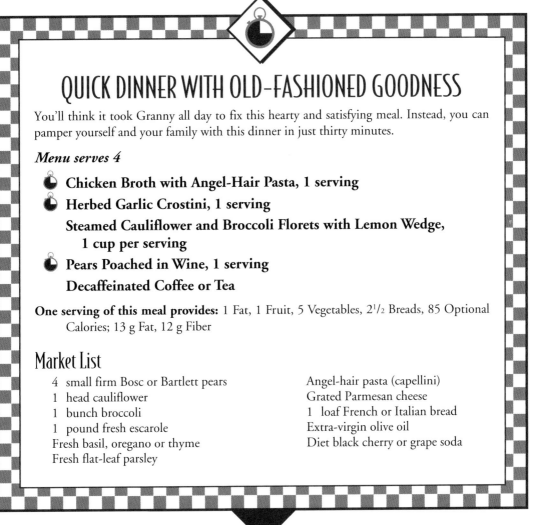

QUICK DINNER WITH OLD-FASHIONED GOODNESS

You'll think it took Granny all day to fix this hearty and satisfying meal. Instead, you can pamper yourself and your family with this dinner in just thirty minutes.

Menu serves 4

- **Chicken Broth with Angel-Hair Pasta, 1 serving**
- **Herbed Garlic Crostini, 1 serving**
   Steamed Cauliflower and Broccoli Florets with Lemon Wedge, 1 cup per serving
- **Pears Poached in Wine, 1 serving**
   Decaffeinated Coffee or Tea

One serving of this meal provides: 1 Fat, 1 Fruit, 5 Vegetables, $2^{1}/_{2}$ Breads, 85 Optional Calories; 13 g Fat, 12 g Fiber

Market List

4 small firm Bosc or Bartlett pears
1 head cauliflower
1 bunch broccoli
1 pound fresh escarole
Fresh basil, oregano or thyme
Fresh flat-leaf parsley

Angel-hair pasta (capellini)
Grated Parmesan cheese
1 loaf French or Italian bread
Extra-virgin olive oil
Diet black cherry or grape soda

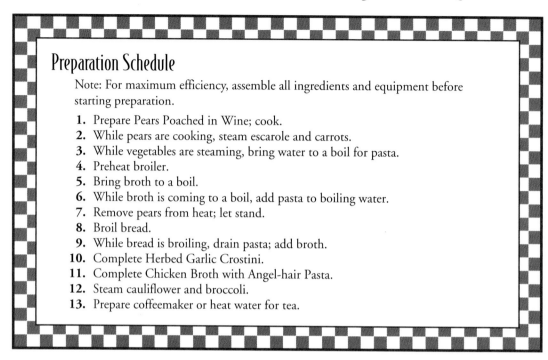

Preparation Schedule

Note: For maximum efficiency, assemble all ingredients and equipment before starting preparation.

1. Prepare Pears Poached in Wine; cook.
2. While pears are cooking, steam escarole and carrots.
3. While vegetables are steaming, bring water to a boil for pasta.
4. Preheat broiler.
5. Bring broth to a boil.
6. While broth is coming to a boil, add pasta to boiling water.
7. Remove pears from heat; let stand.
8. Broil bread.
9. While bread is broiling, drain pasta; add broth.
10. Complete Herbed Garlic Crostini.
11. Complete Chicken Broth with Angel-hair Pasta.
12. Steam cauliflower and broccoli.
13. Prepare coffeemaker or heat water for tea.

CHICKEN BROTH WITH ANGEL-HAIR PASTA

Makes 4 servings

4 cups coarsely chopped escarole	1 tablespoon + 1 teaspoon grated
2 cups sliced carrots	Parmesan cheese
5 cups low-sodium chicken broth	Freshly ground black pepper to taste
4¹/₂ ounces angel-hair pasta (capellini)	

1. Fill medium saucepan with 1" water; set steamer rack in saucepan. Place escarole and carrots on rack. Bring water to a boil; reduce heat to low. Steam vegetables over simmering water, covered, 15 minutes, until tender.
2. In separate medium saucepan, bring broth to a boil. Reduce heat to low; let simmer until ready to use.
3. In large pot of boiling water, cook angel hair 3 minutes, until tender. Drain; return pasta to pot. Add 1 cup of the simmering broth; stir to keep pasta from sticking together.
4. Divide pasta mixture evenly among 4 soup bowls; add an equal amount of escarole, carrots and remaining broth to each bowl. Sprinkle each portion with 1 teaspoon Parmesan cheese, then the pepper.

Each serving (3 cups) provides: 3 Vegetables, 1¹/₂ Breads, 35 Optional Calories

Per serving: 196 Calories, 3 g Total Fat, 1 g Saturated Fat, 0 mg Cholesterol, 130 mg Sodium, 33 g Total Carbohydrate, 4 g Dietary Fiber, 9 g Protein, 69 mg Calcium

HERBED GARLIC CROSTINI

Makes 4 servings

4   ounces French or Italian bread,
    cut into 4 equal slices
1   large garlic clove, halved
1   tablespoon + 1 teaspoon extra-virgin
    olive oil
2   tablespoons chopped fresh basil, oregano
    or thyme leaves or 1 teaspoon dried

1   tablespoon + 1 teaspoon chopped
    fresh flat-leaf parsley
Pinch salt
Freshly ground black pepper to taste

1. Preheat broiler.
2. Place bread slices on baking sheet; broil 4" from heat 1–2 minutes on each side until golden brown.
3. Rub each slice of toast with cut garlic. Drizzle toast evenly with oil, then sprinkle evenly with basil, parsley, salt and pepper.

Each serving (1 crostini) provides: 1 Fat, 1 Bread

Per serving: 120 Calories, 6 g Total Fat, 1 g Saturated Fat, 0 mg Cholesterol, 206 mg Sodium, 15 g Total Carbohydrate, 1 g Dietary Fiber, 3 g Protein, 33 mg Calcium

PEARS POACHED IN WINE

Makes 4 servings

4   small firm Bosc or Bartlett pears, pared,
    cored and cut into 8 wedges each
8   fluid ounces (1 cup) dry red or
    white wine
1   cup diet black cherry or grape soda

Granulated sugar substitute
    to equal $1/4$ cup sugar
2   lemon slices
$1/2$ teaspoon cinnamon

In medium saucepan, combine pears, wine, soda, sugar substitute, lemon and cinnamon. Bring liquid just to a boil; reduce heat to low. Cook, covered, stirring occasionally, 20 minutes, until pears are tender. Remove from heat; let stand, uncovered, until ready to serve.

Each serving (8 pear wedges + $1/2$ cup liquid) provides: 1 Fruit, 50 Optional Calories

Per serving: 144 Calories, 1 g Total Fat, 0 g Saturated Fat, 0 mg Cholesterol, 20 mg Sodium, 26 g Total Carbohydrate, 4 g Dietary Fiber, 2 g Protein, 30 mg Calcium

ITALIAN PASTA AND SALAD DINNER

Linguine is the usual pasta for this old favorite, but try it with small shells or multicolored fusilli pasta for a change. For extra crunch, try serving green beans sauteed with garlic. And for a truly special dessert, add a scoop of frozen yogurt to the luscious liqueur-scented fruit compote.

Menu serves 4

- **Linguine with White Clam Sauce, 1 serving**
- **Endive, Radicchio and Mushroom Salad, 1 serving**
- **Crusty Roll, 1 ounce per serving**
- **Hot Fruit Compote, 1 serving**
- **Dry White Wine, 4 fluid ounces per serving**

One serving of this meal provides: 1 Fat, $2^1/_4$ Fruits, 3 Vegetables, 1 Protein, 3 Breads, 155 Optional Calories; 9 g Fat, 6 g Fiber

Market List

One 12-ounce package fresh mushrooms
2 small Belgian endives
1 small head radicchio
Fresh flat-leaf parsley
Chives
Crusty rolls
8 ounces fresh or drained canned
   whole baby clams

Bottled clam juice
Linguine
Grated Parmesan cheese
Mixed dried fruit
Orange-flavored liqueur

Preparation Schedule

Note: For maximum efficiency, assemble all ingredients and equipment before starting preparation.

1. Chill wine.
2. Prepare Endive, Radicchio and Mushroom Salad; let stand.
3. While salad is standing, combine ingredients for Hot Fruit Compote; simmer.
4. While fruit compote is simmering, cook linguine.
5. Prepare White Clam Sauce.
6. Complete Hot Fruit Compote.
7. Drain linguine; place on platter. Top with sauce.

Italian Pasta and Salad Dinner

LINGUINE WITH WHITE CLAM SAUCE

Makes 4 servings

2 teaspoons olive oil
3 garlic cloves, pressed
Pinch dried red pepper flakes
1 cup clam juice
8 ounces fresh or drained canned
    whole baby clams

¹/₄ cup minced fresh flat-leaf parsley
¹/₂ teaspoon dried oregano leaves
6 ounces linguine, cooked and drained

1. In medium skillet, heat oil; add garlic and red pepper flakes. Cook over medium heat, stirring constantly, 1–2 minutes, until garlic is golden brown. Add clam juice; increase heat to high. Cook 5 minutes, until liquid is reduced in volume to about ¹/₂ cup.
2. Add clams, parsley and oregano to clam juice mixture; remove from heat.
3. Just before serving, place linguine on large decorative platter; top with clam mixture.

Each serving (1 cup linguine + ¹/₃ cup sauce) provides: ¹/₂ Fat, 1 Protein, 2 Breads, 5 Optional Calories

Per serving: 268 Calories, 4 g Total Fat, 0 g Saturated Fat, 38 mg Cholesterol, 197 mg Sodium, 35 g Total Carbohydrate, 1 g Dietary Fiber, 20 g Protein, 80 mg Calcium

ENDIVE, RADICCHIO AND MUSHROOM SALAD

Makes 4 servings

2 teaspoons olive oil
2 cups sliced mushrooms
2 tablespoons low-sodium chicken broth
2 tablespoons fresh lemon juice
2 cups sliced Belgian endive

2 cups shredded radicchio
2 tablespoons grated Parmesan cheese
2 tablespoons chopped chives
Pinch salt
Pinch freshly ground black pepper

1. In large skillet, heat oil; add mushrooms. Cook over medium heat, stirring occasionally, 10 minutes, until lightly browned. Add broth and lemon juice; cook, stirring frequently, 5 minutes longer.
2. Add endive, radicchio, Parmesan cheese, chives, salt and pepper to mushroom mixture; toss to combine. Remove skillet from heat; let salad stand until room temperature.

Each serving (1¹/₄ cups) provides: ¹/₂ Fat, 3 Vegetables, 15 Optional Calories

Per serving: 55 Calories, 3 g Total Fat, 1 g Saturated Fat, 2 mg Cholesterol, 88 mg Sodium, 5 g Total Carbohydrate, 2 g Dietary Fiber, 3 g Protein, 57 mg Calcium

Hot Fruit Compote

Makes 4 servings

6 ounces mixed dried fruit, cut
  into bite-size pieces
$^1/_2$ cup fresh orange juice
2 teaspoons granulated sugar
1 long strip orange zest *

$^1/_4$ teaspoon ground ginger
$^1/_8$ teaspoon cinnamon
1 fluid ounce (2 tablespoons)
  orange-flavored liqueur

1. In small saucepan, combine dried fruit, orange juice, sugar, orange zest, ginger, cinnamon and $^3/_4$ cup water; bring liquid to a boil. Reduce heat to low; simmer, covered, 15 minutes. Remove from heat.
2. Stir in liqueur. Remove orange zest before serving.

Each serving ($^1/_2$ cup) provides: 2$^1/_4$ Fruits, 35 Optional Calories

Per serving: 147 Calories, 0 g Total Fat, 0 g Saturated Fat, 0 mg Cholesterol, 8 mg Sodium, 35 g Total Carbohydrate, 2 g Dietary Fiber, 1 g Protein, 21 mg Calcium

   * *The zest of the orange is the peel without any of the pith (white membrane). To remove zest from orange, use a zester or fine side of a vegetable grater.*

FAST AND FUN FAMILY FARE

This entrée is something like lasagna, but much easier and faster—a real family pleaser! Use fresh fruit in season for the dessert; for fun, add a dollop of plain yogurt or whipped topping.

Menu serves 4

🕐 **Noodle Bake, 1 serving**

Semolina Roll, 1 ounce per serving

🕐 **Mixed Green Salad, 1 serving**

🕐 **Tutti Frutti, 1 serving**

Iced Tea

One serving of this meal provides: 1 Fat, $1^1/_2$ Fruits, 6 Vegetables, $1^1/_4$ Proteins, 3 Breads, 5 Optional Calories; 10 g Fat, 8 g Fiber

Market List

1 cup whole strawberries
1 medium banana
1 small cantaloupe
1 small Granny Smith apple
Grapefruit or orange sections
One 12-ounce package fresh mushrooms
1 medium red bell pepper
Assorted salad greens

Fresh flat-leaf parsley
$1^1/_3$ cups fat-free ricotta cheese
Semolina rolls
Tomato sauce
Grated Parmesan cheese
Broad egg noodles
Dry marsala wine

Preparation Schedule

Note: For maximum efficiency, assemble all ingredients and equipment before starting preparation.

1. Prepare Iced Tea; refrigerate.
2. Prepare Tutti Frutti; refrigerate.
3. Preheat oven.
4. Prepare Noodle Bake; bake.
5. While mixture is baking, prepare salad greens and dressing; refrigerate separately.
6. Just before serving, combine greens and dressing; toss.
7. Just before serving, toss fruit.

NOODLE BAKE

Makes 4 servings

1 teaspoon olive oil	2 cups chopped mushrooms
1 cup minced onions	1¹/₂ cups tomato sauce
¹/₄ cup minced fresh flat-leaf parsley	1 cup chopped red bell pepper
1 teaspoon dried oregano leaves	6 ounces broad egg noodles, cooked
1¹/₃ cups fat-free ricotta cheese	and drained
¹/₄ teaspoon salt	³/₄ ounce grated Parmesan cheese
¹/₄ teaspoon freshly ground black pepper	

1. Preheat oven to 400° F. Spray an 8" square baking pan with nonstick cooking spray.
2. In medium skillet, heat oil; add onions. Cook over medium-high heat, stirring frequently, 3–4 minutes, until golden brown. Remove skillet from heat; stir in parsley and ¹/₂ teaspoon of the oregano.
3. Transfer half of onion mixture to small bowl; stir in ricotta cheese, salt and black pepper. Set aside.
4. To onion mixture remaining in skillet, add mushrooms, tomato sauce, red pepper and the remaining ¹/₂ teaspoon oregano; stir to combine. Place over medium-high heat; bring to a boil. Reduce heat to low; simmer, covered, 5 minutes, until vegetables are tender.
5. Place noodles in prepared baking pan; top with ricotta cheese mixture, then vegetable mixture. Sprinkle evenly with Parmesan cheese; bake 20 minutes, until golden brown and bubbly.

Each serving provides: ¹/₄ Fat, 3¹/₂ Vegetables, 1¹/₄ Proteins, 2 Breads

Per serving: 325 Calories, 5 g Total Fat, 2 g Saturated Fat, 45 mg Cholesterol, 896 mg Sodium, 47 g Total Carbohydrate, 4 g Dietary Fiber, 22 g Protein, 524 mg Calcium

MIXED GREEN SALAD

Makes 4 servings

2 tablespoons red wine vinegar	¹/₈ teaspoon granulated sugar
¹/₂ teaspoon prepared yellow mustard	1 tablespoon olive oil
¹/₈ teaspoon salt	1 garlic clove, lightly crushed (optional)
¹/₈ teaspoon freshly ground black pepper	5 cups torn assorted salad greens

1. To prepare dressing, in large salad bowl, with wire whisk, combine vinegar, mustard, salt, pepper and sugar; continuing to blend with whisk, slowly add olive oil, then garlic if desired.
2. Just before serving, remove and discard garlic clove from dressing.

Each serving (1¹/₄ cups) provides: ³/₄ Fat, 2¹/₂ Vegetables

Per serving: 45 Calories, 4 g Total Fat, 0 g Saturated Fat, 0 mg Cholesterol, 83 mg Sodium, 3 g Total Carbohydrate, 1 g Dietary Fiber, 1 g Protein, 39 mg Calcium

TUTTI FRUTTI

Makes 4 servings

1 cup grapefruit or orange sections	1/2 medium banana, peeled and sliced
1 cup whole strawberries, sliced	1/2 fluid ounce (1 tablespoon) dry marsala wine
1 cup diced cantaloupe	1 teaspoon granulated sugar
1 small Granny Smith apple, cored and diced	

1. In medium bowl, combine grapefruit sections, strawberries, cantaloupe, apple, banana, wine and sugar; toss to combine. Refrigerate, covered, until chilled.
2. Just before serving, toss again.

Each serving (1¹/₄ cups) provides: 1¹/₂ Fruits, 5 Optional Calories

Per serving with grapefruit: 82 Calories, 0 g Total Fat, 0 g Saturated Fat, 0 mg Cholesterol, 4 mg Sodium, 19 g Total Carbohydrate, 2 g Dietary Fiber, 1 g Protein, 20 mg Calcium

Per serving with orange: 84 Calories, 0 g Total Fat, 0 g Saturated Fat, 0 mg Cholesterol, 4 mg Sodium, 20 g Total Carbohydrate, 3 g Dietary Fiber, 1 g Protein, 31 mg Calcium

FULL OF FLAVOR MEXICAN BRUNCH

These hearty, spicy burritos make a great impromptu brunch or lunch for unexpected guests. Serve them with pickled jalapeños and hot pepper sauce for people who like a lot of heat.

Menu serves 4

- **Bean Burritos, 1 serving**
- **Processor Gazpacho, 1 serving**
- **Booze-Berry Sundae, 1 serving**
- **Cappuccino, 1 serving**

One serving of this meal provides: $1/2$ Milk, $1/4$ Fat, $3/4$ Fruit, 3 Vegetables, 1 Protein, $1^1/4$ Breads, 90 Optional Calories; 7 g Fat, 6 g Fiber

Market List

$3/4$ cup blackberries
$3/4$ cup blueberries
$3/4$ cup raspberries
1 head iceberg lettuce
1 bunch scallions
1 medium cucumber
1 medium green bell pepper
$1/2$ cup corn kernels, fresh or frozen
Fresh cilantro
Fresh flat-leaf parsley
$1^1/2$ ounces Monterey Jack or mild cheddar cheese
Nonfat sour cream

Flour tortillas (6" diameter)
Black beans
Canned chipotle peppers in adobo sauce
Low-sodium tomato or mixed vegetable juice
Decaffeinated espresso beans
Corn oil
16 fluid ounces vanilla nonfat sugar-free frozen yogurt
Kirsch or other fruit-flavored brandy

Special Equipment

Espresso or cappuccino maker

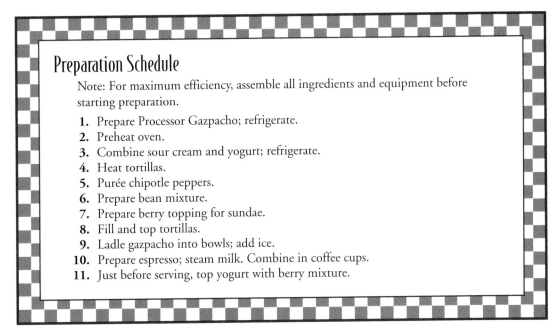

Preparation Schedule

Note: For maximum efficiency, assemble all ingredients and equipment before starting preparation.

1. Prepare Processor Gazpacho; refrigerate.
2. Preheat oven.
3. Combine sour cream and yogurt; refrigerate.
4. Heat tortillas.
5. Purée chipotle peppers.
6. Prepare bean mixture.
7. Prepare berry topping for sundae.
8. Fill and top tortillas.
9. Ladle gazpacho into bowls; add ice.
10. Prepare espresso; steam milk. Combine in coffee cups.
11. Just before serving, top yogurt with berry mixture.

BEAN BURRITOS

Makes 4 servings

2 tablespoons nonfat sour cream
2 tablespoons plain nonfat yogurt
4 flour tortillas (6" diameter)
One 7-ounce can chipotle peppers in adobo sauce
1 teaspoon corn oil
3/4 cup diced onions
2 garlic cloves, pressed

4 ounces drained cooked black beans
1/2 cup fresh or frozen corn kernels
1 1/2 ounces Monterey Jack or mild cheddar cheese, shredded
1/2 cup shredded iceberg lettuce
1/4 cup chopped scallions
1/4 cup chopped fresh cilantro

1. Preheat oven to 350° F.
2. In small bowl, combine sour cream and yogurt; refrigerate, covered, until ready to use.
3. Wrap tortillas in foil; bake 10 minutes, until heated.
4. Meanwhile, in food processor or blender, purée chipotle peppers with sauce until smooth. Set aside 1 teaspoon pureed peppers; refrigerate remaining mixture, covered, for use at another time.
5. In medium skillet, heat oil; add onions and garlic. Cook over medium-high heat, stirring frequently, 4–5 minutes, until lightly golden. Add beans, corn and reserved teaspoon pureed peppers; stir to combine. Reduce heat to low; cook, stirring occasionally, until mixture is heated through and flavors are blended.
6. Just before serving, place 1 warm tortilla on each of 4 plates; divide bean mixture evenly among tortillas. Sprinkle evenly with cheese, lettuce, scallions and cilantro; roll tortillas to enclose filling.
7. Top each tortilla with 1 tablespoon reserved sour cream mixture.

Each serving provides: 1/4 Fat, 3/4 Vegetable, 1 Protein, 1 1/4 Breads, 10 Optional Calories

Per serving: 204 Calories, 6 g Total Fat, 2 g Saturated Fat, 11 mg Cholesterol, 222 mg Sodium, 28 g Total Carbohydrate, 2 g Dietary Fiber, 9 g Protein, 157 mg Calcium

PROCESSOR GAZPACHO

Makes 4 servings

2 1/2 cups low-sodium tomato or mixed vegetable juice
1 medium cucumber, pared, seeded and cut into chunks
1/2 medium green bell pepper, seeded and cut into chunks
1/2 cup fresh flat-leaf parsley leaves

1/4 cup coarsely chopped onion
3 tablespoons red wine vinegar
1/4 teaspoon dried oregano or basil leaves
1/4 teaspoon salt
Freshly ground black pepper to taste
8–12 ice cubes

1. In food processor or blender, combine tomato juice, cucumber, green pepper, parsley, onion, vinegar, oregano, salt and black pepper; with on-off motion, pulse processor 4–5 times, until vegetables are finely chopped. Refrigerate, covered, until chilled.
2. Just before serving, ladle mixture equally into 4 soup bowls; add 2–3 ice cubes to each portion.

Each serving (1 cup) provides: $2^1/_4$ Vegetables

Per serving: 43 Calories, 0 g Total Fat, 0 g Saturated Fat, 0 mg Cholesterol, 155 mg Sodium, 10 g Total Carbohydrate, 1 g Dietary Fiber, 2 g Protein, 34 mg Calcium

BOOZE-BERRY SUNDAE

Makes 4 servings

$^3/_4$ cup blackberries
$^3/_4$ cup blueberries
$^3/_4$ cup raspberries
2 teaspoons granulated sugar

1 fluid ounce (2 tablespoons) kirsch or other fruit-flavored brandy
16 fluid ounces vanilla nonfat sugar-free frozen yogurt

1. In small saucepan, combine blackberries, blueberries, raspberries, sugar and kirsch; cook over low heat, crushing berries with back of wooden spoon, until lukewarm.
2. Divide frozen yogurt evenly among 4 dessert dishes; top each portion with an equal amount of berry mixture.

Each serving provides: $^1/_4$ Milk, $^3/_4$ Fruit, 80 Optional Calories

Per serving: 149 Calories, 0 g Total Fat, 0 g Saturated Fat, 0 mg Cholesterol, 67 mg Sodium, 35 g Total Carbohydrate, 3 g Dietary Fiber, 5 g Protein, 165 mg Calcium

CAPPUCCINO

For each serving, in coffee cup, combine *$^1/_2$ cup hot decaffeinated espresso* and *$^1/_4$ cup steamed skim milk*; sprinkle with *a pinch of cinnamon*.

Each serving provides: $^1/_4$ Milk

Per serving: 24 Calories, 0 g Total Fat, 0 g Saturated Fat, 0 mg Cholesterol, 34 mg Sodium, 4 g Total Carbohydrate, 0 g Dietary Fiber, 2 g Protein, 79 mg Calcium

CUBAN SUPPER

A traditional Cuban combination, rice and beans are not only delicious but are also filled with the goodness of fiber. The hearty cumin-scented beans taste even better the next day, so why not double the recipe to have leftovers on hand?

Menu serves 4

- **Cuban Black Beans, 1 serving**
- **Yellow Rice, 1 serving**
- **Steamed Swiss Chard, 1 cup per serving**
- **Mandarin Orange Sundaes, 1 serving**
- **Iced Tea**

One serving of this meal provides: $1/4$ Milk, $1^1/4$ Fats, 1 Fruit, $3^3/4$ Vegetables, $1^1/4$ Proteins, $1^1/2$ Breads, 70 Optional Calories; 10 g Fat, 3 g Fiber

Market List

1 pound Swiss chard
1 medium red bell pepper
1 medium green bell pepper
1 medium jalapeño pepper
Fresh cilantro (optional)
Black beans
Pimientos (optional)
Long-grain or basmati rice

Chopped walnuts
Canned mandarin orange sections (no sugar added)
16 fluid ounces vanilla nonfat sugar-free frozen yogurt
Frozen light whipped topping (8 calories per tablespoon)
Saffron (optional)

Special Equipment

Microwave oven
Microwave-safe plate

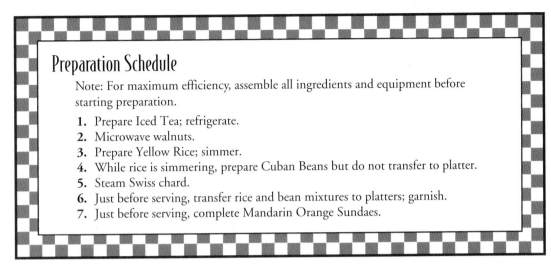

Preparation Schedule

Note: For maximum efficiency, assemble all ingredients and equipment before starting preparation.

1. Prepare Iced Tea; refrigerate.
2. Microwave walnuts.
3. Prepare Yellow Rice; simmer.
4. While rice is simmering, prepare Cuban Beans but do not transfer to platter.
5. Steam Swiss chard.
6. Just before serving, transfer rice and bean mixtures to platters; garnish.
7. Just before serving, complete Mandarin Orange Sundaes.

CUBAN BLACK BEANS

Makes 4 servings

2 teaspoons olive oil	1 medium jalapeño pepper, seeded and finely chopped
1^1/$_2$ teaspoons ground cumin	
1 cup finely chopped onions	8 ounces drained cooked black beans
1 cup chopped red bell pepper	Pimiento strips to garnish (optional)
1 cup chopped green bell pepper	

1. In large nonstick skillet, heat oil; add cumin. Cook over medium-high heat, stirring frequently, 45 seconds, until fragrant.
2. Add onions, red and green peppers and jalapeño pepper to cumin; cook, stirring frequently, 10–15 minutes, until vegetables are soft.
3. Add beans to vegetable mixture; cook, stirring gently, just until heated. Transfer bean mixture to large decorative platter; garnish with pimiento strips if desired.

Each serving (^{3}/$_4$ cup) provides: ^{1}/$_2$ Fat, 1^3/$_4$ Vegetables, 1 Protein

Per serving: 128 Calories, 3 g Total Fat, 0 g Saturated Fat, 0 mg Cholesterol, 4 mg Sodium, 21 g Total Carbohydrate, 3 g Dietary Fiber, 6 g Protein, 35 mg Calcium

YELLOW RICE

Makes 4 servings

1¹/₂ cups low-sodium chicken broth
Pinch saffron (optional)
  1 teaspoon olive oil
  6 ounces long-grain or basmati rice

  1 garlic clove, minced
¹/₂ teaspoon ground turmeric
Fresh cilantro sprigs to garnish
     (optional)

1. In small saucepan, bring ¹/₄ cup of the broth to a boil. Add saffron; remove from heat. Let stand, covered, 5 minutes. *
2. Meanwhile, in medium nonstick skillet, heat oil; add rice and garlic. Cook over medium-high heat, stirring frequently, 2 minutes, until garlic is fragrant (do not brown). Add turmeric, the remaining 1¹/₄ cup broth and reserved saffron mixture; bring liquid to a boil. Reduce heat to low; simmer, covered, stirring occasionally, 15 minutes, until rice is tender and liquid is absorbed.
3. Transfer rice mixture to medium decorative platter; garnish with cilantro sprigs if desired.

Each serving (1 cup) provides: ¹/₄ Fat, 1¹/₂ Breads, 10 Optional Calories

Per serving: 179 Calories, 2 g Total Fat, 0 g Saturated Fat, 0 mg Cholesterol, 22 mg Sodium, 35 g Total Carbohydrate, 0 g Dietary Fiber, 4 g Protein, 14 mg Calcium

   * *If saffron is not used, omit this step.*

MANDARIN ORANGE SUNDAES

Makes 4 servings

  1 ounce chopped walnuts
 16 fluid ounces vanilla nonfat sugar-free
     frozen yogurt
  2 cups drained canned mandarin orange
     sections (no sugar added)

¹/₄ cup thawed frozen light whipped
     topping (8 calories per tablespoon)

1. Line microwave-safe plate with paper towel. Place walnuts in a single layer on prepared plate. Microwave on High (100% power) 2 minutes; stir walnuts. Microwave 1–2 minutes longer, until walnuts are lightly toasted and crisp (do not burn).
2. Just before serving, divide frozen yogurt evenly among 4 dessert dishes; top each portion with ¹/₂ cup mandarin orange sections and 1 tablespoon whipped topping. Sprinkle evenly with toasted walnuts.

Each serving (1 sundae) provides: ¹/₄ Milk, ¹/₂ Fat, 1 Fruit, ¹/₄ Protein, 60 Optional Calories

Per serving: 179 Calories, 5 g Total Fat, 0 g Saturated Fat, 0 mg Cholesterol, 72 mg Sodium, 35 g Total Carbohydrate, 0 g Dietary Fiber, 6 g Protein, 170 mg Calcium

SIMPLE SALAD LUNCHEON

This menu moves from fiber to fire to fun! A healthy dose of beans adds fiber and flavor to the very special spinach salad. The tortilla rolls can be fiery hot by using the pickled jalapeños or cool and piquant by substituting pickled bell peppers. And we're sure you'll enjoy the Berry Slush, a cooling drink/dessert that's easy to make and great fun to eat.

Menu serves 4

- **Spud, Spinach and Bean Salad, 1 serving**
- **Cheese and Chile Rolls, 1 serving**
- **Berry Slush, 1 serving**
  Nonalcoholic Beer, 12 fluid ounces per serving

One serving of this meal provides: $3/4$ Fat, $1^1/4$ Fruits, $3^3/4$ Vegetables, $1^1/2$ Proteins, $1^1/2$ Breads, 75 Optional Calories; 10 g Fat, 11 g Fiber

Market List

4 cups whole strawberries	White kidney (cannellini) beans
Orange juice	Low-sodium chicken broth or
One 10-ounce bag fresh spinach	vegetable broth
10 ounces red potatoes	Pickled jalapeño peppers
1 medium red onion	Flour tortillas (6" diameter)
1 large plum tomato	Nonalcoholic beer
$1^1/2$ ounces sharp cheddar cheese	

Preparation Schedule

Note: For maximum efficiency, assemble all ingredients and equipment before starting preparation.

1. Chill beer.
2. Preheat oven.
3. Prepare Cheese and Chile Rolls; bake.
4. While rolls are baking, prepare salad and dressing; refrigerate separately.
5. Just before serving, combine salad and dressing; toss.
6. Just before serving, prepare Berry Slush.

SPUD, SPINACH AND BEAN SALAD

Makes 4 servings

8 ounces drained cooked white kidney (cannellini) beans
3 tablespoons low-sodium chicken broth or vegetable broth
1 tablespoon olive oil
2 tablespoons red wine vinegar
2 large garlic cloves
$^1/_2$ teaspoon salt

$^1/_2$ teaspoon prepared yellow mustard
$^1/_4$ teaspoon freshly ground black pepper
6 cups packed spinach leaves, rinsed well, dried and shredded
8 ounces cooked sliced red potatoes, chilled
$^1/_2$ medium red onion, thinly sliced

1. To prepare dressing, in food processor or blender, combine 4 ounces of the beans, the broth, oil, vinegar, garlic, salt, mustard and pepper; purée until smooth.
2. To prepare salad, in large salad bowl, combine spinach, potatoes, onion and the remaining 4 ounces beans.
3. Just before serving, pour dressing over salad; toss to coat.

Each serving (2 cups) provides: $^3/_4$ Fat, $3^1/_4$ Vegetables, 1 Protein, $^1/_2$ Bread

Per serving: 181 Calories, 4 g Total Fat, 1 g Saturated Fat, 0 mg Cholesterol, 374 mg Sodium, 29 g Total Carbohydrate, 6 g Dietary Fiber, 9 g Protein, 129 mg Calcium

CHEESE AND CHILE ROLLS

Makes 4 servings

1 large plum tomato, blanched, peeled, seeded and chopped
$1^1/_2$ ounces sharp cheddar cheese, shredded

$^1/_2$ medium pickled jalapeño pepper, drained, seeded and minced
4 flour tortillas (6" diameter)

1. Preheat oven to 350° F. Line a baking sheet with foil.
2. In small bowl, combine tomato, cheese and jalapeño pepper.
3. Divide cheese mixture evenly among tortillas. Roll tortillas to enclose filling; secure with toothpicks. Place on prepared baking sheet; bake 10–15 minutes, until cheese is melted and rolls are piping hot.

Each serving (1 roll) provides: $^1/_2$ Vegetable, $^1/_2$ Protein, 1 Bread

Per serving: 111 Calories, 5 g Total Fat, 3 g Saturated Fat, 11 mg Cholesterol, 190 mg Sodium, 12 g Total Carbohydrate, 1 g Dietary Fiber, 4 g Protein, 103 mg Calcium

Serving suggestion:

Slice baked rolls into bite-size pieces; arrange on medium decorative platter.

BERRY SLUSH

Makes 4 servings

4 cups whole strawberries, sliced
  (reserve 4 whole berries for garnish
  if desired)

1$^1/_2$ cups coarsely crushed ice
$^1/_2$ cup orange juice
2 tablespoons granulated sugar

1. In food processor or blender, combine sliced strawberries, ice, orange juice and sugar; process to a thick slush.
2. Divide slush among 4 individual bowls or tall glasses; serve each portion garnished with a whole strawberry if desired.

Each serving (1$^1/_4$ cups) provides: 1$^1/_4$ Fruits, 25 Optional Calories

Per serving: 84 Calories, 1 g Total Fat, 0 g Saturated Fat, 0 mg Cholesterol, 2 mg Sodium, 20 g Total Carbohydrate, 4 g Dietary Fiber, 1 g Protein, 24 mg Calcium

THE BEST BEAN SOUP SUPPER

If you have always opted for the grated Parmesan cheese that comes in jars or cans, treat yourself to the fresh variety when preparing this hearty soup; you'll be delighted with what it does for the flavor!

Menu serves 4

- **Green and Bean Soup, 1 serving**
- **Brown Bread, 1 serving**
- **Creamy Cucumber Salad, 1 serving**
  Red Delicious Apple, 1 small per serving
  Dry Rosé Wine, 4 fluid ounces per serving

One serving of this meal provides: $1^1/_4$ Fats, 1 Fruit, $5^1/_2$ Vegetables, 1 Protein, $1^1/_2$ Breads, 175 Optional Calories; 10 g Fat, 12 g Fiber

Market List

4 red Delicious apples	Grated Parmesan cheese
1 pound fresh escarole, kale or spinach	Whole-wheat flour
3 medium cucumbers	Molasses
Vegetable broth	Pickled jalapeño peppers
White kidney (cannellini) or red kidney beans	Dry rosé wine

Preparation Schedule

Note: For maximum efficiency, assemble all ingredients and equipment before starting preparation.

1. Chill wine.
2. Preheat oven.
3. Prepare Brown Bread; bake.
4. While bread is baking, prepare Creamy Cucumber Salad; refrigerate.
5. Prepare Green and Bean Soup.

GREEN AND BEAN SOUP

Makes 4 servings

2 teaspoons olive oil
2 cups chopped onions
2 garlic cloves, pressed
4 cups packed escarole, kale or spinach leaves, rinsed well, dried and shredded
2 cups vegetable broth
6 ounces drained cooked white kidney (cannellini) or red kidney beans

1 cup chopped carrot
$^1/_2$ cup chopped celery
$^1/_2$ teaspoon dried oregano leaves
Pinch salt
Pinch freshly ground black pepper
Pinch dried red pepper flakes
2 tablespoons grated Parmesan cheese

1. In medium nonstick saucepan, heat oil; add onions and garlic. Cook over medium heat, stirring frequently, 3–4 minutes, until onions are golden brown.
2. Add escarole, broth, beans, carrot, celery, oregano, salt, black pepper and red pepper flakes to onion mixture; bring liquid to a boil. Reduce heat to low; simmer 10 minutes, until carrot and celery are tender.
3. With slotted spoon, transfer 2 cups solids to food processor or blender; purée until smooth. Return purée to saucepan; stir to combine. Stir in Parmesan cheese.

Each serving (1 cup) provides: $^1/_2$ Fat, 3 $^3/_4$ Vegetables, $^3/_4$ Protein, 25 Optional Calories

Per serving: 155 Calories, 4 g Total Fat, 1 g Saturated Fat, 2 mg Cholesterol, 627 mg Sodium, 24 g Total Carbohydrate, 5 g Dietary Fiber, 7 g Protein, 116 mg Calcium

BROWN BREAD

Makes 4 servings

1 cup + 2 tablespoons whole-wheat flour	$^1/_3$ cup + 2 teaspoons plain nonfat yogurt
1 teaspoon caraway seeds	1 egg, beaten
1 teaspoon double-acting baking powder	1 tablespoon firmly packed dark
$^1/_2$ teaspoon baking soda	brown sugar
$^1/_4$ teaspoon cinnamon	1 tablespoon molasses
$^1/_8$ teaspoon salt	1 tablespoon vegetable oil

1. Preheat oven to 375° F. Spray an 8" round cake pan with nonstick cooking spray.
2. In medium bowl, combine flour, caraway seeds, baking powder, baking soda, cinnamon and salt. In small bowl, with wire whisk, combine yogurt, egg, sugar, molasses, oil and $^1/_4$ cup water. Add wet ingredients to dry; stir with wire whisk just until combined.
3. Transfer batter to prepared pan; bake 20–25 minutes, until golden brown and toothpick inserted in center comes out clean. Serve warm or at room temperature.

Each serving provides: $^3/_4$ Fat, $^1/_4$ Protein, $1^1/_2$ Breads, 40 Optional Calories

Per serving: 207 Calories, 6 g Total Fat, 1 g Saturated Fat, 55 mg Cholesterol, 385 mg Sodium, 34 g Total Carbohydrate, 4 g Dietary Fiber, 8 g Protein, 147 mg Calcium

CREAMY CUCUMBER SALAD

Makes 4 servings

3 medium cucumbers, pared and seeded	$^1/_3$ cup + 2 teaspoons plain nonfat yogurt
1 medium pickled jalapeño pepper,	$^1/_8$ teaspoon cumin seeds, toasted *
drained, seeded and minced (reserve	
2 teaspoons liquid)	

1. With coarse side of 4-sided grater, grate cucumbers onto double layer of cheesecloth; twist and squeeze out as much liquid as possible, discarding liquid.
2. Transfer cucumber pulp to small bowl; stir in jalapeño pepper and reserved jalapeño liquid, yogurt and cumin seeds. Refrigerate, covered, until chilled.

Each serving ($^1/_2$ cup) provides: $1^3/_4$ Vegetables, 10 Optional Calories

Per serving: 25 Calories, 0 g Total Fat, 0 g Saturated Fat, 0 mg Cholesterol, 76 mg Sodium, 4 g Total Carbohydrate, 0 g Dietary Fiber, 2 g Protein, 58 mg Calcium

* To toast cumin seeds, in small nonstick skillet, cook seeds over low heat, stirring constantly, 3 minutes, until fragrant.

CLASSIC COOKBOOK DINNER

This egg entrée, with its mild flavor and creamy texture, is a variation on Eggs Bombay, an old cookbook staple; it is complemented by the fragrant tomatoes and sweet-and-sour slaw. And the pudding cake is a modernized version of an old recipe, too; there's plenty, so enjoy a piece with this meal, and then again later in the week!

Menu serves 4

- **Curried Eggs with Mushrooms, 1 serving**
- **Savory Tomatoes, 1 serving**
- **Processor Carrot Slaw, 1 serving**
- **Chocolate Pudding Cake, 1 serving**
- **Skim Milk, 1 cup per serving**

One serving of this meal provides: 1$\frac{1}{2}$ Milks, 1$\frac{1}{2}$ Fats, 3$\frac{1}{4}$ Vegetables, 1 Protein, 2 Breads, 125 Optional Calories; 16 g Fat, 6 g Fiber

Market List

Apple cider
One 10-ounce package fresh mushrooms
6 firm small plum tomatoes

1 medium green bell pepper
1 medium red onion
Chopped walnuts

Preparation Schedule

Note: For maximum efficiency, assemble all ingredients and equipment before starting preparation.

1. Preheat oven.
2. Prepare Chocolate Pudding Cake; bake.
3. While cake is baking, prepare rice.
4. Prepare Processor Carrot Slaw; refrigerate.
5. Prepare Savory Tomatoes.
6. Sprinkle cake with walnuts; bake.
7. Prepare Curried Eggs with Mushrooms.

Curried Eggs with Mushrooms

Makes 4 servings

1 teaspoon vegetable oil
2 cups sliced mushrooms
1/2 cup chopped onion
1 teaspoon mild or hot curry powder
1 cup evaporated skimmed milk
1/2 cup low-sodium chicken broth or
 vegetable broth

2 teaspoons cornstarch
1/8 teaspoon dried oregano leaves
4 hard-cooked eggs, shelled and halved
3 cups cooked long-grain rice

1. In medium nonstick saucepan, heat oil; add mushrooms, onion and curry powder. Cook over medium heat, stirring frequently, 10 minutes, until liquid is evaporated and onion is softened.
2. In small bowl, with wire whisk, combine milk, broth, cornstarch and oregano, blending until cornstarch is dissolved. Stir milk mixture into mushroom mixture; continuing to stir, cook, until mixture is slightly thickened.
3. Add egg halves to thickened mixture, gently coating; cook until eggs are warm.
4. Just before serving, spoon rice onto medium decorative platter; top with egg mixture.

Each serving (2 egg halves, 3/4 cup sauce and 3/4 cup rice) provides: 1/2 Milk, 1/4 Fat, 1 1/4 Vegetables, 1 Protein, 1 1/2 Breads, 10 Optional Calories

Per serving: 363 Calories, 7 g Total Fat, 2 g Saturated Fat, 215 mg Cholesterol, 147 mg Sodium, 56 g Total Carbohydrate, 1 g Dietary Fiber, 17 g Protein, 236 mg Calcium

Savory Tomatoes

Makes 4 servings

1 teaspoon olive oil
6 firm small plum tomatoes, halved
 lengthwise

2 garlic cloves, pressed
1 tablespoon balsamic vinegar

1. In medium nonstick skillet, heat oil; add tomatoes. Cook over medium-high heat, turning once, until browned on both sides.
2. Add garlic to tomatoes; cook, stirring gently, 15–20 seconds, just until golden brown (do not burn). Stir in vinegar and 1/4 cup water; cook, basting tomatoes constantly, 3 minutes, until liquid is evaporated. Serve at room temperature.

Each serving (3 tomato halves) provides: 1/4 Fat, 3/4 Vegetable

Per serving: 21 Calories, 1 g Total Fat, 0 g Saturated Fat, 0 mg Cholesterol, 4 mg Sodium, 2 g Total Carbohydrate, 1 g Dietary Fiber, 0 g Protein, 5 mg Calcium

PROCESSOR CARROT SLAW

Makes 4 servings

2 medium carrots, cut into chunks
¹/₂ medium green bell pepper, seeded
    and cut into chunks
¹/₄ medium red onion, cut into chunks
¹/₄ cup apple cider

2 tablespoons cider vinegar
¹/₂ teaspoon prepared yellow mustard
¹/₂ teaspoon Worcestershire sauce
¹/₈ teaspoon salt

1. In food processor, combine carrots, bell pepper, onion, cider, vinegar, mustard, Worcestershire sauce and salt; with on-off motion, pulse processor 4–5 times, until mixture is finely chopped and ingredients are blended; do not purée.
2. Transfer carrot mixture to medium bowl; refrigerate, covered, until chilled. Just before serving, toss again.

Each serving (¹/₂ cup) provides: 1¹/₄ Vegetables, 10 Optional Calories

Per serving: 36 Calories, 0 g Total Fat, 0 g Saturated Fat, 0 mg Cholesterol, 103 mg Sodium, 9 g Total Carbohydrate, 2 g Dietary Fiber, 1 g Protein, 19 mg Calcium

CHOCOLATE PUDDING CAKE

Makes 8 servings

1 cup minus 1 tablespoon all-purpose flour
³/₄ cup granulated sugar
¹/₂ cup unsweetened cocoa powder
2 teaspoons double-acting baking powder
¹/₂ teaspoon salt

¹/₂ cup skim milk
2 tablespoons vegetable oil
1 teaspoon vanilla extract
1 cup extra-strength hot coffee *
1 ounce chopped walnuts

1. Preheat oven to 350° F. Spray an 8" round cake pan with nonstick cooking spray.
2. In large bowl, with wire whisk, combine flour, ¹/₃ cup of the sugar, 3 tablespoons of the cocoa, the baking powder and salt. Add milk, oil, vanilla and ¹/₄ cup water, blending with whisk until smooth. Transfer mixture to prepared pan.
3. In small bowl, with wire whisk, combine the remaining sugar, the remaining cocoa and the coffee, blending until sugar and cocoa are dissolved; pour over mixture in pan. Bake 20 minutes.
4. Sprinkle cake with walnuts; bake 10 minutes longer, until firm and a toothpick inserted in center comes out almost clean. Serve warm.

Each serving (¹/₈ of cake) provides: 1 Fat, ¹/₂ Bread, 105 Optional Calories

Per serving: 200 Calories, 7 g Total Fat, 1 g Saturated Fat, 0 mg Cholesterol, 269 mg Sodium, 35 g Total Carbohydrate, 2 g Dietary Fiber, 4 g Protein, 101 mg Calcium

* *If desired, substitute boiling water for the coffee.*

5

Meatless Meals

LIGHT AND LUSCIOUS BRUNCH

Use any of your favorite vegetables in place of the spinach in this pretty Vegetable Frittata to make a dish that suits you perfectly. And feel free to enjoy it often because we've kept the cholesterol low by replacing half of the eggs with egg substitute—you'll never know the difference!

Menu serves 4

Bloody Mary, 6 fluid ounces per serving
Vegetable Frittata, 1 serving
Cheese Toast, 1 serving
Spicy Cucumber Salad, 1 serving

One serving of this meal provides: $^1/_4$ Fat, 4 Vegetables, $2^1/_4$ Proteins, 2 Breads, 75 Optional Calories; 10 g Fat, 4 g Fiber

Market List

1   medium red bell pepper
2   medium cucumbers
1   medium serrano or jalapeño pepper
1   medium red onion
One 12-ounce package fresh mushrooms
1   loaf French or Italian bread

Grated Parmesan cheese
Bloody Mary mix
Egg substitute, frozen or refrigerated
One 10-ounce package frozen chopped spinach
Vodka

Special Equipment

Heat-resistant plate

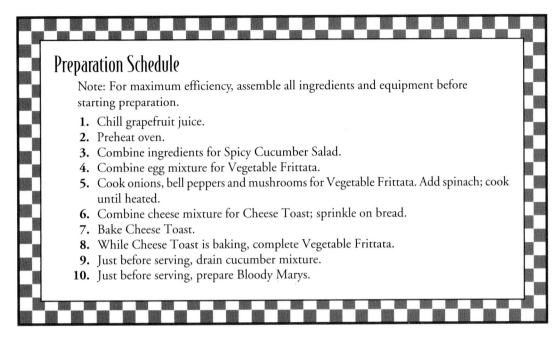

Preparation Schedule

Note: For maximum efficiency, assemble all ingredients and equipment before starting preparation.

1. Chill grapefruit juice.
2. Preheat oven.
3. Combine ingredients for Spicy Cucumber Salad.
4. Combine egg mixture for Vegetable Frittata.
5. Cook onions, bell peppers and mushrooms for Vegetable Frittata. Add spinach; cook until heated.
6. Combine cheese mixture for Cheese Toast; sprinkle on bread.
7. Bake Cheese Toast.
8. While Cheese Toast is baking, complete Vegetable Frittata.
9. Just before serving, drain cucumber mixture.
10. Just before serving, prepare Bloody Marys.

VEGETABLE FRITTATA

Makes 4 servings

4 eggs, beaten
1 cup egg substitute
$^{1}/_{2}$ teaspoon salt
$^{1}/_{4}$ teaspoon freshly ground black pepper
$^{1}/_{4}$ teaspoon dried oregano leaves
1 teaspoon olive oil

1 cup chopped onions
1 cup chopped red bell pepper
1 cup sliced mushrooms
1 cup well-drained thawed frozen chopped spinach

1. In small bowl, with wire whisk, combine eggs, egg substitute, salt, black pepper and oregano; set aside.
2. In medium nonstick skillet, heat oil; add onions, red pepper and mushrooms. Cook over medium-high heat, stirring frequently, 8 minutes, until onions are golden brown. Reduce heat to low; stir in spinach. Cook, stirring frequently, 1–2 minutes, until heated.
3. Pour egg mixture over vegetable mixture; stir quickly, just to combine. Cook, covered, 10–13 minutes, until egg mixture is set.
4. With spatula, loosen edges of frittata. Invert heat-resistant plate over skillet; turn skillet and plate over, allowing frittata to fall onto plate. Cut frittata into quarters; serve hot or at room temperature.

Each serving ($^{1}/_{4}$ frittata) provides: $^{1}/_{4}$ Fat, 2 Vegetables, 2 Proteins

Per serving: 149 Calories, 6 g Total Fat, 2 g Saturated Fat, 213 mg Cholesterol, 459 mg Sodium, 10 g Total Carbohydrate, 2 g Dietary Fiber, 14 g Protein, 119 mg Calcium

CHEESE TOAST

Makes 4 servings

8   ounces French or Italian bread, cut
      into 1" slices
3/4 ounce grated Parmesan cheese

1/8 teaspoon garlic powder
Pinch ground red pepper (optional)

1. Preheat oven to 350° F. Line baking sheet with foil.
2. Place bread on prepared baking sheet. In small bowl, combine cheese, garlic powder and red pepper; sprinkle cheese mixture evenly over bread. Bake 10–15 minutes, until golden brown. Serve immediately.

Each serving provides: 1/4 Protein, 2 Breads

Per serving: 180 Calories, 3 g Total Fat, 1 g Saturated Fat, 4 mg Cholesterol, 444 mg Sodium, 30 g Total Carbohydrate, 2 g Dietary Fiber, 7 g Protein, 116 mg Calcium

SPICY CUCUMBER SALAD

Makes 4 servings

2   medium cucumbers, pared, seeded
      and diced
1   medium serrano or jalapeño pepper,
      seeded and thinly sliced

1/2 cup cider vinegar
1/4 cup diced red onion
1/2 teaspoon caraway seeds, toasted *
1/4 teaspoon salt

1. In small bowl, combine cucumbers, pepper, vinegar, onion, caraway seeds and salt.
2. Just before serving, drain cucumber mixture, discarding liquid.

Each serving (1/2 cup) provides: 1 1/2 Vegetables

Per serving: 14 Calories, 0 g Total Fat, 0 g Saturated Fat, 0 mg Cholesterol, 140 mg Sodium, 3 g Total Carbohydrate, 0 g Dietary Fiber, 1 g Protein, 16 mg Calcium

  * *To toast caraway seeds, in small nonstick skillet, cook seeds over low heat, stirring constantly, 3 minutes, until fragrant.*

LIGHT MEXICAN LUNCH

This menu makes good use of leftover or stale tortillas by shredding them into *migas*, or crumbs. And if you've never tried jicama, this cooling salad will make you a fan of its crisp texture and sweet flavor. Top off the meal with a pineapple-rum treat that will prove the point that dessert can be delicious *and* easy.

Menu serves 2

- **Migas Frittata, 1 serving**
- **Jicama-Lettuce Salad, 1 serving**
- **Coconutty Pineapple, 1 serving**
- **Mexican Beer, 12 fluid ounces per serving**

One serving of this meal provides: 1 Fat, 1 Fruit, $4^{1}/_{4}$ Vegetables, 2 Proteins, 1 Bread, 195 Optional Calories; 7 g Fat, 7 g Fiber

Market List

1 head Romaine lettuce	Shredded coconut
1 small jicama	Egg substitute, frozen or
1 medium jalapeño pepper	refrigerated
1 small plum tomato	Dark rum
Corn tortillas (6" diameter)	
Canned pineapple slices	
(no sugar added)	

Special Equipment

Heat-resistant plate
Toaster oven

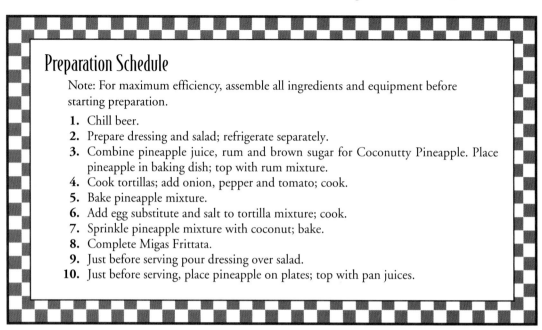

Preparation Schedule

Note: For maximum efficiency, assemble all ingredients and equipment before starting preparation.

1. Chill beer.
2. Prepare dressing and salad; refrigerate separately.
3. Combine pineapple juice, rum and brown sugar for Coconutty Pineapple. Place pineapple in baking dish; top with rum mixture.
4. Cook tortillas; add onion, pepper and tomato; cook.
5. Bake pineapple mixture.
6. Add egg substitute and salt to tortilla mixture; cook.
7. Sprinkle pineapple mixture with coconut; bake.
8. Complete Migas Frittata.
9. Just before serving pour dressing over salad.
10. Just before serving, place pineapple on plates; top with pan juices.

Migas Frittata

Makes 2 servings

2 teaspoons olive oil	1 small plum tomato, blanched, peeled,
2 corn tortillas (6" diameter), day old, torn into pea-size pieces	seeded and chopped
¹/₂ cup finely chopped onion	1 cup egg substitute
1 medium jalapeño pepper, seeded and finely chopped	Pinch salt

1. In medium skillet, heat oil; add tortilla pieces. Cook over medium-high heat, stirring occasionally, 4–6 minutes, until lightly browned and crisp. Add onion, jalapeño pepper and tomato; cook, stirring frequently, 8–10 minutes, until vegetables are softened.
2. Stir egg substitute into tortilla mixture; sprinkle evenly with salt. Reduce heat to medium; cook, covered, occasionally shaking pan vigorously to keep frittata from sticking, until egg substitute is almost set. Uncover.
3. Invert heat-resistant plate over skillet; turn skillet and plate over, allowing frittata to fall onto plate. Transfer frittata back to skillet, bottom side up.
4. Cook frittata 1 minute longer, until firm. To serve, cut frittata in half.

Each serving (¹/₂ frittata) provides: 1 Fat, 1¹/₄ Vegetables, 2 Proteins, 1 Bread

Per serving: 166 Calories, 5 g Total Fat, 1 g Saturated Fat, 0 mg Cholesterol, 269 mg Sodium, 18 g Total Carbohydrate, 2 g Dietary Fiber, 12 g Protein, 94 mg Calcium

Jicama–Lettuce Salad

Makes 2 servings

1 tablespoon + 1 1/2 teaspoons fresh lime juice
1 tablespoon low-sodium chicken broth
1/2 teaspoon mild or hot chili powder

2 cups torn Romaine lettuce
4 ounces pared jicama, cut into 1/8" sticks

1. To prepare dressing, in small bowl, with wire whisk, combine lime juice, broth and chili powder, blending until smooth.
2. Divide lettuce and jicama equally between 2 salad plates; pour half of the dressing over each portion of salad.

Each serving (1 1/2 cups) provides: 3 Vegetables

Per serving: 38 Calories, 0 g Total Fat, 0 g Saturated Fat, 0 mg Cholesterol, 16 mg Sodium, 8 g Total Carbohydrate, 2 g Dietary Fiber, 2 g Protein, 31 mg Calcium

Coconutty Pineapple

Makes 2 servings

4 canned pineapple slices with 1/4 cup juice (no sugar added)
1/2 fluid ounce (1 tablespoon) dark rum
1 teaspoon firmly packed dark brown sugar

1 tablespoon + 1 teaspoon shredded coconut

1. Preheat toaster oven to 400° F. Line a 1-quart shallow baking dish with foil.
2. In small bowl, combine pineapple juice, rum and brown sugar, stirring until sugar is dissolved.
3. Place pineapple slices in a single layer in prepared baking dish; drizzle evenly with rum mixture. Bake 5–8 minutes, until pineapple slices are lightly browned. Leave toaster oven on.
4. Sprinkle pineapple mixture evenly with coconut; bake 3–4 minutes longer, until coconut is lightly browned.
5. To serve, divide pineapple slices equally between 2 plates; top evenly with pan juices.

Each serving (2 pineapple slices + 1/2 the pan juices) provides: 1 Fruit, 40 Optional Calories

Per serving: 114 Calories, 1 g Total Fat, 1 g Saturated Fat, 0 mg Cholesterol, 10 mg Sodium, 23 g Total Carbohydrate, 1 g Dietary Fiber, 1 g Protein, 20 mg Calcium

A PROVENÇAL LUNCHEON

Sunny Provence is only thirty minutes away with this elegant luncheon. Serve it to a few good friends, or your family, and be prepared for the savory flavors of vegetables and herbs to transport you straight to the south of France.

Menu serves 4

- Eggplant, Goat Cheese and Tomato Tart, 1 serving
- Endive and Walnut Salad, 1 serving
  Breadsticks, 1¹/₂ ounces per serving
- Coffee Coupe, 1 serving
  Light White Wine, 4 fluid ounces per serving

One serving of this meal provides: 1¹/₂ Fats, 5 Vegetables, 1 Protein, 2 Breads, 155 Optional Calories; 19 g Fat, 4 g Fiber

Market List

1 medium eggplant
One 12-ounce package fresh mushrooms
Two 4-ounce Belgian endives
1 small head Boston lettuce
Fresh basil
Fresh oregano
Fresh thyme
3 ounces Montrachet (goat cheese)
Breadsticks

Walnut oil
Raspberry vinegar
Chopped walnuts
Bottled capers
Whole coffee beans
8 fluid ounces coffee or chocolate
    nonfat sugar-free frozen yogurt
Coffee-flavored liqueur
Light white wine

Special Equipment

9" ceramic pie plate
Mini food processor
4 wine glasses

A Provençal Luncheon

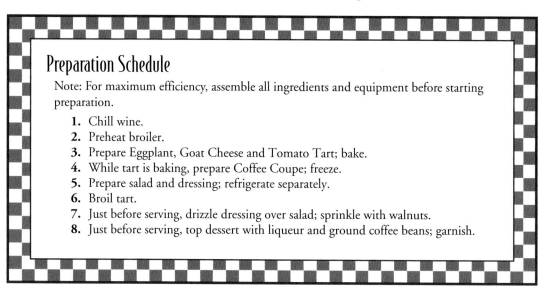

Preparation Schedule

Note: For maximum efficiency, assemble all ingredients and equipment before starting preparation.

1. Chill wine.
2. Preheat broiler.
3. Prepare Eggplant, Goat Cheese and Tomato Tart; bake.
4. While tart is baking, prepare Coffee Coupe; freeze.
5. Prepare salad and dressing; refrigerate separately.
6. Broil tart.
7. Just before serving, drizzle dressing over salad; sprinkle with walnuts.
8. Just before serving, top dessert with liqueur and ground coffee beans; garnish.

EGGPLANT, GOAT CHEESE AND TOMATO TART

Makes 4 servings

1 medium eggplant, cut crosswise into $^1/_4$" slices
$^1/_2$ teaspoon salt
$^1/_4$ teaspoon freshly ground black pepper
2 teaspoons olive oil
3 cups canned plum tomatoes, well drained and chopped
1 cup sliced mushrooms
2 tablespoons chopped fresh basil leaves or 1 teaspoon dried

2 tablespoons drained capers, rinsed
1 tablespoon chopped fresh oregano leaves or $^1/_2$ teaspoon dried
1 tablespoon chopped fresh thyme leaves or $^1/_2$ teaspoon dried
2 garlic cloves, minced
3 ounces Montrachet (goat cheese), cut into $^1/_4$" slices

1. Preheat broiler. Spray large nonstick baking sheet with nonstick cooking spray.
2. Place eggplant slices on prepared baking sheet; sprinkle with $^1/_4$ teaspoon of the salt and $^1/_8$ teaspoon of the pepper. Broil eggplant 4" from heat 5–10 minutes, until lightly browned. Remove eggplant from broiler; set oven temperature at 450° F. Adjust oven rack to divide oven in half.
3. In large nonstick skillet, heat oil; add tomatoes, mushrooms, basil, capers, oregano, thyme, garlic, remaining $^1/_4$ teaspoon salt and remaining $^1/_8$ teaspoon pepper. Cook over medium-high heat, stirring frequently, 5–10 minutes, until mixture is thickened. Remove from heat; set aside.
4. Spray a 9" ceramic pie plate with nonstick cooking spray.

5. Spread prepared pie plate with one-third of the tomato mixture; top with half of the eggplant slices, overlapping as necessary. Top eggplant with half of the remaining tomato mixture, then remaining eggplant; pour remaining tomato mixture over eggplant. Place goat cheese slices evenly over tomato mixture. Bake 10 minutes, until cheese is melted and edges of tart are bubbly. Remove pie plate from oven; set oven control to broil.
6. Broil tart 4" from heat 5 minutes, until cheese is golden brown.

Each serving provides: $^1/_2$ Fat, $3^1/_2$ Vegetables, 1 Protein

Per serving: 179 Calories, 12 g Total Fat, 5 g Saturated Fat, 17 mg Cholesterol, 790 mg Sodium, 14 g Total Carbohydrate, 3 g Dietary Fiber, 7 g Protein, 144 mg Calcium

ENDIVE AND WALNUT SALAD

Makes 4 servings

Two 4-ounce Belgian endives, separated into leaves	$^1/_2$ fluid ounce (1 tablespoon) dry red wine
1 small head Boston lettuce, cut crosswise into thin slices	2 teaspoons olive oil
$^1/_2$ ounce chopped walnuts	1 teaspoon raspberry vinegar
1 tablespoon + 1 teaspoon red wine vinegar	1 teaspoon walnut oil
	Pinch salt
	Pinch freshly ground black pepper

1. To prepare salad, arrange endive leaves and an equal amount of Boston lettuce onto 4 plates.
2. To prepare dressing, in mini food processor or blender, combine $^1/_2$ ounce of the walnuts, the red wine vinegar, wine, olive oil, raspberry vinegar, walnut oil, salt and pepper; purée until creamy.
3. Just before serving, drizzle an equal amount of dressing over each portion of salad; sprinkle each with one-fourth of the remaining walnuts.

Each serving ($1^1/_2$ cups) provides: 1 Fat, $1^1/_2$ Vegetables, 35 Optional Calories

Per serving: 70 Calories, 6 g Total Fat, 1 g Saturated Fat, 0 mg Cholesterol, 40 mg Sodium, 4 g Total Carbohydrate, 2 g Dietary Fiber, 1 g Protein, 23 mg Calcium

COFFEE COUPE

Makes 4 servings

8 fluid ounces coffee- or chocolate-
   flavored nonfat sugar-free
   frozen yogurt
2 tablespoons + 2 teaspoons coffee-
   flavored liqueur

1 tablespoon + 1 teaspoon freshly
   ground coffee beans
Whole coffee beans to garnish
   (optional)

Divide frozen yogurt evenly among 4 wine glasses. Spoon 2 teaspoons liqueur over each portion of yogurt, then sprinkle each with 1 teaspoon ground coffee beans. Serve garnished with whole coffee beans if desired.

Each serving provides: 70 Optional Calories

Per serving: 69 Calories, 0 g Total Fat, 0 g Saturated Fat, 0 mg Cholesterol, 34 mg Sodium, 14 g Total Carbohydrate, 0 g Dietary Fiber, 2 g Protein, 76 mg Calcium

HEARTY SOUP AND CORNBREAD SUPPER

This is a fragrant, hearty meal for a cold night. If you don't have fresh basil on hand, chop 1 teaspoon of dried basil leaves with a handful of fresh parsley to refresh it. And as an added bonus, the cornbread recipe yields enough so you can enjoy some on another day!

Menu serves 4

- **Creamy Tomato Soup with Basil, 1 serving**
- **Cheddar Cornbread, 1 serving**
- **Spinach, Egg and Bacon Salad, 1 serving**
- **Spiced Cider, 1 serving**

One serving of this meal provides: $3/4$ Milk, 2 Fats, 1 Fruit, 6 $1/2$ Vegetables, $1^1/4$ Proteins, $1^3/4$ Breads, 60 Optional Calories; 20 g Fat, 9 g Fiber

Market List

Apple cider
One 10-ounce bag fresh spinach
Fresh basil
2 slices bacon

3 ounces extra-sharp cheddar cheese
Grated Parmesan cheese
Tomato purée

Preparation Schedule

Note: For maximum efficiency, assemble all ingredients and equipment before starting preparation.

1. Preheat oven.
2. Cook hard-cooked eggs for salad.
3. While eggs are cooking, prepare Cheddar Cornbread; bake.
4. While cornbread is baking, prepare Creamy Tomato Soup with Basil; simmer.
5. While soup is simmering, cook bacon for salad.
6. Shell and slice eggs; crumble bacon.
7. Mix dressing for salad.
8. Remove cornbread from oven; cool slightly.
9. Add milk, basil, salt and pepper to soup; heat.
10. Cut cornbread.
11. Add spinach to dressing; toss. Top with bacon and eggs.
12. Just before serving, heat cider; strain into mugs.

CREAMY TOMATO SOUP WITH BASIL

Makes 4 servings

2 teaspoons stick margarine
1 cup chopped onions
1 garlic clove, slightly crushed
4 fluid ounces ($^1/_2$ cup) dry white wine
2 cups tomato purée

$1^1/_2$ cups evaporated skimmed milk
$^1/_2$ cup packed fresh basil leaves, slivered
$^1/_2$ teaspoon salt
$^1/_4$ teaspoon freshly ground black pepper

1. In medium saucepan, melt margarine; add onions and garlic. Cook over medium heat, stirring frequently, 3 minutes, until onion is softened. Add wine; bring liquid to a boil. Cook, stirring occasionally, until most of the wine is evaporated. Remove and discard garlic.
2. Stir tomato purée into onion mixture; bring just to a boil. Reduce heat to low; simmer, stirring frequently, 20 minutes.
3. Stir in milk, basil, salt and pepper; heat thoroughly (do not boil).

Each serving provides: $^3/_4$ Milk, $^1/_2$ Fat, $2^1/_2$ Vegetables, 25 Optional Calories

Per serving: 188 Calories, 2 g Total Fat, 0 g Saturated Fat, 4 mg Cholesterol, 909 mg Sodium, 29 g Total Carbohydrate, 4 g Dietary Fiber, 10 g Protein, 383 mg Calcium

CHEDDAR CORNBREAD

Makes 8 servings

$1^1/_2$ cups yellow cornmeal
3 ounces extra-sharp cheddar cheese, shredded
$^1/_3$ cup + 2 teaspoons all-purpose flour
$^3/_4$ ounce grated Parmesan cheese

2 teaspoons double-acting baking powder
1 teaspoon granulated sugar
$^3/_4$ teaspoon salt
1 cup skim milk
1 egg, beaten

1. Preheat oven to 425° F. Spray a 9" square baking pan with nonstick cooking spray.
2. In medium bowl, combine cornmeal, cheddar cheese, flour, Parmesan cheese, baking powder, sugar and salt. In small bowl, with wire whisk, combine milk and egg. Add wet ingredients to dry; stir just until combined.
3. Pour cornmeal mixture into prepared baking pan; bake 20–25 minutes, until golden brown on top and toothpick inserted in center comes out clean. Cool slightly, then cut into 16 squares.

Each serving (2 squares) provides: $^3/_4$ Protein, $1^3/_4$ Breads, 15 Optional Calories

Per serving: 195 Calories, 6 g Total Fat, 3 g Saturated Fat, 40 mg Cholesterol, 468 mg Sodium, 27 g Total Carbohydrate, 1 g Dietary Fiber, 8 g Protein, 225 mg Calcium

Spinach, Egg and Bacon Salad

Makes 4 servings

2 tablespoons olive oil
2 tablespoons red wine vinegar
1 teaspoon Dijon-style mustard
$^1/_4$ teaspoon salt
Freshly ground black pepper to taste

8 cups packed spinach leaves, well rinsed,
   dried and torn into bite-size pieces
2 slices crisp-cooked bacon, crumbled
2 hard-cooked eggs, shelled and sliced

1. In large salad bowl, with wire whisk, combine oil, vinegar, mustard, salt and pepper.
2. Just before serving, add spinach to oil mixture; toss to coat thoroughly. Sprinkle with bacon, then top with egg slices.

Each serving provides: $1^1/_2$ Fats, 4 Vegetables, $^1/_2$ Protein, 20 Optional Calories

Per serving: 150 Calories, 12 g Total Fat, 2 g Saturated Fat, 109 mg Cholesterol, 365 mg Sodium, 6 g Total Carbohydrate, 4 g Dietary Fiber, 8 g Protein, 152 mg Calcium

Spiced Cider

For each serving, in small saucepan, heat *$^1/_2$ cup apple cider* with *$^1/_2$ cinnamon stick* and *1 clove*; strain into mug.

Each serving provides: 1 Fruit

Per serving: 60 Calories, 0 g Total Fat, 0 g Saturated Fat, 0 mg Cholesterol, 4 mg Sodium, 15 g Total Carbohydrate, 0 g Dietary Fiber, 0 g Protein, 16 mg Calcium

VIVA LAS VEGGIES

Enjoy our magnificent mushroom dish as is, or pile the Broiled Squash and Peppers on top to make a lusciously messy sandwich. And for dessert, this version of the classic Bananas Foster is rich and sweet; for a crowning touch, top it with some frozen yogurt!

Menu serves 4

- **Wild Mushrooms in Toast Boats, 1 serving**
- **Broiled Squash and Peppers, 1 serving**
  Crudités, 1 cup per serving
  Fat-Free Blue Cheese Salad Dressing, 2 tablespoons per serving
- **Bananas Foster, 1 serving**
  Beaujolais, 4 fluid ounces per serving

One serving of this meal provides: 1 Fat, $1^1/_4$ Fruits, $6^1/_2$ Vegetables, 2 Breads, 200 Optional Calories; 8 g Fat, 7 g Fiber

Market List

2 medium bananas
Pineapple juice
Vegetables for crudités
One 12-ounce package fresh mushrooms
3 Portobello mushrooms
1 medium yellow squash

1 medium red bell pepper
1 medium green bell pepper
Fat-free blue cheese salad dressing
Four 3-ounce crusty rolls
Dark rum
Beaujolais

Special Equipment

Large, deep nonstick skillet

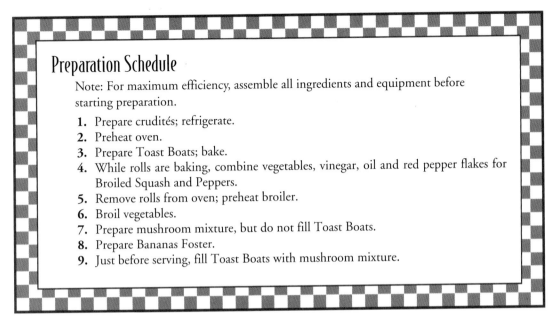

Preparation Schedule

Note: For maximum efficiency, assemble all ingredients and equipment before starting preparation.

1. Prepare crudités; refrigerate.
2. Preheat oven.
3. Prepare Toast Boats; bake.
4. While rolls are baking, combine vegetables, vinegar, oil and red pepper flakes for Broiled Squash and Peppers.
5. Remove rolls from oven; preheat broiler.
6. Broil vegetables.
7. Prepare mushroom mixture, but do not fill Toast Boats.
8. Prepare Bananas Foster.
9. Just before serving, fill Toast Boats with mushroom mixture.

WILD MUSHROOMS IN TOAST BOATS

Makes 4 servings

2 teaspoons olive oil	2 fluid ounces ($^1/_4$ cup) dry red wine
3 cups whole white mushrooms, quartered	2 teaspoons red wine vinegar
3 cups diced Portobello mushrooms (1" dice)	$^1/_2$ teaspoon salt
2 tablespoons minced onion	$^1/_4$ teaspoon dried thyme leaves
2 garlic cloves, pressed	$^1/_4$ teaspoon dried rosemary leaves
$^1/_2$ cup low-sodium chicken broth or vegetable broth	$^1/_4$ teaspoon freshly ground black pepper
	Toast Boats (recipe follows)

1. In large, deep nonstick skillet, heat oil; add white and Portobello mushrooms and onion. Cook over medium heat, stirring frequently, 8–10 minutes, until liquid is evaporated and onion is golden brown.
2. Add garlic to mushroom mixture; cook, stirring constantly, 1 minute.
3. Add broth, wine, vinegar, salt, thyme, rosemary and pepper to mushroom mixture; cook, stirring occasionally, until mixture is reduced in volume to about $^1/_2$ cup.
4. Just before serving, divide mushroom mixture evenly among Toast Boats.

Each serving (including Toast Boats) provides: $^1/_2$ Fat, 3 Vegetables, 2 Breads, 15 Optional Calories

Per serving: 232 Calories, 5 g Total Fat, 1 g Saturated Fat, 0 mg Cholesterol, 594 mg Sodium, 36 g Total Carbohydrate, 3 g Dietary Fiber, 8 g Protein, 69 mg Calcium

TOAST BOATS

Makes 4 servings

Preheat oven to 350° F. Carefully cut tops off *four 3-ounce crusty rolls*; reserve tops. Remove 1 ounce of soft bread from inside of each roll; reserve for use at another time. Place rolls and tops on baking sheet; bake 8–10 minutes, until golden brown.

Each serving provides: 2 Breads

Per serving: 166 Calories, 2 g Total Fat, 0 g Saturated Fat, 0 mg Cholesterol, 308 mg Sodium, 30 g Total Carbohydrate, 1 g Dietary Fiber, 6 g Protein, 54 mg Calcium

BROILED SQUASH AND PEPPERS

Makes 4 servings

1 medium yellow squash, cut into 1" diagonal slices	1 tablespoon balsamic vinegar
1 medium red bell pepper, cored, seeded and quartered	2 teaspoons olive oil
1 medium green bell pepper, cored, seeded and quartered	¹/₄ teaspoon dried red pepper flakes (optional)

1. Preheat broiler. Line baking sheet with foil.
2. In large bowl, combine squash, red and green peppers, vinegar, oil and red pepper flakes, tossing to coat; transfer to prepared baking sheet.
3. Broil vegetable mixture 3–4" from heat, turning once, 5–7 minutes on each side, until lightly charred. Serve hot or at room temperature.

Each serving (³/₄ cup) provides: ¹/₂ Fat, 1¹/₂ Vegetables

Per serving: 39 Calories, 2 g Total Fat, 0 g Saturated Fat, 0 mg Cholesterol, 2 mg Sodium, 4 g Total Carbohydrate, 1 g Dietary Fiber, 1 g Protein, 11 mg Calcium

BANANAS FOSTER

Makes 4 servings

¹/₃ cup pineapple juice
1¹/₂ fluid ounces (3 tablespoons) dark rum
1 tablespoon + 1 teaspoon firmly packed
  dark brown sugar

2 medium bananas, peeled and halved
  lengthwise

1. In medium skillet, combine pineapple juice, rum, sugar and 2 tablespoons water; bring mixture to a boil over medium-high heat. Reduce heat to low; simmer 5 minutes, until slightly syrupy.
2. Add bananas to pineapple juice mixture; cook 1 minute, basting occasionally. Serve warm.

Each serving (¹/₂ banana + 2 tablespoons syrup) provides: 1¹/₄ Fruits, 45 Optional Calories

Per serving: 103 Calories, 0 g Total Fat, 0 g Saturated Fat, 0 mg Cholesterol, 3 mg Sodium, 20 g Total Carbohydrate, 1 g Dietary Fiber, 1 g Protein, 9 mg Calcium

A MAGICAL MOROCCAN MEAL

This menu features the cool, hot and sweet flavors of the traditionally healthy and low-fat cuisine of Morocco. Fiery salad is cooled with refreshing melon for an exotic meal in just minutes.

Menu serves 4

- 🕐 **Marinated Olive and Vegetable Medley, 1 serving**
- 🕐 **Chopped Pepper Salad, 1 serving**
- 🕐 **Vegetable Tagine, 1 serving**
- 🕐 **Spicy Garlic Couscous, 1 serving**
- **Honeydew Slices, 1 cup per serving**
- **Decaffeinated Coffee sprinkled with Cinnamon**

One serving of this meal provides: $1^3/_4$ Fats, 1 Fruit, $7^1/_4$ Vegetables, $1^1/_2$ Proteins, $1^1/_2$ Breads, 25 Optional Calories; 18 g Fat, 22 g Fiber

Market List

1 medium honeydew melon	12 cherry tomatoes
2 medium green bell peppers	Fresh flat-leaf parsley
1 medium red bell pepper	Chick-peas (garbanzo beans)
1 medium Hungarian hot pepper	Couscous
2 medium red onions	Pitted black olives, small
2 medium cucumbers	

Preparation Schedule

Note: For maximum efficiency, assemble all ingredients and equipment before starting preparation.

1. Prepare Chopped Pepper Salad; refrigerate.
2. Prepare Marinated Olive and Vegetable Medley; refrigerate.
3. Prepare Vegetable Tagine; simmer.
4. While tagine is simmering, prepare Spicy Garlic Couscous.
5. Complete Vegetable Tagine.
6. Prepare coffee.
7. While coffee is brewing, slice melon.

A Magical Moroccan Meal

MARINATED OLIVE AND VEGETABLE MEDLEY

Makes 4 servings

 2 cups diced cucumber
 1 cup sliced red onion
12 cherry tomatoes, quartered
20 small pitted black olives

2 tablespoons + 2 teaspoons red wine
    vinegar
2 teaspoons olive oil

In medium bowl, combine cucumber, onion, tomatoes, olives, vinegar and oil; refrigerate, covered, until ready to serve.

Each serving provides: 1 Fat, 2 Vegetables

Per serving: 67 Calories, 4 g Total Fat, 1 g Saturated Fat, 0 mg Cholesterol, 32 mg Sodium, 8 g Total Carbohydrate, 2 g Dietary Fiber, 1 g Protein, 33 mg Calcium

CHOPPED PEPPER SALAD

Makes 4 servings

1¹/₂ teaspoons ground cumin
 ¹/₂ cup chopped fresh flat-leaf parsley
 ¹/₂ cup plain nonfat yogurt
  3 tablespoons fresh lemon juice
  2 garlic cloves, pressed
  2 medium green bell peppers, cored,
       seeded and coarsely chopped

1 medium red bell pepper, cored, seeded
    and coarsely chopped
1 medium Hungarian hot pepper,* cored,
    seeded and coarsely chopped

1. In small skillet, heat cumin over low heat, stirring constantly, 1 minute, until fragrant.
2. Transfer cumin to medium bowl; stir in parsley, yogurt, lemon juice and garlic. Add green, red and Hungarian peppers; stir to combine. Refrigerate, covered, until ready to serve.

Each serving provides: 1³/₄ Vegetables, 15 Optional Calories

Per serving: 51 Calories, 0 g Total Fat, 0 g Saturated Fat, 1 mg Cholesterol, 29 mg Sodium, 10 g Total Carbohydrate, 2 g Dietary Fiber, 3 g Protein, 86 mg Calcium

* If Hungarian hot pepper is not available, substitute poblano, cherry or jalapeño peppers to taste.

Vegetable Tagine

Makes 4 servings

2 teaspoons vegetable oil	1" piece cinnamon stick
1 cup chopped onions	1 bay leaf
1 cup chopped celery	3 cups canned plum tomatoes
3 garlic cloves, minced	(including liquid)
2 cups whole baby or diced carrots	12 ounces drained cooked chick-peas
1 1/2 teaspoons ground cumin	(garbanzo beans)
1/2 teaspoon freshly ground black pepper	1/4 cup chopped fresh flat-leaf parsley

1. In large saucepan, heat oil; add onions, celery and garlic. Cook over medium heat, stirring occasionally, 3–4 minutes, until vegetables are tender.
2. Add carrots, cumin, pepper, cinnamon stick and bay leaf to vegetable mixture; cook 1 minute, stirring constantly.
3. Add tomatoes, chick peas and parsley; bring to a boil. Reduce heat to low; simmer, partially covered, 20 minutes, until carrots are tender. Remove and discard cinnamon stick and bay leaf before serving.

Each serving provides: 1/2 Fat, 3 1/2 Vegetables, 1 1/2 Proteins

Per serving: 498 Calories, 11 g Total Fat, 1 g Saturated Fat, 0 mg Cholesterol, 698 mg Sodium, 86 g Total Carbohydrate, 15 g Dietary Fiber, 22 g Protein, 292 mg Calcium

Spicy Garlic Couscous

Makes 4 servings

1 teaspoon vegetable oil	1/4 teaspoon dried red pepper flakes
2 garlic cloves, minced	6 ounces couscous
2 cups low-sodium chicken broth	

1. In medium saucepan, heat oil; add garlic. Cook over medium heat, stirring constantly, 1 minute, until tender but not browned.
2. Add broth and red pepper flakes to garlic; bring to a boil. Stir in couscous; remove from heat. Let stand, covered, 10 minutes, until liquid is absorbed.

Each serving provides: 1/4 Fat, 1 1/2 Breads, 10 Optional Calories

Per serving: 185 Calories, 3 g Total Fat, 1 g Saturated Fat, 0 mg Cholesterol, 62 mg Sodium, 34 g Total Carbohydrate, 1 g Dietary Fiber, 7 g Protein, 21 mg Calcium

THE PERFECT PIZZA SUPPER

Far more wholesome and delicious than the frozen variety, this homemade pizza is quick to prepare and makes a pleasing light supper. And be sure to use ripe fruit for the soup, as this adds the perfect sweetness and texture.

Menu serves 4

- **Vegetable Pizza Bread, 1 serving**
- **Tossed Salad with Kidney Beans, 1 serving**
- **Berry-Melon Soup, 1 serving**
- **Light Beer, 12 fluid ounces per serving**

One serving of this meal provides: 1 Fat, $1^1/_2$ Fruits, 6 Vegetables, $^3/_4$ Protein, $1^3/_4$ Breads, 125 Optional Calories; 9 g Fat, 9 g Fiber

Market List

1 small cantaloupe	One 8-ounce loaf French or
2 cups whole strawberries	Italian bread
Orange juice	Tomato sauce
One 12-ounce package fresh mushrooms	Grated Parmesan cheese
2 medium red bell peppers	Red kidney beans
1 medium red onion	Dark rum
Assorted salad greens	Light beer

Preparation Schedule

Note: For maximum efficiency, assemble all ingredients and equipment before starting preparation.

1. Chill beer.
2. Preheat oven.
3. Purée cantaloupe mixture for soup; refrigerate.
4. Purée strawberry mixture for soup; refrigerate.
5. Prepare Vegetable Pizza Bread; bake.
6. While pizza is baking, prepare bean mixture for Tossed Salad with Kidney Beans.
7. Just before serving, combine greens and bean mixture; toss.
8. Just before serving, divide cantaloupe mixture into bowls. Top with strawberry mixture; garnish.

VEGETABLE PIZZA BREAD

Makes 4 servings

One 8-ounce French or Italian bread,
  split lengthwise
1   teaspoon olive oil
2   cups sliced mushrooms
2   cups sliced red bell peppers
1   cup sliced onions
1   cup tomato sauce

4   garlic cloves, pressed
$^1/_2$ teaspoon dried oregano leaves
$^1/_2$ teaspoon dried basil leaves
Dried red pepper flakes to taste
  (optional)
$^3/_4$ ounce grated Parmesan cheese

1. Preheat oven to 350° F. Line baking sheet with foil.
2. Evenly remove $^1/_2$ ounce of soft bread from cut side of each bread half; reserve for use at another time. Set bread halves aside.
3. In large nonstick skillet, heat oil; add mushrooms, red peppers and onions. Cook over high heat, stirring frequently, 5 minutes, until vegetables are softened.
4. Add tomato sauce, garlic, oregano, basil and red pepper flakes to vegetable mixture; remove from heat.
5. Spoon an equal amount of vegetable mixture onto each bread half; sprinkle evenly with cheese. Place bread on prepared baking sheet; bake 15–18 minutes, until top is golden brown.

Each serving ($^1/_4$ bread) provides: $^1/_4$ Fat, $3^1/_2$ Vegetables, $^1/_4$ Protein, $1^3/_4$ Breads

Per serving: 231 Calories, 5 g Total Fat, 2 g Saturated Fat, 4 mg Cholesterol, 774 mg Sodium, 40 g Total Carbohydrate, 4 g Dietary Fiber, 9 g Protein, 145 mg Calcium

TOSSED SALAD WITH KIDNEY BEANS

Makes 4 servings

4   ounces drained cooked red kidney beans
2   tablespoons minced red onion or
      scallions
2   tablespoons red wine vinegar
1   tablespoon olive oil
2   garlic cloves, pressed

$^1/_2$ teaspoon prepared yellow mustard
Pinch salt
Pinch freshly ground black pepper
5   cups coarsely shredded assorted
      salad greens

1. In medium bowl, combine beans, onion, vinegar, oil, garlic, mustard, salt and pepper.
2. Just before serving, add greens to bean mixture; toss to combine.

Each serving provides: $^3/_4$ Fat, $2^1/_2$ Vegetables, $^1/_2$ Protein

Per serving: 83 Calories, 4 g Total Fat, 0 g Saturated Fat, 0 mg Cholesterol, 48 mg Sodium, 10 g Total Carbohydrate, 2 g Dietary Fiber, 4 g Protein, 49 mg Calcium

BERRY–MELON SOUP

Makes 4 servings

1 small cantaloupe, pared, seeded and diced	2 cups whole strawberries, sliced (reserve 4 whole berries for garnish if desired)
1 tablespoon fresh lime juice	2 tablespoons orange juice
$^1/_2$ fluid ounce (1 tablespoon) dark rum *	1 tablespoon granulated sugar

1. In food processor or blender, combine cantaloupe, lime juice and rum; purée until smooth. Transfer to medium bowl; refrigerate, covered, until chilled.
2. In same food processor, combine sliced strawberries, orange juice and sugar; purée until smooth. Transfer to small bowl; refrigerate, covered, until chilled.
3. Just before serving, divide cantaloupe mixture evenly among 4 soup bowls. Carefully top each portion of cantaloupe mixture with $^1/_4$ of the strawberry mixture; serve garnished with whole strawberries if desired.

Each serving (1 cup) provides: $1^1/_2$ Fruits, 25 Optional Calories

Per serving: 87 Calories, 1 g Total Fat, 0 g Saturated Fat, 0 mg Cholesterol, 11 mg Sodium, 19 g Total Carbohydrate, 3 g Dietary Fiber, 2 g Protein, 24 mg Calcium

If desired, rum may be omitted; reduce Optional Calories to 15.

Per serving: 79 Calories, 1 g Total Fat, 0 g Saturated Fat, 0 mg Cholesterol, 11 mg Sodium, 19 g Total Carbohydrate, 3 g Dietary Fiber, 2 g Protein, 24 mg Calcium

Serving Suggestion:

Create a star pattern in each portion of soup by drawing a knife from center to edge of bowl, making 6 to 8 star points; garnish center of each with a whole strawberry.

Metric Conversions

If you are converting the recipes in this book to
metric measurements, use the following chart as a guide.

Volume		Weight		Length		Oven Temperatures	
1/4 teaspoon	1 milliliter	1 ounce	30 grams	1 inch	25 millimeters	250°F	120°C
1/2 teaspoon	2 milliliters	1/4 pound	120 grams	1 inch	2.5 centimeters	275°F	140°C
1 teaspoon	5 milliliters	1/2 pound	240 grams			300°F	150°C
1 tablespoon	15 milliliters	3/4 pound	360 grams			325°F	160°C
2 tablespoons	30 milliliters	1 pound	480 grams			350°F	180°C
3 tablespoons	45 milliliters					375°F	190°C
1/4 cup	50 milliliters					400°F	200°C
1/3 cup	75 milliliters					425°F	220°C
1/2 cup	125 milliliters					450°F	230°C
2/3 cup	150 milliliters					475°F	250°C
3/4 cup	175 milliliters					500°F	260°C
1 cup	250 milliliters					525°F	270°C
1 quart	1 liter						

Dry and Liquid Measurement Equivalents

Teaspoons	Tablespoons	Cups	Fluid Ounces
3 teaspoons	1 tablespoon		$^{1}/_{2}$ fluid ounce
6 teaspoons	2 tablespoons	$^{1}/_{8}$ cup	1 fluid ounce
8 teaspoons	2 tablespoons plus 2 teaspoons	$^{1}/_{6}$ cup	
12 teaspoons	4 tablespoons	$^{1}/_{4}$ cup	2 fluid ounces
15 teaspoons	5 tablespoons	$^{1}/_{3}$ cup minus 1 teaspoon	
16 teaspoons	5 tablespoons plus 1 teaspoon	$^{1}/_{3}$ cup	
18 teaspoons	6 tablespoons	$^{1}/_{3}$ cup plus two teaspoons	3 fluid ounces
24 teaspoons	8 tablespoons	$^{1}/_{2}$ cup	4 fluid ounces
30 teaspoons	10 tablespoons	$^{1}/_{2}$ cup plus 2 tablespoons	5 fluid ounces
32 teaspoons	10 tablespoons plus 2 teaspoons	$^{2}/_{3}$ cup	
36 teaspoons	12 tablespoons	$^{3}/_{4}$ cup	6 fluid ounces
42 teaspoons	14 tablespoons	1 cup plus 2 tablespoons	7 fluid ounces
45 teaspoons	15 tablespoons	1 cup minus 1 tablespoon	
48 teaspoons	16 tablespoons	1 cup	8 fluid ounces

Note: Measurement of less than $^{1}/_{8}$ teaspoon is considered a dash or a pinch.

Index